# Qualitative Research in
# Counselling and Psychotherapy

# Qualitative Research in Counselling and Psychotherapy

John McLeod

**SAGE Publications**
London • Thousand Oaks • New Delhi

First published 2001

 SAGE Publications Ltd
6 Bonhill Street
London EC2A 4PU

SAGE Publications Inc
2455 Teller Road
Thousand Oaks, California 91320

SAGE Publications India Pvt Ltd
32, M-Block Market
Greater Kailash – I
New Delhi 110 048

**British Library Cataloguing in Publication data**

A catalogue record for this book is available
from the British Library

ISBN 0 7619 5505 4
ISBN 0 7619 5506 2 (pbk)

**Library of Congress catalog card record available**

Typeset by Mayhew Typesetting, Rhayader, Powys
Printed in Great Britain by Biddles Ltd, Guildford, Surrey

*For Julia*

# Contents

# Preface

Qualitative research has much to offer counsellors and psychotherapists, in terms of generating new understandings of the complexities of the therapeutic process, and in enabling the experience of different participants in therapy, particularly clients, to be heard. Many practitioners are critical of the existing quantitative research, arguing that in controlling and measuring 'variables' the researcher is left with results that may be statistically significant but are clinically superficial and which do not represent or reflect their everyday work with clients.

Qualitative research, or what has in recent years been called 'qualitative inquiry', is a hugely interesting, engaging, challenging and rewarding activity. At its heart, qualitative research involves doing one's utmost to map and explore the meaning of an area of human experience. If carried out with integrity, this is a process that can result in unique learning both for the person who is the inquirer, and for those who are his or her audiences. We live in a culture which is built on thin and superficial descriptions of experience. We can 'surf' across innumerable websites, flick through television channels, listen to 'sound bites', know ourselves and others in the context of life compartments (work, the sports club, this year, today). By contrast, good qualitative research requires an *immersion* in some aspect of social life, in an attempt to capture the wholeness of that experience, followed by an attempt to convey this understanding to others.

My experience has been that many counsellors and psychotherapists are drawn towards qualitative inquiry because they can recognise its potential. Many of the techniques and skills used in qualitative research are similar to those used in therapy: eliciting people's stories, sensitive listening, building up an understanding, checking it out. The knowledge generated by qualitative research – holistic, nuanced, personal, contextualised, incomplete – is a knowing that is familiar to therapists. Nevertheless, it seems to me that very often therapists become frustrated and disillusioned when they carry out qualitative studies or read qualitative papers. The promise and potential of qualitative research is not matched by the actuality.

The goal of this book is to build some bridges between the world of therapy and the world of qualitative inquiry. For example, counsellors and psychotherapists who sign up for qualitative methods courses are generally confronted with an array of texts which offer sets of (somewhat contradictory) guidelines for conducting qualitative studies of different types. These guidelines may be perfectly valid in themselves, but can be difficult to follow in the absence of context or concrete examples. Although some sets of procedures are indeed included in various chapters of this book, I have given more emphasis to looking at examples of how researchers have used these frameworks in the context of actual studies. It is essential to consider what researchers are trying to achieve when they do research, and how they position themselves in relation to philosophical and practical issues.

When counsellors or psychotherapists cross the bridge into the territory of qualitative inquiry they find a world with many wonders. I do not think that sufficient attention has been paid in the past, within psychotherapy research, to the enormous diversity and richness of the qualitative or 'human science' tradition. Specifically, there are big philosophical questions around the nature of knowledge and truth which are unavoidable once one enters that world. I hope in this book to be able to open up some of these questions in at least an introductory manner.

This book seeks to do three things:

- introduce and describe the methods that have been used to carry out qualitative research in counselling and psychotherapy;
- summarise and discuss examples of qualitative research in counselling and psychotherapy;
- review the issues and controversies associated with this area of work.

I make no claim that this book can provide a comprehensive and authoritative review of the field of qualitative research in counselling and psychotherapy; I am aware of how much I do not know and do not fully understand. Readers are encouraged to regard this book as an invitation to a conversation, rather than as a definitive statement about the truth of these matters. The book is a continuation of a line of work which has come to light in two earlier books, and a number of papers. In *Doing Counselling Research* (1994) I attempted to map out what seemed to me to be the key elements of a pluralistic approach to research in counselling and psychotherapy. *Practitioner Research in Counselling* (1999) sought to describe an approach to research and inquiry that took as its starting-point the everyday work of therapy practice. I am sure that a capacity to both conduct and learn from appropriately focused qualitative research is essential to the future development of counselling and psychotherapy. However, although more qualitative research has been carried out in recent years, most of it is still dominated by the assumptions and validity criteria associated with mainstream positivist, quantitative methods. Personally, while I have no difficulty in acknowledging the value of quantitative methods, I believe that qualitative or 'human science' research is a fundamentally different endeavour. If this book is taken as an invitation to a conversation, then we need to understand that it is also a bid to move the ground of the conversation, and introduce some new topics into it, for example around such issues as the necessity of a philosophical perspective, and the centrality of personal commitment and integrity.

Some sections of Chapter 10 were first published as 'Human experience on trial: power and exclusion in psychotherapy research', *Universities Psychotherapy Association Review*, No. 7, pp. 15–25, 1999.

My thanks and appreciation are extended to those who have helped me to learn about qualitative research and who have shared in the struggle of how to make sense of data and method, and how best to put knowing into words: Lynne Angus, Sophia Balamoutsou, Mike Beaney, Linda Berman, Maurice Bond, Sue Cowan, Dee Danchev, Robert Elliott, Joerg Frommer, Soti Grafanaki, Kenneth Hamilton, Kate Kirk, Sharon McDonald, Dave Mearns, Mary Reid, David Rennie, Cathy Riessman, Iain Steele, Clifford Stott, Gill Tuckwell and William West. Alison Poyner at Sage has been consistently supportive as editor.

My deepest debt is to my family – my wife Julia and daughters Kate, Emma and Hannah – who continue to teach me more than I will ever know.

# 1

# Qualitative Inquiry and the Reconstruction of Counselling and Psychotherapy

In recent years, qualitative research, or what has become known as *qualitative inquiry*, has become increasingly influential within social science, education and health care research. For many people wishing to do research into real-life topics and problems in these fields, qualitative inquiry offers a set of flexible and sensitive methods for opening up the meanings of areas of social life that were previously not well understood. Qualitative inquiry holds the promise of discovery, of generating new insights into old problems, and producing nuanced accounts that do justice to the experience of all those participating in the research.

The domain of counselling and psychotherapy research has been a relatively late addition to the qualitative inquiry movement. Psychotherapy research has steadily expanded since the 1950s, largely driven by the pressure to evaluate the clinical effectiveness of different therapies. However, psychotherapy research has been dominated by the methods of inquiry used within the disciplines of psychology and psychiatry, such as standardised measurement instruments (tests), diagnostic categories and experimental designs. It has not been easy for qualitative researchers to break down the resistance that many in the psychotherapy research establishment feel in relation to methods which appear (to them) to lack rigour and generalisability.

If qualitative research in counselling and psychotherapy is to flourish, and make a significant contribution to the quality of services that are offered to users, it is essential for researchers to possess a clear idea of what they are trying to do when they carry out a qualitative study. Qualitative research is not merely 'quantitative research without numbers'. Qualitative research has its own *distinctive* role to play in the creation of a knowledge base for practice and policy. The aim of this chapter is to examine the nature of that role, by locating the practice of qualitative research within its historical, social and cultural context. It is only by understanding where qualitative research has come from, and how it has developed, that qualitative researchers in counselling and psychotherapy can appropriately position themselves in relation to the topics and issues they wish to study.

## A definition of qualitative research

Why do research? What is the point or purpose of conducting qualitative research into an activity such as counselling or psychotherapy? The answer to this question is obvious. The purpose of research is to enhance knowledge, to enable us to know more about the way counselling and psychotherapy operate and how or why they are effective (or perhaps not effective). But what do we mean by 'knowing' and 'knowledge'? In order to carry out useful qualitative research it is important to be clear about the types of knowledge that it can produce. Qualitative methods contribute a particular kind of knowledge about the world, which is different from the knowledge generated by other methods of inquiry. The nature of qualitative research can be summed up in these terms:

The primary aim of qualitative research is to develop an understanding of how the world is constructed

The notion of the world being 'constructed' implies that we inhabit a social, personal and relational world that is complex, layered, and can be viewed from different perspectives. This social reality can be seen as multiply constructed. We construct the world through talk (stories, conversations), through action, through systems of meaning, through memory, through the rituals and institutions that have been created, through the ways in which the world is physically and materially shaped.

The various qualitative methodologies that have been devised all seek to contribute to an understanding of how the world is constructed, but each of them takes on a different facet of this task. For example, grounded theory and phenomenology focus, for the most part, on the meanings through which people construct their realities. Ethnography has a particular concern with the way that worlds are constructed through action such as ritual and social practices. Discourse, conversational and narrative analysis are mainly designed as ways of making sense of how reality is constructed through talk and language use. Hermeneutic research seeks to uncover historical and cultural horizons of meaning through which the world is experienced.

There is a paradox at the heart of qualitative research. We understand the world already (Ossorio, 1985). On almost any occasion, in response to almost any event or experience, the majority of people would be able to offer some kind of common-sense explanation or understanding of why and how that event or experience happened. Much of the time, we are so confident about our 'grasp' of what is going on that we do not feel any need to explain things. Much of human experience is 'taken for granted'.

Why, then, is there any necessity for qualitative research? If we already *know*, then what is the point of going to all the trouble of carrying out interviews, analysing transcripts, writing papers and all the other time-consuming tasks involved in qualitative research? There are at least two interlocking reasons why it can be worthwhile to pursue qualitative inquiry. These can be summarised as *knowing*, and *becoming a knower*. The first of these, the goal of *knowing*, is acknowledged as central by most people involved in research, at least in public.

Everyday, common-sense knowledge in the modern world is far from being coherent and consistent. Quite possibly there were times in the past when people lived according to a fixed set of well-known rules and axioms, but those days are long gone. Now, there exist several contrasting images of the good life, along with their associated values and guidelines for action. The way we talk about things changes too. New elements of common sense becoming re-worked, appropriated by different groups, or outmoded, and all this has an effect on language, not only on the words that are used but also on the ways these words are brought together in texts. So, for example, while novels and plays from the eighteenth century represent a world that is recognisably human and somehow connected to contemporary experience, the way that they are written, and many of the assumptions that they rely upon, may appear strange.

Those of us working in the broad area of human services (not only counsellors and psychotherapists but also teachers, health professionals, managers and many others) have to be able to find our way around this constructed world of common-sense understandings. Specifically, we need to be able to claim some kind of understanding of what is going on that is somehow better or more insightful than ordinary, everyday understanding. It is on such claims that professional status and expertise can be justified.

Qualitative research is a process of careful, rigorous inquiry into aspects of the social world. It produces formal statements or conceptual frameworks that provide new ways of understanding that world, and therefore comprises knowledge that is practically useful for those who work with issues around learning and adjustment to the pressures and demands of the social world. There are basically three areas within which qualitative research can produce new forms of knowing. The first can be described as *knowledge of the other*. A second branch of qualitative research seeks to develop *knowledge of phenomena*. The third category of research aims at the production of *reflexive knowing*.

Knowledge of the other is generated by research which takes a category of person (such as psychotherapy client, hospital patient, gang member) who is of interest to members of a professional group, and seeks to describe, analyse and interpret the world-view, experiences and language of a sample of people who represent that category. Much qualitative research in counselling and psychotherapy (and in other professional fields such as social work, nursing and education) is of this type. This kind of knowledge is enormously useful for practitioners. Characteristically, practitioners are socialised into somewhat stereotyped views of clients or service users, and may have little time to explore in depth how their clients feel about things.

In addition, there may be barriers of gender, class, ethnicity and power that inhibit professionals gaining a rich understanding of the world of their clients. Qualitative research which gives clients a 'voice', which allows their experiences and life stories to be documented, is therefore invaluable to the smooth, efficient and humane running of human services agencies. It allows professionals to know much more about the construction of that segment of their world that is represented by their clients.

The second field of qualitative research, which aims to develop *knowledge of phenomena*, is directed toward categories of event that are of interest to professional groups. For example, in the area of research in counselling and psychotherapy, qualitative studies have been conducted into a wide range of phenomena that are considered significant from a practitioner standpoint, such as change events, or the use of figurative language in therapy. Qualitative studies of the phenomena of counselling and psychotherapy have made a major contribution to expanding practitioners' awareness of the process of therapy.

Research that aims to develop *reflexive knowing* is much harder to carry out and is found somewhat less frequently in the research literature. Reflexive knowing occurs when researchers deliberately turn their attention to their own process of constructing a world with the goal of saying something fresh and new about that personal (or shared professional) world. For example, some reflexive research has attempted to examine the historical development of aspects of professional practice, thereby opening up an understanding of the social, cultural, political and economic 'archaeology' of practice. Other reflexive research has focused on language, by analysing the assumptions that underpin professional terms such as 'schizophrenia' or other psychiatric categories. Some reflexive studies have looked at the way language is used, for example the various types of rhetorical and discursive devices that are employed in constructing convincing professional 'cases'. Yet other reflexive studies have explored the everyday experience of professionals – 'people like us', rather than clients. The outcome of reflexive research is usually uncomfortable for the reader. Many researchers within the various traditions and genres that are here being characterised as 'reflexive' use terms like 'deconstruction' and 'critical' to describe what they are trying to do. This is research which is intended to subvert everyday ways of seeing.

Each of these forms of knowing is temporary. Implicit in any form of qualitative inquiry is the realisation that, ultimately, we can never *really* know how the world is constructed. We can never achieve a complete 'scientific' understanding of the human world. The best we can do is to arrive at a truth that makes a difference, that opens up new possibilities for understanding. This understanding is forever incomplete. The best we can do is perhaps to make a temporary 'clearing' within which some things may be better understood, at least for a while. After a while, the images and ideas around which this fresh understanding has been constructed themselves become appropriated and assimilated into everyday common-sense ways of thinking. They no longer make a difference. There is a sense in which qualitative research can never be truly cumulative and is therefore fundamentally different from, for example, biological research. The highly productive medical research industry painstakingly builds up a model of a disease entity like cancer which is the accumulation of thousands of studies carried out in dozens of laboratories. Qualitative research does not function like this.

Also implicit in qualitative inquiry is the idea that there is someone doing the constructing: the world is constructed by and through the collective activities of *people*. Qualitative research does not assume a billiard-ball cause-and-effect reality constituted by scientific laws. Nor does it assume that our actions are ultimately controlled by the will of a Deity. Qualitative research is humanistic, in the broadest sense of that term. Like other fields of humanistic inquiry, it proceeds on the basis that, individually and collectively, we create the world we live in, must take responsibility for it, and can choose to make it different.

It is perhaps worth reflecting on how and why qualitative research has itself been constructed. Qualitative research has not always existed. No one has ever claimed that ancient civilisations employed qualitative social scientists. Qualitative research is associated with the shift from a tradition-based, largely rural society into a modern, urbanised, largely secular society which occurred around the end of the eighteenth century. In traditional societies, the nature of the social world is for the most part fixed and given. People are born into particular roles, and *know their place*. In modern societies, people are socially and geographically mobile. There are many 'identities' on offer. A modern city offers a confusing array of roles, identities and life-styles. As a result, it is no longer possible just to live a life. It becomes necessary to have some means of figuring out what is happening, what the rules are. Qualitative research, along with other cultural forms such as life-style magazines, psychotherapy, the Oprah Winfrey show, have functioned as ways of mapping and exploring this world.

Who does qualitative research, and why do they do it? Up to now, qualitative research has been carried out by people in professional roles, usually employed by the knowledge industry (mainly universities and market research companies). Most of the qualitative research that is publicly accessible (that is, published) derives from academic sources; market research qualitative studies are seldom published, for commercial reasons. Qualitative studies yield knowledge 'products' in the form of conference papers, journal articles and books. To some extent these products are used to inform policy and practice in areas such as health and social care, although it is widely acknowledged that the links between research and application are diffuse and uncertain. At best, qualitative research products can be viewed as feeding into a dialogue between practitioners and researchers. But research also has a more direct and precise function in society. The successful completion of a piece of research operates as a *rite de passage* for the researcher, signifying his or her suitability to receive a degree (and thereby join the white-collar workforce) or a Doctorate (and thereby be regarded as suitable to teach and ultimately to 'profess'). Most of the time, qualitative research is carried out by those of higher status on and about those with lower status. For example, health professionals study the experiences of patients, criminologists study the experiences of both criminals and victims of crime. The completion of the study is a means of confirming the status and 'expertise' of the researcher. It is in this sense that one of the key goals of research is that of *becoming a knower*. Researchers in universities and other organisations are allocated a social role that ascribes to them the capacity to possess knowledge, and even actively to promote that knowledge within society.

It is apparent to many people that, in relation to research in counselling and psychotherapy, a gap has opened up between the dissemination of 'knowing', and the interests of those who seek to 'become knowers' (that is, work in universities). Those who are authorised to create 'knowledge', through PhD research and becoming faculty members in universities, seem to have lost the knack of transmitting this knowledge to those who practise in the field (the majority of counsellors and psychotherapists) (see Cohen et al., 1986; Morrow-Bradley and Elliott, 1986). An important reason for the emergence of this 'gap' lies in the way that psychotherapy research has evolved over the last 50 years. An account of the historical development of research in counselling and psychotherapy is offered in a later section of this chapter.

## The diversity of qualitative research

So far, the nature and contribution of qualitative 'knowing' has been described in general terms. However, qualitative research is not a unitary, unified activity or approach. One of the distinctive characteristics of the field of qualitative research is the existence of a complex set of competing traditions. There are many different ways of doing qualitative research. Grounded theory, content analysis, narrative analysis, participant observation, ethnomethodology, feminist analysis, and phenomenology are just some of the many alternative genres of qualitative inquiry that are alive and thriving.

It is important to understand *why* qualitative research practice is so diverse. Behind the mainstream, quantitative research tradition, there lies a philosophical belief in a unitary, knowable, objective reality (von Wright, 1993). There is therefore *one science*, one single best way of gaining knowledge about that reality. Qualitative inquiry is built on a different philosophical stance. It assumes that, at least in human affairs, reality is *constructed*. There are, therefore, many alternative or complementary definitions or understandings of reality, reflecting the backgrounds and interests of those involved. The idea of *pluralism* is therefore intrinsic to the qualitative approach to research. From the perspective of most qualitative researchers, the idea that one single way of knowing could be regarded as privileged or foundational would be highly suspect. On what basis could that 'method' make such a claim? It is this intrinsic pluralism (and relativism) that makes the existence of different genres of qualitative research inevitable.

The recent classic overview of developments in qualitative research, the *Handbook of Qualitative Research* (Denzin and Lincoln, 1994a), describes the different approaches to qualitative research, and attempts to explain their inter-relationships. In that book, Denzin and Lincoln (1994b) offer a useful way of making sense of the diversity of qualitative methods. They suggest that there have been five discrete stages in the evolution of qualitative research. These are:

1 *The traditional period*. This phase began in the early 1900s and continued until the 1940s (although, like all the other stages, it continues to have its supporters and adherents even in present times). The typical qualitative studies carried out in this era were anthropological fieldwork investigations of tribal peoples, such as Malinowski's study of the Trobriand Islanders or the well-known work of Gregory Bateson or Margaret Mead. These researchers believed that they were able to arrive at an objective, verifiable truth through the application of their methods of inquiry. Denzin and Lincoln (1994b: 7) write that:

> the field-worker, during this period, was lionised, made into a larger-than-life figure who went into and then returned from the field with stories about strange people . . . this [was] the period of the Lone Ethnographer . . . the man-scientist who went off in search of his native in a distant land . . . underwent his rite of passage by enduring the ultimate ordeal of 'fieldwork' . . . [and demonstrated] a commitment to objectivism, a complicity with imperialism, a belief in monumentalism (the ethnographer would create a museumlike picture of the culture studied) . . . a belief in timelessness (what was studied never changed) . . . [and a capacity to] write complex, dense theories.

Crucial to the traditional school of qualitative research was the power and authority vested in the researcher to represent the experience of the subject of the research.

2 *The modernist phase*. Denzin and Lincoln argue that the second stage in the history of qualitative research stretched through the postwar years up to the 1970s, although again the themes and methods introduced in this

phase continue to influence much current work. The modernist phase was characterised by an attempt to *formalise* the methodology of qualitative research, through the publication of standardised 'how-to-do-it' methodology textbooks outlining techniques for carrying out grounded theory, phenomenological and ethnographic studies. The highly influential texts by Glaser and Strauss (1967) and Lofland (1971) date from this era. One of the main goals of the researchers fronting these developments was the desire to prove that qualitative research could be as valid and rigorous as its positivist quantitative counterpart. Denzin and Lincoln (1994b: 9) describe this era as a 'golden age' of qualitative research, wherein researchers behaved as 'leftist cultural romantics' who valued 'villains and outsiders as heroes to mainstream society'. More recent books by Strauss and Corbin (1990) and Miles and Huberman (1994) represent the resilience of this tradition.

3   *The moment of blurred genres*. By the beginning of the third phase of qualitative inquiry (1970-86), researchers working in this area had available to them a broad repertoire of paradigms, methods, strategies and techniques that could be applied in their work. Denzin and Lincoln suggest that two books by the anthropologist Clifford Geertz – *The Interpretation of Cultures* (1973) and *Local Knowledge* (1983) – served to define this phase. Geertz produced a series of very powerful interpretive accounts of cultures that blurred the distinction between the humanities and social sciences. Both the humanities and social sciences could be regarded as dealing in the hermeneutic interpretation of texts. Not only that, but the voice of the researcher began to appear in qualitative reports. The establishment of an increasing number of specialist qualitative journals made it easier for researchers to allow themselves to turn away from the battle against positivism and openly espouse a constructivist/constructionist epistemology within which no single genre or research tradition could be seen as 'privileged'.

4   *The crisis of representation*. What Denzin and Lincoln call the 'fourth moment' occurred in the mid-1980s. The 'crisis of representation' can be seen as an unfolding of the consequences of the blurring of genres, a process that inevitably led to a kind of methodological nihilism. On what basis could a researcher now make a decision about which approach to take? On what basis could a researcher claim veracity or validity for his or her findings? How can a researcher, in practice, write himself or herself into the text? The answers to these questions have emerged slowly, and have necessitated a rethinking of basic issues. It no longer seems at all obvious to many researchers that they can capture in their field notes and interview tapes the actual lived experiences of 'informants'. Instead, the lived experience is created in and through the writing undertaken by the researcher. As a result, qualitative researchers have started to experiment

with new forms of representation, such as poems, images, dialogues and drama (Richardson, 1994).

5  *The fifth moment.* Denzin and Lincoln define the present as a 'fifth moment', characterised by a more action-oriented, political and pluralistic approach to qualitative research. They claim that the publication of their *Handbook* has helped to define and create this moment. However, one might suggest that it is always difficult to categorise what is happening in the present, particularly if one is a protagonist. Perhaps all that can be said is that there *is* a fifth moment.

The five-stage scheme proposed by Denzin and Lincoln needs to be seen as a heuristic device, rather than as an eternal truth. Indeed, they soon decided that they could identify a 'sixth moment' (Lincoln, 1995), characterised by postmodern relativism (Denzin, 1997). The implication of their model is that one stage is, to a large extent, replaced by the next, that the modernist tendency is swept away by the age of blurred genres. This has not happened, or at least not in such a clear-cut manner. The styles of qualitative inquiry associated with earlier periods – traditional and modernist – are alive and well, continuing to sustain many careers and generate large numbers of publications. Denzin and Lincoln perhaps underestimate the potential for conflict between the alternative styles of qualitative research. They downplay the tensions and debates within the qualitative movement by presenting its history in terms of a series of stages of development.

The Denzin and Lincoln framework can be applied to the body of qualitative research into counselling and psychotherapy. It seems very clear that the traditional stage in qualitative therapy research centred around the work of the writers of the early psychoanalytic case studies. Just like the 'Lone Ethnographer', the brave psychoanalyst would venture into dangerous and unknown territory, to return with objective data that could be spun into dazzling theory. Just like the ethnographer, the psychoanalyst underwent his or her own initiation in the field, and was able to claim immense personal authority. Just like the ethnographer, the psychoanalyst created classic, eternal, 'museumlike' studies that could be revisited again and again by new generations of students.

The second stage in the development of qualitative research, the modernist phase, is also clearly represented in the therapy qualitative research literature. In the 1980s, several researchers constructed systematic, rigorous approaches to qualitative research into therapy process. The most important of these have been the Comprehensive Process Analysis of Robert Elliott (see Chapter 8), the work of David Rennie (Chapter 6) on applying grounded theory analysis to therapy data, and the methods of empirical phenomenology as expressed in the work of the Duquesne University group (see Chapter 3). In the 1990s, Clara Hill has also been developing a rigorous system for qualitative therapy research (Chapter 9). The modernist tenor of the work of this group of researchers can be seen in their collaborative attempt to define a set of quality criteria on qualitative research that could be employed by editors of psychotherapy and counselling journals (Chapter 11). What has been happening has been very much an effort to *formalise* the methods of qualitative research into therapy.

Qualitative therapy research does not appear to have progressed beyond the modernist phase to any significant degree. Because of the domination of psychotherapy research by medically and psychologically trained researchers, and the importance of medical funding, the progress of qualitative research into therapy has been much slower than in disciplines such as nursing, teaching and management. In addition, the power, status and influence of psychoanalysis, including the use of the psychoanalytic case study as a research method, has exerted a strong pull on the field. While ethnography has evolved more or less continuously over the last century as succeeding generations of researchers have reflected on the nature of ethnographic inquiry, this has not happened to any degree in psychoanalysis. In many ways psychoanalytic and psychodynamic therapeutic *practice* has grown and developed, but the method of advancing knowledge through case studies written by clinicians from their process notes has remained basically unchanged.

'Blurring of genres' and the 'crisis of representation' have not hit therapy research yet. It can only be assumed that all this is yet to come, that the current uneasy calm that pervades the little world of counselling and psychotherapy qualitative research is about to be shattered by the clamour of the voices of reflexivity, feminism, hermeneutics and so on.

It seems likely that therapy research will follow other areas of qualitative research in moving in these directions. This is not just because other disciplines have followed this path, but because there is an inevitability about blurring and crisis. The act of carrying out qualitative research, if it is done in the spirit of 'human science', inevitably leads researchers into a realm of critical reflexivity. The apparent certainties of modernist methodological formulations just do not work. Qualitative inquiry generates uncertainty, ambiguity, a sense of the unknowability of things, a loss of boundary between self and other. These are experiences that cannot easily be contained within a set of standardised research procedures, or, to put it another way, *should not* be so contained. It is the willingness to enter fully into a process of inquiry, a willingness to draw upon (or risk) one's integrity as a person, that gives the best qualitative research its 'edge'. There is an echo here of the risks taken by 'Lone Ethnographers'. Yet while it is not helpful to over-romanticise this aspect of research, neither is it useful to deny the importance of the personal meaning of this kind of work, and the links between the degree of personal investment – at all levels – and the quality of the final product.

# The historical development of research in counselling and psychotherapy

The growing interest shown by counsellors and psychotherapists in qualitative methods of inquiry is not accidental, or mere fashion, or only a by-product of wider trends within psychology and social science. Rather, the increased attention being paid to qualitative inquiry reflects a basic shift in the nature of psychotherapy. Therapists are drawn to different ways of exploring their practice because the practice itself is changing.

There is a necessary relationship between the historical development of a profession or academic discipline and the methods of inquiry which it espouses. At the beginning of the formation of a discipline, the requirement is for descriptive research, usually in the form of case studies, which function to establish the parameters of the discipline, define its key questions and knowledge domain, introduce concepts, document what pioneers are up to, and generally persuade the appropriate audiences that this new discipline is something distinctive and worthwhile and deserving of support. As the discipline or profession becomes established, research moves toward consolidating the status quo. Kuhn (1962) has called this 'normal science'. The basic product is known, the task now is to look at some of its properties with the aim of refining and improving it. The criterion for good 'normal' research is not that it is persuasive or innovative (as in the previous stage in the history of the discipline) but that it is reliable and repeatable.

The movement from stage one (forming the discipline or profession) to stage two (consolidation and routinisation) is only possible if institutional and statutory approval is obtained. Danziger (1990, 1997a) has documented some of the moves in this process in relation to the establishment of psychology as an academic discipline in the period from 1870 to about 1930. Danziger points out that at the beginning of this period there existed a diversity of approaches to psychological inquiry, whereas by the end the method of laboratory experimentation and statistical analysis of data was dominant. For example, in the 1870s Wundt and other German investigators were carrying out studies in which the roles of researcher and 'subject' were interchangeable. By the 1930s very few studies of this type were being conducted or reported. Psychology had established itself by adopting the methods of the natural sciences, which included the assumption of passive 'objects' of investigation.

A similar process can be seen to have taken place in psychotherapy, but over a more extended period of time. The pioneers of psychotherapy, such as Freud and Rogers, used case reports both to explore the nature of how they worked with clients, and to publicise their approach. In their early publications there is no sense that what is happening is the routine application of a fixed method of inquiry; different methods are used in different papers. It was only in the 1950s and 60s that research into both client-centred and psychoanalytic psychotherapy became 'routinised' in the form of the widely adopted process and outcome measures which are still in use today. A useful account of historical trends in the evolution of psychotherapy research can be found in Russell (1994).

It is remarkable how little attention has been given to the history of counselling and psychotherapy (although, see Cushman, 1995). However, it is clear that, although psychotherapy existed in the period 1890–1950, its main expansion took place in the latter half of the twentieth century. From the 1940s through to the 1970s the main professional associations were formed, and the principal models of practice and settings for practice were established. During this time, leading figures and institutional groups in counselling and psychotherapy have continuously worked to demonstrate their legitimacy in the face of professional rivalry from psychiatrists, social workers and to some extent clergy, and in the face of a background of scepticism from some sectors of the public (see Hasenfeld, 1992). In this struggle, the legitimacy of psychotherapy has been reinforced by its allegiance to key values of modernity such as individualism, progress, and belief in science. Nevertheless, psychotherapy has needed to fight hard to keep its place in a culture where many people believe also in biological explanations of character and conduct, or equate emotion with weakness.

At the same time, psychotherapy has been internally divided, into competing approaches or schools of thought. These schools have sought legitimacy in relation to each other in a variety of ways, including the use of research findings to demonstrate their effectiveness, to signal their acceptance of rational, scientific values, and to ease their entry into the academy.

The importance for the counselling and psychotherapy community of these two forms of legitimacy – external and internal – has resulted in a preference for forms of knowledge-making that have been primarily concerned with being able to convince other people of the truth of statements already believed by the inquirer to be true. Therapy research has sought to establish the plausibility of statements such as 'therapy relieves the symptoms of depression in the majority of cases' or 'the type of therapy we practise here is particularly effective because . . .'. Although everyone knows that research cannot 'prove' anything, and that there are no 'facts' in the social sciences, the kinds of research articles that have been published on therapy (the official scientific knowledge base) rely heavily on a rhetoric of facticity and objectivity, with the methods section often being the lengthiest part of a research paper. It is seldom that psychotherapy researchers report 'discoveries' such as new phenomena or new theoretical models. In psychotherapy, the discoveries, such as they are, arise in practice, and the role of research has been to verify or 'test' them.

All research in the psychological and social sciences can be viewed as comprising an interplay between verification and discovery. The motivation for embarking on a piece of research arises from some mix of a wish to be able to demonstrate that already known propositions are true (verification) and a wish to generate new propositions about the world (discovery). Even in the most hypothesis-driven experimental research a failure to support the hypothesis can be seen as a discovery, a first step in the direction of a new proposition about the phenomenon being studied. Even in the most tightly controlled experimental studies, there are always some findings that defy categorisation within the explicit conceptual framework of the study, and require a search for ad hoc explanation. Conversely, in even the most discovery-oriented qualitative studies, findings will not be plausible unless they are to some degree 'obvious', in affirming at least some aspects of taken-for-granted everyday reality. Radical qualitative inquiry which seeks to deconstruct everyday reality must still verify enough of the routine and the familiar to make sense to readers. However, although verification and discovery are *both* present in all research, the relative emphasis given to one or the other differs according to the aims of the investigators. In psychotherapy research, the goal of verification has prevailed for a considerable period of time.

There are at least three reasons why verificationist, rather than discovery-oriented, research has dominated the therapy field. First, as already mentioned, verificationist research is an effective strategy for building legitimacy. Second, the academic disciplines that have hosted the bulk of therapy research – psychology and psychiatry – have been dominated by hypothesis-testing, experimental research designs. Third, the majority of therapists have received training which does not encourage, prepare or motivate them to become involved in research. Training is mainly oral and practical, with much time being given to socialisation into the set of practices and world-view represented by the training institute. On the whole, counsellors and psychotherapists learn to have little interest in research, and have low expectations that research might actually help them in their everyday work with clients.

But things are beginning to change. It is difficult to know the extent to which these changes arise from a general shift in the direction of what has been called a 'postmodern' culture, or whether they are specific to the world of therapy. The pressure to prove legitimacy certainly still exists, most recently in the pressure to conform to state health policies in Europe and the USA over the restriction of funding to 'evidence-based' or 'empirically-validated' forms of care. What has changed in this domain is the realisation that, if more than 1,000 controlled trials of the efficacy of therapy cannot convince people that it works then maybe it is time to try other ways of making the case. The rigidity of the divisions within therapy, into competing schools or approaches, is dissolving as more and more practitioners describe themselves as 'integrationist' in theoretical orientation. The consolidation of counsellor and psychotherapist training in universities has meant that staff members have been exposed to a variety of different modes of research and inquiry through contact with colleagues in other faculties and departments.

These factors have contributed to the adoption of a rhetoric of 'pluralism' in the psychotherapy research community. Beginning with a paper by Howard (1983), many counsellors, psychotherapists and researchers have apparently accepted that it is important to acknowledge the value of a diversity of research approaches, encompassing qualitative as well as quantitative methods. A highly significant signal of the acceptability of qualitative methods came in the fourth edition of the authoritative *Handbook of Psychotherapy and Behavior Change*, published in 1994, in which the editors and some contributors publicly asserted the value of methodological pluralism (Bergin and Garfield, 1994a).

Curiously, despite this kind of high-level support, qualitative research remains on the margins of the counselling and psychotherapy research enterprise. Few qualitative papers are being published, relative to the number of quantitative studies, and its proponents have needed to promote the cause of qualitative inquiry through the medium of special issues of journals rather than merely waiting for these journals to respond in the normal way to a flood of qualitative submissions which has never materialised. Suspecting that perhaps some journal editors might be prejudiced against qualitative papers, the champions of qualitative psychotherapy research have even sought to help journal editors treat qualitative papers equitably by providing them with guidelines for assessing the merit of qualitative research (see Chapter 11). There have also been special conferences, workshops and training events of qualitative research in counselling and psychotherapy. None of this seems to have made much of a difference: few qualitative papers are being published.

## The problem with qualitative research in psychotherapy

The *Handbook of Qualitative Research*, published in 1994 (Denzin and Lincoln, 1994a) has already been cited several times in this chapter. This book is generally considered to provide a definitive picture of the field of qualitative research in the 1990s. The journals *Qualitative Inquiry* and *Qualitative Health Research* are widely accepted as publishing at the 'cutting edge' of qualitative research. There is an absence of papers and chapters on counselling and psychotherapy research in these important publication outlets. While other applied disciplines such as education, social work, nursing and management studies are amply represented, there is no sign of qualitative writing on therapy. Why is this? What is the problem with qualitative research in psychotherapy?

There are several problems associated with qualitative psychotherapy research. These can be divided into two broad categories: practical and basic. Practical problems are associated with a range of everyday operational hassles that prevent people from doing qualitative therapy research. Basic problems relate to the underlying meaning of the research, and its social and institutional significance.

It is possible to generate a list of practical problems surrounding qualitative therapy research. This list might include:

- collecting qualitative data from clients or patients, for example through interviews, can be intrusive and demanding, and therefore ethically questionable; reporting rich qualitative data (for example client narratives) may compromise confidentiality;
- the majority of those who carry out research (such as postgraduate students in clinical or counselling psychology) will probably have received excellent training in experimental design and statistics, but minimal training in qualitative methods;
- it is difficult, and takes a long time, to write qualitative papers; it is hard to condense qualitative findings into the word limits usually imposed on journal articles; journal reviewers may be unfamiliar with qualitative research and inappropriately apply judgement criteria drawn from a quantitative paradigm;
- to be good at qualitative research it is useful to have a background in literary or cultural studies, sociology or philosophy;
- therapy research has been dominated by the question of outcome – qualitative methods do not appear to be suited for this kind of research question.

These are all very significant problems. On the other hand they have been addressed in a variety of ways, which are discussed in later chapters. It is evident that there are some individuals and groups who are able successfully to pursue qualitative therapy research and can be presumed to have managed to overcome these practical barriers. It seems reasonable to speculate, therefore, that the low volume and impact of qualitative research in counselling and psychotherapy can be attributed to more basic issues.

Qualitative research introduces a different set of relationships between therapy, society and 'knowledge'. It was argued earlier that the 'golden age' of therapy research, the period from the 1960s through to the mid-1980s which saw the accumulation of large numbers of controlled studies of outcomes, was characterised by social pressures to produce knowledge that could be used to consolidate, legitimate and verify the role of therapy in society. The basic problem with qualitative research is that it undermines these attempts to consolidate, legitimate and verify. Good qualitative research is intrinsically *discovery-oriented* and *critical*.

## The seventh moment: the relationship between qualitative research and psychotherapy practice

The five (or six) 'moments' of qualitative research suggested by Denzin and Lincoln (1994b), and summarised earlier in this chapter, refer for the most part to strands of qualitative inquiry that have been carried out for 'academic' purposes, with the aim of producing theoretical knowledge. Qualitative research in counselling and psychotherapy is fundamentally different from these previous qualitative traditions, because it necessarily addresses an area of *practice* with the goal of changing that practice. Qualitative research in counselling and psychotherapy differs from qualitative studies in other applied fields, such as nursing or education, in that the activity of doing qualitative research (identifying and clarifying meaning; learning how the meaning of aspects of the social world is constructed) is highly concordant with the activity of doing therapy (making new meaning, gaining insight and understanding, learning how personal meanings have been constructed). So, while qualitative research in domains such as nursing and education can focus on and 'separate off' the specific aspects of the professional work that are being investigated, qualitative research in therapy tends to lead in the direction of a questioning of basic assumptions and accepted practices. The application of qualitative methods to topics within counselling and psychotherapy inevitably leads in the direction of the deconstruction and reconstruction of therapy theory and practice.

It seems likely that the historical development of counselling and psychotherapy has reached a point where there is an awareness of the need for deconstruction and reconstruction of practice. The increasing popularity of qualitative methods among counselling and psychotherapy researchers (despite formidable practical and institutional barriers) reflects the perceived relevance of qualitative methods in a situation where therapy is being 're-invented' in response to cultural change. Such a development would also be significant for the broader field of qualitative research itself. Up until now, it has been sufficient for qualitative researchers to write largely for each other. The challenge of adapting qualitative methods to generate knowledge-for-practice brings a new edge to debates over relativism, generalisability, reflexivity and communicability in respect of the products of qualitative inquiry.

The 'problem' with qualitative therapy research delineated earlier, the absence of published qualitative studies despite vigorous championing, can be understood as resulting from a reluctance to embrace the possibilities of this approach, for fear of where it might lead. It is clear, to both the researchers themselves and the readers of their work, that qualitative research which adopts a verificationist, objectivist stance yields results that are not very interesting. Compelling and memorable qualitative research requires a willingness to step into what David Rennie (Chapter 6) has described as a 'period of darkness'. A recurring theme in later chapters of this book is the view held by key figures in qualitative research, from many different approaches, that the act of qualitative inquiry involves suspending and questioning the beliefs and 'pre-understandings' that one brings to the topic. This is a hard thing for therapy researchers who are also therapists to do.

To characterise qualitative research in counselling and psychotherapy as contributing to the deconstruction and reconstruction of therapy practice may seem an empty assertion. What does it mean to 're-invent' therapy? The role of qualitative research in therapy can be understood more concretely in terms of a number of discrete tasks.

## Reconfiguring therapy in response to social and cultural change

Counselling and psychotherapy are the contemporary versions of forms of healing, reconciliation, adjustment and meaning-making that exist in all cultures. Any approach to psychotherapy consists of some combination of the set of healing elements described by Jerome Frank (1974) and Carl Rogers (1961). The task of psychotherapy research is that of determining how best these elements can be configured to meet the needs of different clients, social groups, practitioners and settings. There are few, if any, fundamental new discoveries to be made in psychotherapy research. The contribution of research and inquiry lies in finding the most suitable ways to assemble and deliver a set of largely known therapeutic activities. In some situations, the contribution of research may involve rediscovering or re-emphasising therapeutic approaches and ideas that have been lost.

## Documenting and exploring the interface between therapy and other cultural forms

Modern society is characterised by a literate citizenship and open access to information. In addition, commercial interests (including the mass media) tend to appropriate ideas and symbols in the interest of making profit. As a result of both of these factors, the language and concepts developed by counsellors and psychotherapists become incorporated into everyday discourse, and as a consequence lose their capacity to provide therapy clients with a fresh and challenging vantage point from which to view their problems. In parallel, therapy itself appropriates and re-works the dominant and silenced discourses of the culture within which it is located. It is essential that therapy continues to 're-invent' itself. Research can play a part in documenting, stimulating and evaluating this on-going, dynamic, cultural process.

## Drawing attention to the structures of power and control

Counselling and psychotherapy exist at the intersection of liberation and social control. The unique personal / professional relationship that develops between client and therapist contains within it the potential to assist the person to be fully human in the sense of getting closer to the values and relationships that reflect their idea of the good life, and to participate meaningfully as a citizen. However, the intensity of this relationship also introduces the potential for manipulation and control. There are social forces, including both the state and commercial organisations, who may have an interest in co-opting therapy and therapists as agents of social control. There is a steady drift in the direction of further regulation, professionalisation and state licensing that brings with it increased pressure for therapy to become a means of social control. The continual reconstruction of therapy involves devising ways of resisting this external control and appropriation, and retaining the liberatory potential of counselling and psychotherapy. As will be seen in the following chapters, qualitative research in therapy has already opened up important new understandings of the power relationship between client and therapist.

## Creating a space for an affirmatory, pluralistic conception of therapy

For the most part, the types of counselling and psychotherapy that are practised today are the products of modernity, and reflect the values and world-view that have driven the expansion of modern industrial society: rationality, the primacy of scientific knowing, individualism, globalism, progress, militarism, avoidance of risk, heterosexism, mastery. It is becoming increasingly apparent to many people that this constellation of beliefs and constructs omits many central aspects of humanity: emotionality, faith, spirituality, community, tradition, mystery, respect for the natural environment, diverse sexualities. The reconstruction of therapy involves finding ways of incorporating these 'pre-modern' areas of experience into therapeutic practice. Here, the contribution of qualitative research lies in its capacity to approach research topics from a perspective of openness to different voices, a willingness to examine the historical 'archaeology' of therapeutic knowledge and an ability to deconstruct therapeutic language.

## The development of an interdisciplinary, 'postpsychological' therapy

Counselling and psychotherapy have prospered as components of what has been variously labelled the 'psy-complex' (Rose, 1990), or 'mental health industry' (Kovel, 1981). This is an international institutional network that is built around defining and explaining people's 'troubles' or 'problems in living' in psychological and psychiatric terms, and supplying forms of specialist professional intervention to resolve these troubles. Deregulation, improvements in consumer access to information, the emergence of new forms of professional roles, and the increasing importance of multi-culturalism, have all served to threaten different elements of this structure. Specifically, the idea that a 'therapeutic' relationship should solely or necessarily be built on the use of psychological terminology and under-standings has been questioned. There can be seen the beginnings of a *postpsychological* approach to counselling and psychotherapy (McLeod, 1999b), which appreciates the value of psychology but also knows its dangers, and which therefore seeks to operate from a fuller understanding of what it means to be human. Qualitative methods of inquiry are intrinsically both social (in demanding that the researcher takes account of the social and historical context of their work) and philosophical (in demanding that researchers position themselves in relation to core issues of being and knowledge). The adoption of qualitative methods thereby facilitates the spread of postpyschological thinking in counsellors and psychotherapists.

The relationship between counselling/psychotherapy and society is one in which therapy is continually reconstructed in response to changes in culture and society. Qualitative research is a form of knowing that is particularly attuned to the study of how aspects of social life (such as counselling and psychotherapy) are constructed and reconstructed. As the reconstruction of therapy has become more pressing, resulting from the impact of forces such as postmodernism, multiculturalism, consumerism and changes in health care governance, the need for qualitative research has grown. It can be argued that the present era in counselling and psychotherapy research is beginning to move beyond legitimation and verification and into a stage of discovery, adaptation and innovation.

Qualitative research in counselling and psychotherapy is a method of analysing the ways in which the 'world' of therapy is constructed. In doing so it has the potential to facilitate critical deconstruction and recon-struction of existing assumptions about what therapy is and how it works. The following chapters in this book trace the implications of this view through an examination of the methods and issues existing within present-day qualitative research in counselling and psychotherapy. The aim is to explore the ways in which different styles of qualitative research and inquiry operate in practice, and the types of contribution to knowledge which they make.

This chapter has presented an outline of the nature, context and goals of qualitative research in counselling and psychotherapy. The central themes explored in this chapter can be summarised in terms of a set of core questions:

- All qualitative research or inquiry is basically attempting to fulfil the same aim, which is that of developing an understanding of how the world is constructed. When reading a study, the following types of questions are relevant: How does the study contribute to an understanding of how this aspect of the world is constructed? What does the study highlight, but what processes of construction might it conceal or downplay?
- It is important to take into account the social and historical context within which qualitative research is carried out. An awareness of context leads to questions such as: What does the study *do*, in relation to the social world? Why was it carried out, and to what use will it be put?
- A postmodern perspective presents strong challenges to the qualitative research 'establishment', in particular by raising difficult questions about method and purpose, such as: Where is the authority? Whose story is being told, and who is telling it?

Behind these questions is an even more fundamental question: What is involved in doing *good* qualitative research? This opening chapter has set out the background to qualitative research in counselling and psychotherapy. In the following chapters the focus moves to a consideration of how to do qualitative research, and, a more challenging target, how to do it well.

# 2

# The Relevance and Contribution of Hermeneutics

Interpretation, in the sense relevant to hermeneutics, is an attempt to make clear, to make sense of an object of study. This object must, therefore, be a text, or text-analogue, which in some way is confused, incomplete, cloudy, seemingly contradictory – in some way or another, unclear. The interpretation aims to bring to light an underlying coherence or sense.

(Taylor, 1971: 3)

Hermeneutic human sciences study the objectivications of human cultural activity (texts, etc.) with a view to interpreting them, to find out the intended or at least the expressed meaning, in order to establish a co-understanding or possibly even consent which has not (yet) been obtained or repairing the same . . .; and in general, to mediate traditions so that the historical dialogue of mankind may be continued or reassumed, and also deepened. . . .

Texts, etc., will be judged important to the degree in which they are relevant for the practice of life, on the grounds that the heart of the human sciences is co-understanding and possibly also consent about the possibilities and norms of being-in-the-world. The interest in co-understanding about the phenomenon intended in the text . . . is, of course, not limited to contemporaries but will include the communication of the living with past generations through the transmission and mediation of traditions.

(Radnitzky, 1970: 22)

Hermeneutics is concerned with the interpretation of texts. In Greek mythology, Hermes was the messenger of the gods. Hermeneutics became established in the context of Scriptural interpretation: what was God's message as mediated by often incomplete or ambiguous fragments of Biblical text? A hermeneutic approach has subsequently been applied to a wide range of other texts, in fields such as literature, history and the law. In the twentieth century, hermeneutics has come to be seen by some commentators as a method, or perhaps even *the* method, of the social sciences. The philosopher Paul Ricoeur has argued that any human action can be regarded as a text, and interpreted. The influence of psychoanalysis, as a method of therapy and inquiry that relies strongly on interpretation, has been influential in relation to the acceptance of interpretive approaches within the social sciences.

This chapter examines the relevance of hermeneutics for qualitative research in counselling and psychotherapy. The nature of the relationship between qualitative psychotherapy research and hermeneutics has enormous implications for the conduct of research in this area. At the heart of this relationship is what is meant by the term 'hermeneutics'. The quotations from Taylor (1971) and Radnitzky (1970) presented above have been chosen to illustrate a central tension within discussions of hermeneutic approaches to psychology and social science: is hermeneutics merely a matter of using interpretation? The excerpt from Charles Taylor does not do justice to the richness of his thought on this matter, but captures one sense in which hermeneutics is understood. Hermeneutics is defined as an act of interpretation which 'bring[s] to light an underlying coherence or sense' within the actions, behaviour or utterances of a person or group. This view defines hermeneutics as 'interpretive' social science, which takes as its goal the achievement of 'understanding', without specifying any further what is implied by the act of interpreting, or the experience of understanding. In this usage of 'interpretive', the distinction is made between 'interpretive' social science and 'hypothetico-deductive' scientific method. Interpretive social scientists read texts and develop understandings; natural scientists carry out experiments to test hypotheses that are derived from explanatory models or theories. However, the notion of interpretation is kept broad, loose and unspecified.

It can be argued that what is properly meant by hermeneutics goes far beyond interpretation. At the risk of over-simplifying a complex and difficult area of intellectual endeavour, there would appear to be two main ways in which a true hermeneutic approach differs from an interpretive approach. First, hermeneutics is essentially a culturally and historically informed method. Second, to work properly as a system for producing reliable and practical knowledge, hermeneutics requires the existence of publicly accessible data. Neither of these factors is necessary to conduct an inquiry that is simply 'interpretive'.

The quotation from Radnitzky (1970) is a distillation of centuries of philosophical debate over how to arrive at valid interpretations, and the meanings of truth, validity and understanding in this context. Scholars of hermeneutics are aware of a line of methodological development stretching back to the Middle Ages (Mueller-Vollmer, 1985). In the course of these discussions, a broad agreement has emerged, exemplified in the writings of Gadamer (1975), that hermeneutics involves the appreciation that a successful interpretation is from a perspective, takes place from a position within history, requires sensitivity to the use of language, and leads to a shift (or learning) on the part of the person making the interpretation.

Some of this is captured in Radnitzky's (1970) encapsulation of the aim of hermeneutics: 'to mediate traditions so that the historical dialogue of mankind may be continued or reassumed, and also deepened'.

The argument here is that any text is created in a cultural-historical context, and is then interpreted in a different context. If we shared the same context as the originator of the text, we would presumably understand it well enough: it is the dislocation in time and place that makes interpretation necessary. Our attempt to understand the text is framed by what Gadamer (1975) has called 'historical consciousness'. Our understanding of anything, whether text or event, is built up from a set of cultural constructs, embodied in language. The act of understanding, for Gadamer, involves the coming together of the historical understanding or world of the interpreter, and that of the text. This 'fusion of horizons' may represent a moment of insight and transformation for the interpreter, but, more crucially, it signifies an act of continuing and deepening, or enriching, the cultural-historical tradition of which the interpreter is a member. As Gadamer (1975: 290) has put it: 'understanding is to be thought of less as a subjective act than as participating in an event of a tradition'.

It is this insistence on *tradition* that distinguishes hermeneutics from a broader interpretive social science. Hermeneutics can be understood as 'tradition-informed' inquiry, in the sense that questions that are being investigated are always viewed not only in their cultural-historical context but from the context or tradition of the researcher. We cannot step outside culture and history. We can only make sense of action in terms of the value, virtues and story of the good life that prevail within our cultural world. Hermeneutics insists that we accept and embrace these realities, rather than pretending that we can achieve a knowledge of human affairs that somehow transcends culture and history. The way we can achieve useful understandings of human affairs is to enter fully into dialogue.

Gadamer (1975) identifies the Enlightenment as a crucial turning point in European cultural life. The Enlightenment promoted rationality and empiricism as antidotes to tradition. Anything traditional was regarded with suspicion and subjected to close critical re-examination. In Gadamer's phrase, the Enlightenment saw the beginnings of a 'prejudice against prejudice', and the construction of a modern world in which social life could apparently be re-invented on rational, social-scientific grounds. But this is impossible if we live within history, and in communities which perpetuate traditions. Every act of hermeneutic understanding begins with a pre-understanding, which orients the inquirer in relation to the text or topic. One of the tasks of the hermeneutic scholar is to become aware of and reflexively to explicate this pre-understanding in a way that creatively feeds in to the process of understanding itself.

It is essential to appreciate that hermeneutics is not just interpretation, but is tradition-informed interpretation. This characteristic marks hermeneutics out from all the other principal approaches to qualitative research in counselling and psychotherapy (for example, phenomenology, grounded theory and discourse analysis) that are discussed in subsequent chapters of this book. In a later section of this chapter, an example of a piece of hermeneutic psychotherapy research is discussed. It will be seen that this is a radical method, whose results challenge many of the prevailing assumptions of the therapy profession.

The second basic difference between hermeneutics and interpretation lies in the nature of the data or text being analysed. Interpretivist psychotherapy research can be carried out in relation to virtually any kind of text: therapy session transcripts, interview material, ethnographic fieldwork notes, client written accounts of the most helpful event in a therapy session, etc. Hermeneutic inquiry, on the other hand, is a method that has been developed to enable the study of documents (texts) that are in the public domain, or at least are sufficiently accessible to be known to at least some of the readers of a research report. The classical application of hermeneutics has been within Biblical exegesis. Clearly, anyone reading the interpretive writings of Biblical scholars would be highly familiar with the original text (Scripture) that was being analysed. Later, when hermeneutic ideas began to be applied to literary and legal texts, it could still be assumed that the audience for the interpretation would have read the original object of the interpretation.

The story that is always told about hermeneutics, as a kind of introduction to the approach, is that it originally developed within the field of Biblical scholarship, in the efforts of theologians to interpret the meaning of Scriptural texts. The task of the hermeneuticist was to uncover God's true message within the pages of the Bible. There are several observations one can make about the specificity of this research situation. First, the text itself is clearly sacred, and possesses meaning that is of great importance. Second, not only does the hermeneutic inquirer come to the text with a strong set of pre-understandings, but *so does the reader of the hermeneuticist's eventual interpretation or findings.* These two aspects of what might be called an original hermeneutic method carry with them a number of consequences that do not sit easily alongside contemporary research practice. The sacredness of a Biblical text, or indeed other texts studied by early hermeneuticists, such as myths, plays and legal cases, meant that the inquirer adopted, at least in principle, an attitude that there might be something worth discovering that might take him or her beyond their current framework of understanding. As Gadamer (1975) has put it, the text asks questions of the inquirer. (In conventional qualitative research it is the reverse.) This 'sacredness' meant also that many different inquirers were willing to have a go at the task, leading to a multiplicity of competing or contrasting readings. The criticism that is often made of contemporary qualitative research, that it produces one-sided, subjective or biased accounts of phenomena, is less compelling in a situation where there already exist many alternative accounts of the same phenomenon. The concept of 'sacredness' also inverts conventional current thinking about sampling procedures in research. For a Biblical scholar, as far as Biblical texts are concerned, n = 1. There is no escape from interpretive difficulties in arguing that the case is not representative and that a larger sample is required.

The position of the reader of a hermeneutic study likewise raises a number of difficulties for current research approaches. If I am a Shakespeare scholar and I read a new interpretation of Hamlet, then I am in a position of both knowing the original text inside out, and of possessing my own interpretive pre-understanding of the play, which I would have worked out for myself well in advance of reading the new interpretive study. Thus, when I read a new study I am in a good position to evaluate this new interpretation in the light of my criteria for interpretive plausibility. Most of the time, none of this is true for readers of psychotherapy research. Readers of psychotherapy research are fed selected bits of the text. Even when the research is carried out within narrative analysis or discourse analysis traditions (see Chapter 7), which recommend the presentation of extended extracts of text within a paper, readers do not have the time to arrive at their own understanding of the text before being presented with the analysis carried out by the author. Even in an explicitly hermeneutic study, such as Walsh et al. (1999), despite the best efforts of the researchers to present informants' 'texts' to the reader, there is an insufficient basis for the reader to make up his or her own mind about it: the researcher/author remains in control. A way of looking at the positioning of the reader in 'original' hermeneutic inquiry and in contemporary qualitative research is depicted in Figure 2.1. For those of us reading qualitative research papers today, rather than actually being in a position directly to evaluate whether the author's interpretation has enhanced *our* understanding of the text, we are largely limited to witnessing the author's assertion that the interpretation has enhanced *his* or *her* understanding. The elaborate methodological details that are provided by most writers of qualitative psychotherapy research can be viewed as forms of rhetoric designed to convince us of the truth-claims, or understanding-claims, made by the author(s) of research papers. The qualitative researcher is engaged in a kind of covert battle with his or her readers, trying to defend himself or herself against anticipated claims that findings are not supported by evidence, that the 'paper-trail' is not convincing. But a truly hermeneutic approach allows the author to do without much of this type of rhetoric, and concentrate his or her rhetorical skills on conveying just what the interpretation is that they are offering; readers can make up their own minds how useful it is for them. This is why, within psychotherapy research, the most successful examples of hermeneutic analysis have been studies where the 'text' has been in the public domain, as with Cushman's (1995) historical research and Greenberg's (1994) exploration of the meaning of the self-help literature.

For these two reasons – tradition-informed inquiry and public preknowledge of the text – it is clear that a merely interpretivist approach does

In qualitative research

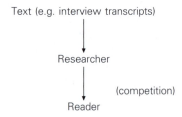

In hermeneutic inquiry

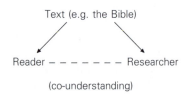

Figure 2.1   Positioning of researcher, reader and text

not do justice to hermeneutics of the kind envisaged by Gadamer and other philosophers. Hermeneutics is basically a form of cultural inquiry that seeks to construct a historical understanding of the experience and realities of other persons. The success of hermeneutic studies, in terms of producing knowledge that can lead to action, depends on the existence of a community of scholars willing and able to engage in dialogue over alternative interpretations of 'sacred' texts. It is only within such a collective framework of inquiry that research and scholarly activity can effectively inform tradition.

## Main principles of a hermeneutic approach to inquiry

Given its philosophical origins, it is not hard to see why there have been few attempts to systematise hermeneutics into a set of step-by-step methodological procedures. Nevertheless, it is possible to extract a number of key methodological principles that can be used to guide hermeneutic research. These are briefly outlined below.

### *Hermeneutic inquiry is a process of interpreting a text*

This is the core idea that underpins hermeneutics; it is reinforced by frequent references to the origins of hermeneutics in the myth of Hermes, messenger of the gods, and the use of hermeneutics in revealing the meaning of Biblical texts.

## The hermeneutic circle

Inquiry proceeds by building up an interpretation, through moving back and forth between the part and the whole. This involves: gaining a sense of the meaning of the whole text, and then using that as a framework for understanding fragments of the text; carrying out micro-analysis of the possible meanings of small sections of text, and using these to challenge or re-interpret the overall sense of the total text.

## Use of empathy

Sensitive interpretation requires developing a personal sense of under-standing of the emotional and interpersonal worlds, and cultural-historical situation of the person(s) who generated the text.

## Achieving a comprehensive, coherent interpretation

The end-point of an effective hermeneutic analysis is a reading which encompasses all aspects of the text.

## Speaking from within a tradition

The researcher is a member of a community or tradition, and his or her reading of the text is informed and shaped by the values, beliefs and 'prejudices' of that tradition ('no knowledge without foreknowledge'). The aim of hermeneutic inquiry includes not only that of assimilating the text into the tradition, but also that of expanding and enriching the 'pre-understandings' of members of the tradition:

> Long before we understand ourselves in retrospective reflection, we understand ourselves in self-evident ways in the family, society and state in which we live. The focus of subjectivity is a distorting mirror. The self-reflection of the individual is only a flicker in the closed circuits of historical life. (Gadamer, 1975: 245)

> The world of human experience must be studied from the point of view of the historically and culturally situated individual. (Denzin and Lincoln, 1994a: 512)

## Innovation and creativity

Hermeneutics is not merely a matter of imposing a pre-existing set of interpretive concepts or categories on a text, but requires a genuine act of discovery: 'the interpretation goes beyond the immediately given and enriches the understanding by bringing forth new differentiations and interrelationships in the text, extending its meaning' (Kvale, 1996: 50).

## Fusion of horizons

The criterion of a satisfactory hermeneutic study is that both text and researcher are changed: 'understanding . . . involves a transformation of the initial positions of both "text" and "interpreter" in a "fusion of horizons" or consensus over meaning' (Warnke, 1987: 107). The emphasis on fusion of horizons and arriving at consensus over meaning reflects the *dialogical* nature of hermeneutic work. There is always on openness to hermeneutic inquiry, in the awareness that whatever accont the hermeneutic researcher has to offer is in response to earlier interpretive endeavours, and will itself in turn be assimilated into later turns in the conversation.

These principles can be seen as reflecting a combination of both *ontological* and *epistemological* hermeneutic ideas. Ontology refers to ways of understanding the basic nature of persons, their core being. Ontological hermeneutics is a way of understanding that views people as existing within multiple horizons of meaning, as striving to make sense of their experience, as constituted by their cultural and historical context, as engaged in dialogue. Epistemology, on the other hand, refers to the way in which people gain knowledge about the world and come to regard some beliefs as true and others as false. Epistemological hermeneutics, therefore, is a body of philosophical writing that has examined the value and limitations of an interpretive approach to knowledge creation. For example, the notion of the hermeneutic circle is an important element of epistemological hermeneutics. A hermeneutic methodology for social science relies on both ontological and epistemological hermeneutic principles.

## Social constructionism as a contemporary expression of hermeneutics

Social constructionism, as exemplified in the work of Kenneth Gergen (1985, 1994a, b, 1997), represents a contemporary approach to social science which honours the spirit of the hermeneutic tradition. Moreover, the writings of philosophers such as Gadamer provide a valuable added dimension to social constructionist inquiry. A social constructionist approach is basically *critical* and non-foundational, in the sense of opening up all aspects of a phenomenon to interpretive scrutiny. A good social constructionist study, therefore, will strive to deconstruct the concepts used by both researcher and researcher participants, may question why the research was carried out, may look at the implications of how a paper is written. There is no basis on which anyone can claim a privileged position in relation to knowledge. Any such claims can be seen as unwarranted strategies to gain power and control over the phenomenon in question. Second, social constructionist research widens the interpretive horizon to include the cultural and historical context within which the study is located. Social constructionism seeks to understand the ways in which the world is co-constructed by persons living within a cultural tradition. Again, both research informants/participants and researchers are embedded within cultural traditions. The researcher cannot claim a uniquely objective, 'God's-eye' view of things. Third, a social constructionist perspective opens up for reflection and consideration the ways in which people *use* psychological concepts such as 'the self'. The notion of the self as an entity, as an autonomous, boundaried locus of decision-making and intention, may be the way that many people in western societies make sense of who they are, but from a social constructionist perspective this can be understood as constructed, as mediated through many different forms of cultural practice. Psychotherapy itself is viewed as a cultural practice which sustains the idea of an autonomous, bounded self.

## An example of hermeneutic inquiry: the work of Philip Cushman

The research by Philip Cushman into the development of a historical awareness of the rise of psychotherapy in the USA represents the single most significant example of hermeneutic inquiry in the field of counselling and psychotherapy. In a series of publications, Cushman (1990, 1992, 1995) has examined the social and cultural factors which have shaped the evolution of therapy. His key book, *Constructing the Self, Constructing America: A Cultural History of Psychotherapy* (Cushman, 1995) provides the best illustration of his method. To understand Cushman's approach, it is helpful to begin with his opening statement in the book, where he sets out the 'problematic' as he sees it:

> We take psychotherapy for granted today. It is such a normal, everyday aspect of our lives that we rarely look at it, wonder about it, question it. It is certainly true that we criticize psychotherapy and make jokes about it, but we criticize it as we would the weather. For late twentieth-century urban Americans, psychotherapy is a given; it is an unquestionable part of our world . . . When social

> artefacts or institutions are taken for granted it usually means that they have
> developed functions in the society that are so integral to the culture that they
> are indispensable, unacknowledged, and finally invisible. So what, then, *are*
> psychotherapy's sociopolitical functions? What part does psychotherapy play
> in the complicated cultural landscape of late twentieth-century America? How
> does psychotherapy either add to or challenge the status quo . . .? (Cushman,
> 1995: 1)

Here, it can be seen that Cushman takes as his 'text', the everyday
experience of psychotherapy within American urban life. This 'text' is
something that is accessible to all of his readers, to a greater or lesser extent,
and all of them could claim to have an understanding of the meaning of that
text (that is, an understanding of what therapy is and what it aims to
achieve). But Cushman, as with the classical Biblical hermeneuticists,
suggests that the meaning of the text is not clear. Beyond our taken-for-
granted understanding of this text there is, potentially, a deeper and richer
understanding to be revealed. And, following Gadamer, the best way to
acquire that richer understanding is to study the phenomenon both from a
historical perspective and from the perspective of its current horizons: 'in
order to understand American psychotherapy, we must study the world into
which it was born and in which it currently resides' (Cushman, 1995: 4).
The basis of his approach in a social constructionist philosophical hermeneutics is succinctly explained on pages 17–23 of *Constructing America*.

The scope of the hermeneutic analysis attempted by Cushman (1995)
stretches from the 1730s (Protestant revival meetings) to the 1960s (self-
liberation through consumerism: post-World War II object relations
theory, self psychology, and the empty self). Even the briefest reflection on
the scale of this undertaking brings an appreciation of the difficulties of
this kind of work. Where to begin? How to organise the mass of cultural
and historical material that might be collected? How to decide what
was relevant and what was not? In order to structure his research,
Cushman decided to divide up the 250-year period in which he was
interested into a series of separate eras, so that each era could be described
and discussed in turn. To facilitate his identification of eras, and to orient
his exploration of the main cultural themes relevant to psychotherapy
within each era, Cushman organised his data collection and analysis
around four 'signposts':

1   the predominant configuration of the self of a particular cultural or
    historical 'clearing';
2   the illnesses with which that self was characteristically afflicted;
3   the institutions or officials most responsible for healing those illnesses;
4   the technologies that the particular institutions or practitioners have
    used in order to heal that self's characteristic illnesses. (Cushman,
    1995: 25)

These 'signposts' can be seen as a device for enabling the researcher to move backward and forward between the figure and ground, detail and context (the hermeneutic circle). They provided the specification for the kinds of detailed textual evidence that needed to be collected, but in a manner that was always consistent with the overall aims and 'sense' of the study as a whole. 'Signposts' are a practical means of productively focusing analytic time and energy.

The cultural and historical material used by Cushman (1995) almost entirely consists of secondary sources. He draws mainly on books and articles written by cultural, social and economic historians, rather than carrying out primary research in archives or through the collection of oral histories. It would not be practicable to undertake a study on the scale of *Constructing America* based on primary sources. One advantage of Cushman's use of secondary sources, from a hermeneutic perspective, is that the texts he used are readily at hand in the public domain. His work can also be used, hopefully, by subsequent researchers, as a guide to areas or topics for further primary research.

*Constructing America* concludes with two chapters which return to Cushman's initial question: 'what are psychotherapy's sociopolitical functions?' These chapters, on 'Psychotherapy as moral discourse' and 'The politics of the self', return the reader to an examination of the meaning of psychotherapy in contemporary society. The purpose of the kind of hermeneutic research carried out by Cushman is not to 'do history' but to develop an appreciation of the historical construction of a 'text' that exists now. The aim is to expand the 'historical consciousness' through which we read that text. In doing so there is a 'fusion of horizons', as the horizon of understanding with which we began the quest opens to assimilate and accommodate ideas and sensibilities from the other (historical and cultural) horizons encountered along the way.

Other examples of psychotherapy research conducted from a social constructionist hermeneutic stance include Greenberg's (1994) study of the self-help literature, and my own case analysis presented in McLeod (1997, chapter 7). The concept of 'hermeneutics' that has been adopted by some other psychotherapy researchers, for example in the studies by Jackson and Patton (1992), Packer (1985) and Walsh et al. (1999), seems to derive from a more limited definition of the term, concentrating more on a narrowly conceived interpretive approach rather than on critical, culturally sensitive, 'tradition-informed' work in the spirit of Gadamer and Gergen. The edited collection by Messer, Sass and Woolfolk (1988) provides insight into the contested nature of hermeneutic approaches to research in psychology and psychotherapy. The essay by Woolfolk, Sass and Messer in that book gives a clear account of the interplay between the different positions that exist within thinking about hermeneutics. Packer and Addison (1989) represents another important source for those interested in exploring more deeply the application of a hermeneutic perspective in psychology.

## Hermeneutics and psychoanalysis

For counsellors and psychotherapists, it may be of particular relevance to examine the tension between an interpretive and a fully hermeneutic approach to inquiry in the context of debates over the role of psycho-analysis as a form of research. As Kvale (2000) has pointed out, psy-choanalysis has made an enormous contribution to the development of psychology and psychotherapy. He suggests that, if psychoanalytic or psychoanalytically inspired ideas were deleted from standard psychology textbooks, there would be little left to read. And yet, despite the theoretical generativity and heuristic value of psychoanalytic ideas, few members of the counselling and psychotherapy research community would accept that the psychoanalytic case study could be regarded as a valid (in any sense of that term) research method.

One of the most influential critics of the psychoanalytic case study has been the psychoanalyst Donald Spence (1989). In an important paper examining the relationship between psychoanalysis and hermeneutics, Spence (1993) makes clear the difference between imposing an interpretive framework on 'data' that are not open to public scrutiny, and are selected to conform to the assumptions of the interpreter, and a hermeneutic approach which takes cultural context, personal reflexivity and the possi-bility of alternative 'readings' into account. He characterises psycho-analytic inquiry in the following terms:

> . . . we have no public archive of clinical happenings that is open to any interested party, our 'data', largely stored as memories, [are] all the time shaped by whatever theory is most popular. And because the 'data' are largely illusory, we have no chance to build theory from the bottom up, the usual way. Psychoanalysis is a top-down science, pure and simple. With no data to contra-dict them, theories run wild, and their rhetorical voice – and not their content – plays a large role in their persuasive appeal. (Spence, 1993: 3)

In practice, a 'top-down' approach means that debate is stifled and the accuracy of an interpretation is established and mantained by force of authority rather than through open, reasoned dialogue. The field therefore keeps coming back to the core ideas promulgated by authority figures, rather than making genuine intellectual progress: 'repeated references to Freud are not the same as a growing body of replicated findings' (Spence, 1993: 2). The only way to break out of this cycle is to adopt a radical hermeneutic approach:

> Until we can appreciate the extent to which our theory is the projection of the zeitgeist, we will always be at the mercy of our context. Here is where the hermeneutic left has the most to contribute, because until this point is recog-

nised, we will continue to make 'discoveries' that are little more than projections. (ibid.: 7)

Finding ways *not* to produce 'discoveries that are little more than projections' was just what Schleiermacher, Gadamer and other hermeneutic methodologists have been trying to do for the last several centuries. Any interpretive methodology that restricts its horizons within the limits of a single system of ideas lacks the possibility for critical inquiry. No matter how powerful the initial set of ideas might be, all that can happen in a purely interpretive approach is that they become reproduced over and over. It is only when the interpretive framework is forced to engage with the messy, ambiguous cultural context within which it seeks to operate that a creative 'fusion of horizons' can take place.

In a commentary on Spence's (1993) paper, Jerome Bruner (1993) argues that the effect of the interpretive stance taken by psychoanalysts has been to 'bind them in a common secret'. How much better it would have been, he suggests, if Freud had bestowed upon his colleagues 'the gift for ensuring that there were always interesting strangers in the house'.

## Conclusion: hermeneutics, social constructionism, and the reconstruction of psychotherapy research

Hermeneutics is an approach to human science which has been around for a long time. As a result, there exist many contrasting understandings of what hermeneutics is about, and how it can be applied. The term 'hermeneutic' has been generally adopted to describe any approach to qualitative inquiry that places particular emphasis on the act of interpretation. In this chapter, it has been argued that a generalist definition of hermeneutics runs the danger of denying and losing many of its most valuable characteristics. It has been suggested that the form of hermeneutics described by Gadamer, which uses a culturally and historically informed, or 'tradition-informed' approach to the interpretation of texts that are common cultural property is not only more true to the hermeneutic tradition as a whole, but has a great deal to offer those pursuing research in the areas of counselling and psychotherapy. This approach to understanding hermeneutics has a close affinity to the social constructionism of Kenneth Gergen: the work of Philip Cushman represents an impressive example of what can be achieved using this methodology.

The adoption of a hermeneutic social constructionist approach implies a new direction for psychotherapy research, and for the practice of therapy itself. The potential of a hermeneutic approach to counselling and psychotherapy has been described by Christopher (1996), Sass (1988), and by Cushman (1995) in the closing chapters of his book, in a positive and hopeful light. A hermeneutic stance allows the inquirer freedom from many of the polarised oppositions which have stifled dialogue:

> The hermeneutic position is attempting to do without certain dimensions or binary oppositions in which philosophy and psychology have for centuries been rooted, and which have largely informed our questions, our techniques, and our abiding arguments: e.g., inner versus outer, self versus world, subjective versus objective, act versus system, individual versus society, and freedom versus determinism. . . . Hermeneutics would encourage in the psychologist an ironic and self-critical, but by no means despairing, awareness of both the value and danger of presuppositions – and with this, a realisation that though truth can never be value-free, it is not naïve to seek truth. (Sass, 1988: 263, 265)

# 3

# The Phenomenological Approach

It is not possible to write about the phenomenological approach to qualitative research without mentioning the name of Husserl. The invention and continued domination of phenomenology by Husserl represents a great strength but also, perhaps, a fatal weakness. Edmund Husserl was born in 1859 to middle-class Jewish parents, in Moravia, then part of the Austrian Empire. Husserl studied mathematics at the Universities of Leipzig, Berlin and Vienna. Between 1884 and 1886 he attended lectures at the University of Vienna delivered by the philosopher Franz Brentano, and as a result decided to devote his life to philosophy. Husserl then pursued a career as a university professor in philosophy, at Halle, Göttingen and finally Freiburg. He died in 1938. Culturally and historically, Husserl was a contemporary of Sigmund Freud.

During his life Husserl wrote many books and articles, but also left behind 45,000 pages of manuscript written in shorthand, which are to this day still being studied by scholars of phenomenology. Husserl's body of work is not only vast, but is acknowledged as complex and difficult. This is because the task he set himself, that of creating a phenomenological understanding of the world, was both enormously ambitious and ultimately impossible.

It is important to locate Husserl within the tradition of European thought and culture. This is clearly a massive undertaking in itself, and can only be attempted in a very preliminary fashion here. Nevertheless, one way of understanding Husserl is to appreciate that his approach can be seen as a working out of the implications of the Enlightenment. Europe had been dominated by a Christian world-view until the seventeenth and eighteenth centuries. These centuries can be regarded as a period of transition between the traditional, feudal beliefs and ways of life of the medieval world, and the new beliefs and ways of life that characterised the modern, industrial, scientific world of the twentieth century. One of the most significant driving forces of the transition into modernity was the effort made by philosophers and scientists all over Europe to create new ways of thinking about the world. The scientific studies of Copernicus and Galileo had demonstrated that Earth was not the centre of the universe. In similar fashion, philosophers such as Descartes, Hume and Kant set about challenging the Bible and religious dogma as the sole source of truth about the human condition.

There was a real sense among these philosophers that their job was to *enlighten* people by enabling them to arrive at rational answers to problems, rather than relying on prejudice and unexamined religious beliefs. There was also a sense that it was possible to start again, to build an understanding of the world from rational first principles. The idea of the *Renaissance* captures this hope that it would be possible to build a new world, and of course at this time in history new worlds were being discovered by explorers and scientists.

One of the key figures in European philosophy was René Descartes (1596–1650). Descartes set about the job of arriving at ultimate rational truth through applying the method of systematic doubt. He believed that by questioning and doubting all his beliefs and values that he would eventually arrive at the truth. Whatever remained following the application of systematic doubt would be indubitable, and could therefore be taken as the starting point for a framework for living. Descartes is best known for the *cogito*: 'I think, therefore I am.' For him, this statement is indubitably true, and can be used as the fundamental basis for a philosophical understanding of persons. In fact, this idea has resonated throughout western civilisation, and has contributed to the notion that *mind* (and therefore psychology) represents the defining characteristic of persons.

Husserl shared some of this philosophical agenda, but also questioned aspects of it. Specifically, Husserl was seeking to find a method of arriving at ultimate truth. As one of the most influential contemporary phenomenologists, Maurice Natanson, has put it, Husserl was committed to the 'search for radical certitude':

> Philosophy, for Husserl, is the search for radical certitude. It is the effort to locate in experience the kind of necessity which mathematics has, but a necessity which is a function of our life in the world rather than of the postulations and definitions of an axiomatic method . . . Husserl was searching for a certainty of roots, of conditions which underlie experience and make it possible. (Natanson, 1973: 5)

And here can be seen the immensity of the phenomenologist's task. How can we ever know the 'conditions which underlie experience and make it possible'? In attempting to carry out this task, our only tools are our experience itself, and the language which has evolved within a culture to account for that experience. This is what makes reading Husserl so difficult. He was forcing language to do something that it had hardly been made to do. Phenomenology involves using language to describe what lies beyond language, and in so doing invites the criticism that it is attempting the impossible, that what can be known is what can be said. There are clearly profound issues here concerning the nature of being human, and the role of language and culture in our human-ness.

Where Husserl departed from Descartes was that he did not accept that certitude could be achieved solely through the use of rationality and logic. Husserl argued that it was necessary to examine the bedrock of everyday experience, because it was there, in our emotions, actions and perceptions of things and relationships, that an ultimately true understanding could be derived. Phenomenology strives to describe the *essence* of everyday experience. For Husserl, the attempt to engage with the process of identifying this essence placed a great demand on the inquirer, because it could only be achieved by the individual rigorously examining their own personal experience of the world:

> Anyone who seriously intends to become a philosopher must . . . withdraw into himself and attempt, within himself, to overthrow and build anew all the sciences that, up to then, he has been accepting. Philosophy, wisdom . . . is the philosopher's quite personal affair. It must arise as *his* wisdom, as his self-acquired knowledge. (Husserl, 1960: 2)

Phenomenology requires a kind of withrawal from the world, and a willingness to lay aside existing theories and beliefs. This is risky, and takes an act of courage. It can be viewed as a journey during which one leaves familar places and then returns and sees these places in a fresh light.

Before moving to a discussion of just what phenomenologists do to arrive at 'radical certitude' it is perhaps worth considering the meaning of Husserl's work alongside other developments occurring during the period of time when he was formulating his ideas. In Europe, there were at least three other groups of people who were engaging in the kind of rigorous and systematic examination of personal experience that Husserl advocated. At Leipzig, from the 1870s, Wilhelm Wundt and his followers were using the method of introspection as a means of exploring psychological phenomena. In Vienna, from the 1890s, Freud and his group were employing free association in order to uncover 'unconscious' material. And in Switzerland, Jung, with the word-association technique, and then Hermann Rorschach, with the inkblot test, had developed methods of opening up the quality of individual experience for analysis. In their different ways, all of these groups were attempting to create 'knowledge from first principles', to 'overthrow and build anew' by using accounts of patterns of personal experience as their primary data. There are certain aspects of these parallel developments that are significant. There was a strong focus on the individual as the source of knowledge. There was also a curious and unacknowledged (except later, by Jung) incorporation and re-working of religious practices such as meditation and the confessional. Finally, there was a confidence, characteristic of the late nineteenth-century professional classes, that the products of this type of inquiry were objectively true. The idea of relativism, and that descriptions of experience might be understood as versions, as socially constructed, does not appear to have been part of the dominant world-view of Husserl or any of these other intellectual pioneers.

This commitment to 'certitude', which is central to Husserl's approach, represents a critical issue in relation to the adoption of phenomenological methods by qualitative researchers in the fields of counselling and psychotherapy. On the whole, contemporary qualitative researchers are comfortable with a constructionist or constructivist position which acknowledges that the 'findings' being reported are reflexively contextualised and comprise *a* truth rather than *the* truth. Strictly speaking, phenomenology as conceived by Husserl does not take this view. The assumption that what is being sought is an 'essence' is intrinsic to the phenomenological method. This creates problems for researchers, because as a consequence the phenomenological method tends not to include much in the way of strategies for contextualising findings, and this in turn can make it difficult to integrate findings from studies of the same or similar phenomena. If two phenomenological researchers independently study 'empathy', for example, and arrive at somewhat different accounts, the lack of contextual information makes it pretty well impossible to integrate or reconcile their findings, or even make sense of how they came to different conclusions. It is my impression that phenomenological researchers have in the main avoided carrying out investigations of phenomena which have previously been studied, thus sidestepping this particular dilemma. But more of this later.

## The principles of phenomenological method

There are many writers who have offered interpretations of Husserl's ideas on phenomenological methods. The following discussion draws heavily on the work of Natanson (1973) and Moran (2000).

The aim of phenomenology is to produce an exhaustive description of the phenomena of everyday experience, thus arriving at an understanding of the essential structures of the 'thing itself', the phenomenon. Husserl used the phrase 'natural attitude' to describe the network of assumptions that we usually employ to make sense of our everyday world. Phenomenology seeks to go beyond this natural attitude by adopting a *transcendental attitude*, which is achieved by 'bracketing-off' such assumptions. This process was described by Husserl as *eidetic seeing* (seeing essence, seeing the essential nature of things). Rather than accept a description or account of a phenomenon at face value, a phenomenologist would consider it from all angles and perspectives ('imaginative variation') in order to be able to separate off those aspects of the phenomenon that were contingent on particular circumstances, and those which remained constant (the essence). The term *phenomenological reduction* or *epoche* was also employed to describe the work of phenomenology, reflecting the goal of 'reducing' the phenomenon to its essential qualities, in the sense of the Latin *reducere* (to lead back). A phenomenological reduction *leads back* to the essence of the phenomenon by peeling off the layers of assumptions and projections that have obscured this essence. All this has been summed up well by Moran:

> Husserl characterised the practice of *epoche* in many different ways: 'abstention' . . . 'dislocation' from, or 'unplugging', or 'exclusion' . . . of our normal unquestioning faith in the reality of what we experience. He speaks of 'withholding', 'disregarding', 'abandoning', 'parenthesising', 'putting out of action' and 'putting out of play' all judgements which posit a world in any way as actual or as 'there'. . . . But the essential feature is always to effect an alteration or 'change of attitude', to move away from naturalistic assumptions about the world, assumptions both deeply embedded in our everyday behaviour towards objects. . . . The change of orientation brings about a 'return' to a transcendental standpoint, to uncover a new transcendental domain of experience . . . the transcendental must not be thought to be simply a dimension of my own mind, reached through psychological reflection. . . . To experience the reduction is to experience an enrichment of one's subjective life – it opens infinitely before one. (Moran, 2000: 147; all references to original German-language terminology omitted)

What is being attempted here is challenging, disturbing, radical and critical. Husserl was *not* trying to develop a way of gaining access to the 'phenomenal field' (Rogers) or the 'construct system' (Kelly). He was striving to break through to a 'transcendental domain of experience' in which the essential nature of phenomena would become self-evidently true. In setting out on this kind of intellectual and personal journey, Husserl or any other phenomenologist would have to be willing to question and 'bracket' all and every assumption they might hold, in the hope of finding something new, real and worthwhile at the end.

## From Husserl to phenomenological research

Husserl himself appeared to be far from convinced that phenomenology methods could appropriately be transferred from philosophy into social science disciplines such as psychology or sociology. For Husserl, the point of phenomenological description was to contribute to a better understanding of fundamental human categories such as intentionality, time, colour and number. This understanding was achieved by the individual applying phenomenological methods to their own personal experience. There was also a holistic aspect to the Husserlian approach: no specific domain of experience could be examined without an appreciation of the nature of personal experience as a whole. Husserl did not himself attempt to work out how it might be possible to study the way that another person, or a group of people, might experience a phenomenon. His approach was 'egological', grounded in the self-reflection of the individual philosopher-inquirer. Also, most of the concepts that might be considered to be of interest to social scientists, for example empathy, social class, power, memory, gender, etc., can be considered to be themselves elements of a 'natural attitude' and would presumably dissolve once subjected to phenomenological reduction.

It is therefore by no means obvious that philosophical phenomenology, as understood by Husserl, can be applied to the majority of topics in which social scientists might be interested. There are, however, two domains of social science where phenomenology seems to be readily applicable. The first of these is the study of the psychology of perception, in the work of Albert Michotte, J.J. Gibson and others.

Another applied field with which phenomenology seems to have an easy affinity is counselling/psychotherapy. There are points in therapy where most therapists will encourage their clients to bracket off their assumptions about their problems, describe their experiences in detail, express their sense of their experience in fresh language, and in general 'overthrow and build anew' their understanding of self and relationships. There are also, certainly, many ways in which therapy is *not* a phenomenological enter-prise (some forms of therapy more than others). But the point is that, in seeking to bring to light the experiential data that constitute the 'problem' and its 'solution', and in finding ways to uncover the 'essence' of the problem, the therapist can be seen as teaching, guiding or coaching the client in the self-application of phenomenological principles which were first identified by Husserl.

But all this is still a long way from the kinds of broader psychological and social scientific phenomenological research that has been carried out in recent years. By 'broader' research is meant studies in which specific areas of experience of 'subjects' or research participants (rather than that of the investigator) are examined. There have been three main traditions of this broader use of phenomenological principles. These are: the Duquesne school of empirical phenomenology; the post-Lewinian method of 'con-ceptual encounter' developed by Joseph de Rivera; and the existential-phenomenological investigations of R.D. Laing and others. These recent traditions of phenomenological research are now explored in turn, in relation to their contribution to therapy research and with particular focus on the type of research output that each of them produces.

## The Duquesne school of empirical phenomenology

The Department of Psychology at the Duquesne University has for many years tended the flame of phenomenology within the hostile environment of North American empiricist psychology. It is generally agreed that the key figure in the early development of the Duquesne approach was Amadeo Giorgi, now based at the University of Montreal. Giorgi's (1970) book remains a seminal text within this tradition. More recently, important contributions to therapy research have been made by several other members of the Duquesne group, including Constance Fischer (1984), Fred Wertz (1984) and Chris Aanstoos (1984).

Possibly the most significant factor behind the success of the Duquesne school has been its willingness to codify and systematise the phenomenological method so that it can be taught to students, applied by researchers in other centres, and generate publishable research papers. There are several different versions of the 'Duquesne method', but possibly the most widely adopted has been the set of procedures described by Colaizzi (1978), and further elaborated by Bullington and Karlsson (1984), Wertz (1984), Hycner (1985), Polkinghorne (1989) and Moustakas (1994). The general protocol outlined by these authors specifies a number of steps to be followed by phenomenological researchers:

Ultimate research goal: To elucidate the essence of the phenomenon being studied, as it exists in participants' concrete experience.

Step 1   Collect verbal or written protocols describing the experience.
Step 2   Read them through carefully to get a sense of the whole.
Step 3   Extract significant statements.
Step 4   Eliminate irrelevant repetition, discarding statements 'not revelatory of the phenomenon' (Wertz, 1984).
Step 5   Identify the central themes or meanings implicit in these statements.
Step 6   Integrate these meanings into a single 'exhaustive description' of the phenomenon.

*Throughout this process the researcher should:*

Seek to develop an attitude of open-ness and wonderment in relation to the phenomenon.
Strive to 'bracket off' assumptions (phenomenological reduction').
Adhere to the principle of horizontality: no one meaning is considered more important than any other.
Engage in imaginative variation – (What would need to change to make this into a different phenomenon? What are the limits of the phenomenon?) – thus distinguishing the essential from the inessential features of the phenomenon.
Develop an empathic presence to the described situation. The researcher uses the description to enter and immerse herself in the situation just as it was lived by her subject.
Slow down and patiently dwell on the topic. The researcher spends time lingering 'in' the described situation.
Magnify, amplify and pay special attention to detail. The researcher allows each detail of the situation to be fully contacted, to loom large for her consideration.

Turn from objects to immanent meanings. The researcher attunes herself particularly to the meaning of objects and events as they are lived by the subject. (Summarised and condensed from Colaizzi, 1978; Wertz, 1984)

It is clear that this kind of research 'manual' is balanced somewhere between a set of methodological rules that specify exactly what to do to produce phenomenological research findings, and a more philosophically oriented set of general principles. For instance, in discussing the step of identifying meanings, Colaizzi (1978: 59) acknowledges that here the phenomenological researcher is engaged in 'that ineffable thing known as creative insight'; Wertz (1984) admits that this process draws on 'intuition'.

To gain a better understanding of how phenomenological research of the Duquesne school operates in practice, two representative studies are briefly summarised next.

The first exemplar study selected to represent the Duquesne tradition is the investigation of 'the experience of being criminally victimized' carried out by Connie Fischer and Fred Wertz. Although this study does not specifically address issues of therapy process or outcome, it has been used to inform the design of a model of therapy intended to help victims of crime. There have been two published reports based on this study: Fischer and Wertz (1979) give more methodological detail, while Fischer (1984) offers an extended discussion of the practical implications of the research. However, both reports contain basically similar accounts of methods and findings. Interviews were carried out with individuals identified by the Police Department as having been recent victims of crimes such as assault, robbery, burglary, theft, attempted rape, vandalism and harrassment. Open-ended interviews were conducted with 50 victims of crime, reflecting a broad range of age, social class and ethnicity. Before carrying out the interviews, the investigators (two primary researchers and four Doctoral students in psychology) individually wrote about and collectively discussed their own personal experiences of being victims of crime, as a means of sensitising themselves to the topic and identifying presuppositions regarding the phenomenon. Interviews were transcribed and initial analysis was carried out by all members of the research team.

The material collected in the interviews was analysed in a number of different ways, to meet the needs of diverse audiences and also to enable the researchers to 'cull from the description its essential psychological constituents' (Fischer and Wertz, 1979: 136). The stages in the analyses were:

1   *Individual case synopses.* A reading of the transcripts guided by the question: 'What is revealed here, is essential, to *this person's* experience of being criminally victimised?' The synopsis was written in the person's own words, or in a close approximation to their words.

2 *Illustrated narrative.* Identifying personal meanings and sequences of events present across cases. The generalised narrative that emerged was illustrated by excerpts from individual informants.
3 *General condensation.* A summary statement of the essential meanings identified in the previous stages of inquiry.
4 *General psychological structure.* A statement reflecting the psychological organisation of the experience of victimisation.

Fischer and Wertz (1979) note that there are many different ways of reporting on the findings of phenomenological research. An important aspect of their own paper, as an exemplar study, is that they are open about the multiple methodological choice-points faced by phenomenological researchers – they do not claim that there is one single best way of doing good work within this research tradition.

The yield of the criminal victimisation study is most readily accessed through their *general condensation*:

> Being criminally victimized is a disruption of daily routine. It is a disruption that compels one, despite personal resistance, to face one's fellow as predator and oneself as prey, even though all the while anticipating consequences, planning, acting, and looking to others for assistance. These efforts to little avail, one experiences vulnerability, separateness, and helplessness in the face of the callous, insensitive, often anonymous enemy. Shock and disbelief give way to puzzlement, strangeness, and then to a sense of the crime as perverse, unfair, undeserved. Whether or not expressed immediately, the victim experiences a general inner protest, anger or rage, and a readiness for retaliation, for revenge against the violator.
>
> As life goes on, the victim finds him/herself pervasively attuned to the possibility of victimization – through a continued sense of reduced agency, of the other as predatory, and of community as inadequately supportive. More particularly, one continues to live the victimization through recollection of the crime, imagination of even worse outcomes, vigilant suspiciousness of others, sensitivity to news of disorder and crime, criticalness of justice system agents, and desires to make sense of it all.
>
> But these reminders of vulnerability are simultaneously efforts toward recovery of independence, safety, trust, order, and sense. One begins to get back on top of the situation through considering or taking precautions against crime, usually by restricting one's range of activities so as not to fall prey again. During this process, the victim tries to understand not only how a criminal could have done and could again do such a thing, but also how he or she (the victim) may have contributed to the criminal's action. Also, one's intermittent readiness for retaliation provides a glimpse of one's own potential for outrageous violence. The victim thus is confronted with the paradoxical and ambiguous character of social existence: the reversible possibilities we all share, such as being agent or object, same or different, disciplined or disruptive, predator or prey. One may move from this encounter toward a more circumspect attitude toward personal responsibility.

However, the person's efforts toward such an integration of the victimization are not sufficient. The environment must over time demonstrate that the victim's extreme vigilance is no longer necessary. And other persons must respond with concern and respect for the victim's full plight, including his or her efforts toward sensemaking. All three components are essential for recovery of one's prior life as well as for development of a fuller sense of responsibility, reciprocity, and community. The absence of any of them eventuates in a deepened victimization of isolation, despair, bitterness, and resignation. (Fischer and Wertz, 1979: 149)

It is worth reproducing the Fischer and Wertz (1979) 'general condensation' in full because this type of statement represents the 'bottom line' of a phenomenological research report – the ultimate statement of what has been found. It is perhaps significant that these investigators choose to call their statement a 'condensation', which carries with it an implicit reference to a natural process, rather than designating it as a more socially made 'construction' or 'representation'. The phenomenological 'condensation' needs to fulfil contradictory purposes. It must be 'obvious' in the sense of describing a slice of experience which the reader can recognise. Yet at the same time it must be 'revelatory'; it should challenge and somehow reach beyond the 'natural attitude' of the reader. The condensation must be detailed enough to carry a sufficient sense of the complexity and texture of the phenomenon, but also brief enough to communicate with and be assimilated by readers.

How are we to assess the value of such research findings? Stiles (1993) and others have mapped out various criteria that can be employed in assessing the quality of qualitative research (see Chapter 11). However, the work of Fischer and Wertz is an attempt to capture the sense of an experience in which all of us have shared, to some extent, and therefore it calls forth a personal and subjective response from the reader. Personally, I was struck by how central the theme of predator and prey was in the Fischer and Wertz condensation. This did not quite resonate with my sense of the experience of being victimised. And for me, fear for myself and fear for my family members (particularly my children) are central to this experience; these elements seemed muted in the Fischer and Wertz account. But does this matter? In other respects the victimisation paper certainly seems to do an admirable job in bringing together the various strands of this experience. How important is it that a phenomenological analysis should illuminate the personal experience of the reader? Surely Fischer and Wertz (1979) interviewed a good sample of crime victims, faithfully reflected what their informants said to them, and did a painstaking job of analysing this material. Isn't that enough?

Consideration of a study by Fessler (1983) may provide another perspective on this question. In this investigation, tape recordings were taken of therapy sessions between experienced therapists and clients who had been in treatment for at least six months. The researcher made a written transcript of a 5–10 minute segment of the tape, and met separately the following day with both therapist and client to conduct interviews around their experiences of this portion of the therapy session. This study is, in its general outline, similar to the Interpersonal Process Recall (IPR) research carried out by Elliott (1986) and Rennie (1992). Fessler (1983) asked each interviewee first to recall what had taken place during that section of the therapy session. Then the tape was played, with the research participant reading along from the transcript, and encouraged by the researcher to recapture the experience of the session by responding to questions such as 'What had he been trying to say, and why?', 'What had he thought the other person was trying to say or do, and why?', 'What thoughts had he had but not expressed?' Each interview lasted for more than one hour. Tape recordings of the interviews were transcribed and analysed.

There are two points of interest in relation to the results of this study. First, Fessler found major differences between what therapists and clients recalled *before* hearing the tape and their recollected experience of the session stimulated by listening to the recording. Fessler (1983: 41) concluded that 'both the therapists and the patients, in living through the session a second time by way of the tape, *were able to see things they knew that they had not seen at the time*' (italics added). This finding can be viewed as a direct affirmation of the contribution that phenomenology can make. For these clients and therapists, there was a profound difference between their 'natural attitude' account of their experience and the much more detailed and illuminating account that they were able to give when assisted by an investigator inviting them to engage in a form of supported *epoche*.

The second point of interest arising from Fessler's approach is that, having generated a rich description of the phenomenon, he was able to go on to articulate his understanding of this material in such a way as to challenge the taken-for-granted assumptions of his readers regarding the process of therapy. In one particularly luminous passage, he writes:

Therapist and . . . patient do not take turns speaking and listening. Rather they participate in a speech that is taking place between and through them – a speech that is both spoken and listened to simultaneously. Each speaks in response to what he hears the other expressing, and each tries to express himself in a way that the other can hear and understand. When one participant speaks, he does not speak randomly but speaks in a particular way – *to* the other that he experiences, articulating his response to what he heard the other say. And his expressions in turn are heard by the other, who then responds to what *he* hears. They may have completely different experiences of what is being said, but despite that each is lead on by the other's words to a further elaboration and articulation of his own experience and to a further unfolding of what he thinks the other is trying to express. As the session continues, the evolution of each subject's experience and the articulation of that experience contribute to the

> evolution of the *other's* experience and articulation, even if it is not in the way that each thinks or intends. Therapy is not done by one and received by the other; it is a shared speech that participates in a 'sculpting' of a developing meaning for each participant – a meaning that does not originate *in* either one of them but through their parallel attempts to be heard and understood. (Fessler, 1983: 44)

There are few, if any, better descriptions of the co-constructed nature of therapy. Certainly, for me as a reader, Fessler has captured *something* of the essence of therapy that is immediately recognisable and yet, up to that point, was hardly capable of expression. However, in terms of the adequacy of his description of his method, the Fessler paper is sadly lacking. There is no explanation of how the analysis was carried out step by step. His findings seem to be generated less by method and more by intuition and passion. In this sense, Fessler (1983) represents both the promise and the limitations of the Duquesne approach. It has the potential to generate powerful new understandings. But perhaps these under-standings do not wholly rely on the application of the method.

## The method of conceptual encounter

*Conceptual encounter* is an approach to phenomenological research devised by Joseph de Rivera. Conceptual encounter builds upon the 'human science' perspective of the Duquesne group, and is also influenced by the 'field theory' methods of the German social psychologist Kurt Lewin (de Rivera, 1976). The primary goal of conceptual encounter is to produce a 'map of personal experience'. At the heart of the method is the encounter between the investigator and a person who has agreed to act as a research partner. The investigator has decided to study some aspect of human experience, and has carried out some preliminary reflections on his or her personal experience of the topic, as well as reading relevant scientific and fictional literature. As a result of this reading and reflection, the investi-gator enters the study sensitised to the topic and in possession of their own tentative ideas about the contours of the phenomenon. The research partner is invited to recount a specific example of whatever is being studied. The investigator may ask facilitative questions to assist the partner to draw out different aspects of the experience, and strives to make sure that he or she fully appreciates the uniqueness of the informant's personal experience. Following this stage, the investigator shares with the partner his or her abstract ideas about the nature of the phenomenon, checks that these ideas have been understood, and asks the partner how well this framework fits the specific concrete experience that was described earlier. Through the ensuing dialogue, the investigator gets confirmation of some of the features of his or her abstract model of the phenomenon, but finds that other elements may be strongly challenged and require revision or further differentiation. By carrying out this procedure with a series of research partners, the investigator converges on a final version of the essential features of the phenomenon being studied. The early studies carried out by de Rivera and the other members of his group focused on the experience of emotions such as anger, love, shame, guilt, distance and elation (de Rivera, 1981, 1989, 1991; Lindsay-Hart, de Rivera and Mascolo, 1995). A more recent application of the method has investigated the phenomenon of recovered memories of childhood sexual abuse (de Rivera, 1997). Guidelines for how to carry out a conceptual encounter study can be found in de Rivera (1981), particularly Chapter 1.

Conceptual encounter is therefore a dialectical process through which the researcher does not rely solely on their own personal experience (as in classical Husserlian phenomenology) or on informant accounts (as in Duquesne empirical phenomenology) but sets up a dynamic interplay between the two:

> An adequate conceptualization usually takes a long time to develop. At first the investigator may not be aware of any particular pattern in the different experiences that are examined. Then, a pattern may suddenly emerge . . . or there may be a sudden grasping of a pattern, the report of one experience may be a revelation, an insight into the essential structure of the phenomenon . . . regardless of personal style the formation of a good conceptualization is a continual making process as the researcher moves back and forth between interviews, observations, literature and reflection, gradually becoming more alert to the nuances and patterns of the phenomenon. (de Rivera, 1981: 6–7)

This sense of a 'continual making process' pervades de Rivera's writings on method. The investigator is not engaging in a meditation, but is actively checking one piece of description against another, one source against another, and throughout all this being open to others about his or her hunches and emerging formulations and in turn open to their rebuttals and new angles.

A good exemplar study within the conceptual encounter tradition is the investigation of shame and guilt by Lindsay-Hart et al. (1995).

## Existential-phenomenological research

There is a strong connection between phenomenology and existentialism. Existentialism can be defined as a philosophical perspective which takes as its goal the understanding of the experience of being-in-the-world. Existential philosophers and psychotherapists use phenomenology as the method through which they explore the meanings of existential concepts.

The term *existential-phenomenological* has been applied to these practitioners and scholars (see Valle and Halling, 1989).

One of the most powerful programmes of human inquiry carried out
within the existential-phenomenological tradition was the study of schizophrenia conducted by the Scottish psychiatrist R.D. Laing and his
colleagues between 1958 and 1963 at the Tavistock Institute for Human
Relations in London. This research was based first on therapeutic work
with 'schizophrenic' people, and then with formal research interviews with
'schizophrenic' patients and their family members. The results of this
research were published in four books. Laing (1960, 1961) presents the
'theoretical' interpretation of what was found. Laing and Esterson (1964)
provide a descriptive phenomenological account of the interpersonal
worlds of the families studied. Laing, Phillipson and Lee (1966) give an
outline of the method. There are two main reasons why this research is
important. The first is the quality of phenomenological description that
was achieved by Laing and his colleagues. The second is that, unlike other
phenomenological studies which concentrated on interesting but nevertheless mundane aspects of everyday life (being angry, being anxious,
feeling misunderstood), Laing chose to address a concept with profound
political implications. 'Schizophrenia' was (and is) a concept that can have
great significance in relation to the politics of family life. For some families,
the meaning of 'schizophrenia' is that one of their members is 'ill' and can
therefore be hospitalised in good faith. 'Schizophrenia' is also a concept
that has meaning in relation to law and state institutions. There are state-
funded organisations, professions and statutes built around a medical
definition of this phenomenon. Schizophrenia is embedded in a set of
commercial meanings associated with activities of drug companies.
Because of the political sensitivity of the topic, the research carried out
by Laing and his collaborators has probably had more impact than any
other phenomenological study. Laing's books remain in print, and remain
influential, even though Laing himself was subsequently to drift away from
an existential-phenomenological approach. This research therefore offers
an example of the potential of phenomenological methods to influence
professional and, more widely, cultural ideas and practices.

How did Laing set about investigating the phenomenology of
'schizophrenia'? His goal, from the start, was to go 'as directly as possible
to the patients themselves' (Laing, 1960: 18). In doing this, Laing is
following Husserl's precept to return to 'the things themselves'. However,
to attend directly to the experiences of 'schizophrenic' patients is no easy
matter:

> as a psychiatrist, I run into a major difficulty at the outset: how can I go straight
> to the patients if the psychiatric words at my disposal keep the patient at a
> distance from me? How can one demonstrate the general human relevance and
> significance of the patient's condition if the words one has to use are specifically

designed to isolate and circumscribe the meaning of the patient's life to a particular clinical entity? . . . It will be convenient, therefore, to start by looking at some of the words in use. (Laing, 1960: 18)

The method of inquiry that emerged from this perspective emphasised careful exploration of the meanings of the words used by those involved in co-constructing the phenomenon of 'schizophrenia' in individual cases: the patient, family members, mental health professionals. In Laing and Esterson (1964) and Laing, Phillipson and Lee (1996) the attributions of family members are carefully teased apart. In Laing (1960, 1961) the language through which psychiatry and psychoanalysis construct the experience of schizophrenia is subjected to critical analysis. It is only when all of these 'taken-for-granted' ways of understanding are 'bracketed-off' in this way that the experience of the person defined as schizophrenic can become visible.

What is it that becomes visible? Laing provides two ways of making sense of the experience of 'schizophrenia' – one narrative and the other paradigmatic. He constructs narrative life histories that are compiled largely from the words of the person and other members of his or her family, with little overt researcher interpretation. One of the most compelling of these phenomenological histories is 'The ghost of the weed garden' in Laing (1960). His other means of representing the experience of schizophrenia is through a series of existential concepts: ontological insecurity, embodiment, falseness, collusion, elusion, pretence, etc. (Laing, 1960, 1961). In the best of his writing, narrative and conceptual accounts are woven together.

What comes out of this kind of research is that the 'natural attitude' way of understanding the phenomenon dissolves. Within late twentieth-century society it is 'natural' to view schizophrenia as an illness that is primarily genetically and biologically caused. Laing's research leads to a completely different way of 'seeing' schizophrenia. For example, what was senseless (the apparently meaningless language of schizophrenic speech) becomes a metaphoric and highly meaningful way of trying to say something about relationships and a state of being. Eventually, the very notion of 'schizophrenia' becomes questionable, and it begins to appear in quote marks, along with terms like 'mental illness'. And on the back of this new way of seeing come new forms of therapeutic practice.

Laing and his colleagues use the term *demystification* to describe what they are trying to achieve. They examine situations where everyday, taken-for-granted assumptions (the 'natural attitude') have operated not only to obscure the true nature of what is going on ('back to the thing itself') but have done so in the interests of powerful groups (psychiatrists, psychoanalysts). They are practising a kind of *critical* phenomenology, which employs the methods of phenomenology to challenge the moral basis on which certain actions are being carried out. In so doing, they are in effect operating from a *hermeneutic* standpoint, as described in the previous chapter. That is, they are using a phenomenological approach to broaden and change the description of the phenomenon under investigation (schizophrenia, transference) and are then using that re-description or new 'way of seeing' to support a new interpretive account. It is important to recognise, however, that this set of methodological moves would not work in the absence of a powerful and convincing phenomenological analysis that serves to jolt the reader/audience out of their previously existing attitude to the topic. The effectiveness of Laing's research depends on the combination of phenomenological and hermeneutic strategies advocated by Heidegger (1962).

## An appraisal of the phenomenological approach

In summing up the contribution that phenomenology has made to psychotherapy research, and might make in the future, it is necessary to begin by emphasising that phenomenology is one of the basic tools of qualitative research (Osborne, 1994). Whatever else they are up to, all qualitative researchers, at some point in their research, apply the procedures originally identified by Husserl: bracketing-off of assumptions, horizontalisation, careful and exhaustive description, searching for the essence of the phenomenon. I also believe that Husserl is correct in his view that, ultimately, human science is a personal quest: 'the philosopher's quite personal affair'. Even when working in a group or team, a qualitative researcher needs to become immersed in, and challenged by, the topic. De Rivera (1981: 13) has stated that his approach is 'completely dependent on the personal qualities of the researcher'.

It seems to me that phenomenology represents a way of knowing that has always been a crucial part of human culture. As a language-using and culture-building species we need to have ways of renewing and reconstructing our language and culture in order to keep it alive. We need to have some way of getting to the very edge of what we can say. One means of doing this is through some kind of almost meditative withdrawal from the world. Another way is to seek to describe the world as exhaustively as possible. The existence of an exhaustive description may act at the very least as a bulwark against those who would seek to impose partial descriptions.

Nevertheless, despite the central position which phenomenology must have within the human sciences, there are a number of fairly substantial problems and limitations associated with the way that phenomenological research is currently practised in relation to psychotherapeutic topics.

Much contemporary phenomenological research is characterised by an over-reliance on procedural manuals. It is hard to believe that anyone can learn to carry out a phenomenological study on the basis of the kind of step-by-step guidelines published by Colaizzi (1978). An understanding of what is being attempted in a phenomenological inquiry requires a proper grasp of the underlying philosophical arguments that support the approach. Given that, for most counsellors and therapists, the philosophical literature is complex and difficult, it is certainly helpful to learn about how phenomenological researchers such as Colaizzi, Fischer and Wertz, and others have 'operationalised' their understanding of a phenomenological approach. But surely it is misleading to suggest that copying out 'phrases and sentences that directly pertain to the investigated phenomenon' (Colaizzi, 1978: 59) is how phenomenological reduction is carried out. It is more appropriate to novice researchers to grasp the notion that Colaizzi himself understood the concept of 'phenomenological reduction', and in a particular study found that the procedures he used represented a suitable way of engaging with the phenomenon to this end. For readers accustomed to a prescriptive, rule-governed conception of method, this point perhaps gets lost when set alongside a set of step-by-step instructions. The key point here is that the *epoche*, the act of suspending the taken-for-granted assumptions of the everyday natural attitude, is a radical act that is perhaps better understood as a discipline that takes time to master, rather than a technique that can be 'manualised' and switched on and off.

There is an absence of cumulative knowledge within the phenomenological literature. The phenomenological psychology literature appears to be, to a remarkable extent, populated by one-off studies. It is almost as though the very existence of a previous study on a topic is enough to deter subsequent students from carrying out an investigation into the same phenomenon. There are possibly three factors at work here. First, phenomenological research has been marginalised in North American psychology and social science, with the result that relatively little research is being carried out. Second, the Husserlian emphais on an 'egological', personal and individual style of research probably leads students to seek out topics where they can clearly demonstrate that they are generating knowledge based on their own personal investigative journey. Third, it could be argued that the way in which most phenomenological studies are written for publication makes it hard for future researchers to know the extent to which they agree or disagree with what has been found. For 'second-generation' phenomenological researchers there are dangers involved in presenting findings which agree with a previous study (nothing new has been found, or they were over-influenced by the findings of the first study) or disagree (they have missed something). The work of de Rivera (1981) and Lindsay-Hart et al. (1995) shows that it is possible to write phenomenological research in a form that invites replication and further elaboration. However, I suspect that the emphasis in phenomenology on the phenomenon itself, as opposed to the context of the phenomenon, acts as an inhibiting factor in relation to replication of studies. If, for example, the Fischer and Wertz study of the experience of the criminally victimised had been explicitly situated in terms of place, ethnicity, gender, age or social class, one imagines that other researchers might well have responded by taking their paper as an implicit invitation to replicate the study in different places, with different ethnic groups, etc. But because Fischer and Wertz adopted the typical phenomenological strategy of seeking some kind of Husserlian universal 'certitude', they stifled the emergence of potential lines of future studies that would have extended the reach of their work. Ultimately, the effect would be to diminish the impact of their study, since policy-makers are understandably more comfortable acting on the findings of programmes of research rather than investing resources on the basis of one-off studies, no matter how insightful these individual studies might be. On the other hand, signs of a productive future for phenomenological research in counselling and psychotherapy can be found in the growing number of published studies which have used phenomenological methods, for example Bachelor (1995), Pogge and Dougher (1992) and Worthen and McNeill (1996). In addition, Fischer, Eckenrod, Embree and Jarzynka (2000) have recently compiled a review of previously unpublished Duquesne research dissertations in psychotherapy.

There also appears to be a general lack of interest in social context within recent phenomenological research. Subsequent generations of scholars have understood Husserl's injunction to return to the 'things themselves' as an invitation to turn away from the social world. Yet it is clear that phenomenology does not necessarily involve an avoidance of social, historical and cultural dimensions of experience. The marvellous studies carried out by van den Berg (1961, 1972, 1974) demonstrate convincingly that a phenomenological approach can be applied to cultural and historical material.

No one can doubt that the claims and aspirations of Husserl regarding phenomenology have not been actively pursued in a century of work using this approach. For anyone seeking to make discoveries about the ways in which personal and social worlds are constructed, it is *necessary* to adopt a phenomenological stance. Yet the yield of a purely phenomenological approach is, in many cases, disappointing. Why is this? One of the leading recent writers on phenomenological research, the late Michael Crotty, has argued that there are *two* phenomenologies. There is the mainstream phenomenology of Husserl and Merleau-Ponty. And there is the new, empirical phenomenology used by researchers in psychology and health. Crotty argues that the radical tradition represented by Husserlian phenomenology has been lost:

> something is lost when one is content to accept the new phenomenology and looks no longer to mainstream phenomenology. That so-called phenomenology simply describes the state of affairs instead of problematising it. It looks to what

is taken for granted but fails to call it into question: on the contrary, it per-petuates traditional meanings and reinforces current understandings. It remains preoccupied with 'what is' rather than striving, however laboriously and tenta-tively, towards 'what might be'. At best, this entails a failure to capture new meanings and a loss of opportunities for revivifying the understandings that possess us. (Crotty, 1996: 7)

For Crotty, Husserlian and empirical phenomenology are 'far apart'. The 'new' phenomenology, associated with van Kaam, Giorgi and the Duquesne school, developed in the 1960s as an adjunct to North American humanistic psychology, and represented a 'distortion' of Husserlian ideas. Specifically, the new phenomenology is *subjective*, in seeking to explore the subjective experience of people, whereas mainstream phenomenology is a study of phenomena, of the *objects* of human experience. So, for example, Fischer and Wertz (new phenomenology) report on the experience of being victimised, whereas de Rivera reports on the structure of shame, as a thing in itself. For Crotty (1996), the new phenomenology also lacks a *critical* edge, it 'remains preoccupied with "what is"'. Mainstream phenomeno-logy, he argues, was always intended as a critical approach. The very act of phenomenological reduction is one of *questioning* taken-for-granted assumptions.

# 4

# Hermeneutics and Phenomenology: the Core of Qualitative Method

This chapter is intended as a bridge between earlier and later sections of the book. Hermeneutics and phenomenology are long-established approaches to knowing, which have their origins in some of the main currents of western intellectual life. The chapters which follow introduce and discuss a set of methods which have for the most part emerged in the latter half of the twentieth century: ethnography, grounded theory, discourse analysis and others. These more recent methods have generally been specified in terms of sets of procedural guidelines, or practical techniques, rather than in terms of philosophical principles. It will be argued that method can never be enough. As Walsh (1995) has put it, a qualitative researcher does not merely apply a method, but works from within an *approach*. The researcher's 'approach' comprises an appreciation of the conceptual and historical meanings implicit in the research act.

Anyone who has ever completed a piece of qualitative research knows that doing *good* qualitative research is not merely a matter of following a set of procedural guidelines. The principal source of knowing in qualitative inquiry is the researcher's engagement in a search for meaning and truth in relation to the topic of inquiry. It is the struggle to know that generates new and useful insights. There is no methodological 'sausage machine' where one can set the controls, feed data in one end, crank the handle, and produce the goods (sausages, or, in this case, useful research findings). Step-by-step method guides like those produced by Strauss and Corbin (1990) or Colaizzi (1978) (and many other methods teachers) give useful hints regarding how best research tasks may be structured and organised in order not to dissipate time and energy. These methods books can be seen as a way of passing on practical wisdom. But in the end it is the capacity of the inquirer to see and understand that makes the difference. A method like grounded theory, empirical phenomenology or discourse analysis does not work unless the person doing the research knows *why* these steps and procedures make sense, and what they are intended to achieve. To produce good work, qualitative researchers need to reflect on *how* they see and understand, to reflect on the process of knowing itself.

The process of knowing involves employing a practical method, that is derived from an epistemology (theory of knowledge) which is in turn grounded in an ontology (set of assumptions about the nature of life). Routine decisions made by qualitative researchers, for example relating to sampling strategies, ways of collecting data, ways of analysing data, and selecting a format for communicating findings, can only be resolved by recourse to underlying epistemological and ontological principles. The interconnection of methodology, epistemology and ontology can be represented in terms of three key questions:

1  *The ontological question.* What is the form and nature of reality, and, therefore, what is there that can be known about it? For example, if a 'real' world is assumed, then what can be known about how it is, 'how things really are' and 'how things really work'. Then only those questions that relate to matters of 'real' existence and 'real' action are admissible; other questions, such as those concerning matters of aesthetic and moral significance, fall outside the realm of legitimate scientific inquiry.

2  *The epistemological question.* What is the relationship between the knower and would-be knower and what can be known? The answer that can be given to this question is constrained by the answer already given to the ontological question; that is, not just *any* relationship can now be postulated. So if, for example, a 'real' reality is assumed, then the posture of the knower must be one of objective detachment or value freedom in order to be able to discover 'how things really are' and 'how things really work'. (Conversely, assumption of an objectivist posture implies the existence of a 'real' world to be objective about.)

3  *The methodological question.* How can the inquirer (would-be knower) go about finding out whatever he or she believes can be known? Again, the answer that can be given to this question is constrained by answers already given to the first two questions; that is, not just *any* methodology is appropriate. For example, a 'real' reality pursued by an 'objective' inquirer mandates control of possible confounding factors, whether the methods are qualitative (say, observational) or quantitative (say, analysis of covariance). (Conversely, the selection of a manipulative methodology – the experiment, say – implies the ability to be objective and a real world to be objective about.) The methodological question cannot be reduced to a question of methods; *methods must be fitted to a predetermined methodology* (emphasis added): (Guba and Lincoln, 1994: 108)

The point being emphasised by Guba and Lincoln concerns the importance of achieving consistency between practical method and underlying epistemological and ontological assumptions. This consistency can only be attained by qualitative researchers in counselling and psychotherapy by developing an appreciation of the philosophical issues implicit in their research. It could be argued that, for positivist, quantitative researchers, the concordance between ontology and methodology has long since been established. The same argument cannot currently be made in relation to qualitative research in therapy. Qualitative therapy researchers have on the whole been trained and employed within psychology and psychiatry departments in which epistemological and ontological questions are not encouraged. They have had little opportunity or requirement to study philosophy. They have published in journals that demand empirical detail and method specificity, rather than conceptual analysis. There is an absence of awareness and discussion of what qualitative research is really about.

## The roots of all qualitative research lie in hermeneutics and phenomenology

For qualitative researchers operating within the tradition of western social science, there are two basic epistemologies that have informed research practice: phenomenology and hermeneutics. Phenomenology seeks to set aside any assumptions about the object of inquiry, and build up a thorough and comprehensive description of the 'thing itself'. Phenomenology is almost a meditative practice, and involves an 'in-dwelling' in the phenomenon until its essential features reveal themselves. Hermeneutics takes the opposite tack. In hermeneutics, understanding is always from a perspective, always a matter of interpretation. The researcher can never be free of the pre-understandings or 'prejudices' that arise from being a member of a culture and a user of a language. We can never get beyond our language – all the questions we ask and words we use to articulate our understandings are embedded in culture. What we can do in research is to extend the horizon of our culture-based understanding, or achieve a *fusion* of horizons through allowing ourselves to learn from our immersion in the 'text' being studied and thereby permitting the world expressed by the text to speak to our world.

In Chapter 1, it was proposed that the aim of qualitative research is to develop understandings of how the world is constructed. Phenomenology and hermeneutics represent opposite and alternative ways of doing this. Phenomenology does not contextualise its knowledge in a social or historical moment. It pushes at the edge of language, trying to find words for what is beyond our everyday ways of speaking about whatever it is we are studying. Hermeneutics is all about context, about placing the topic of inquiry into historical and cultural perspective.

Can phenomenology and hermeneutics be reconciled or combined, or do these epistemological traditions represent utterly different ways of knowing? This is a central question for anyone undertaking qualitative research. For those pursuing qualitative research in counselling and psychotherapy the question has a double resonance, because the positions that can be taken in relation to these two traditions in research apply equally well to an understanding of therapy practice itself.

There are a number of ways of looking at the question of the tension between phenomenology and hermeneutics, and it is helpful to address them one at a time.

## The underlying affinity between phenomenology and hermeneutics

No matter how different phenomenology and hermeneutics may be, they possess significant areas of convergence when compared to the approach to knowledge which underpins natural science. Phenomenology and hermeneutics both assume an active, intentional, construction of a social world and its meanings by reflexive human beings. This is quite different from the model of causality and image of the world found in natural science. Phenomenology and hermeneutics both deal mainly with linguistic material, or with language-based accounts of other forms of representation (e.g., numbers, pictures, physical objects). Natural science (at least as it is normally practised) is, by contrast, largely concerned with the *numerical* representation of qualities and characteristics of objects or with visual displays (e.g., graphs) only in so far as these function as expressions of underlying numerical structures. Natural science depends in fundamental ways on the use of mathematics and on the development of technologies (e.g., measuring instruments) through which mathematical data can be collected. There is also an important sense in which natural science is concerned with the construction of *explanatory* theories that have the capacity to *predict* future events. Hermeneutics and phenomenology, by contrast, are concerned with the development of *understandings* which may assist people to anticipate events, by sensitising them to possibilities. However, this kind of anticipation occurs with an appreciation that the field of the possible may include will and choice. The object of the human sciences (hermeneutics and phenomenology) is a being that is capable of reflection, choice and language use. The object of natural science is not constituted in this way at all. There are, therefore, many dimensions of similarity between phenomenology and hermeneutics that are highlighted when a comparison is made with the approach taken by the natural sciences.

## One is right and the other is wrong

It is possible to construct arguments that either phenomenology or hermeneutics can claim epistemological priority. The aim of these arguments is to show that one can, in effect, be assimilated into the other, or indeed that one of them is fundamentally a mistake. At the heart of the tension between phenomenology and hermeneutics are two positions. Phenomenologists argue that their method of 'bracketing' allows them to note but then lay aside existing interpretive frameworks in order to gain access to a truth that lies *beyond* these frameworks (the 'essence' of the phenomenon). By this procedure, phenomenology transcends hermeneutics. From a hermeneutic perspective, by contrast, the basic argument is that to be human is to live in an 'interpreted world', a world in which experience is constructed in terms of language. For the hermeneutic analyst, an attempt to 'transcend' language merely leads to another set of statements or propositions that are themselves linguistic and interpretive.

Probably the most compelling attack on Husserlian phenomenology, in relation to work in the domain of psychology and psychotherapy, can be found in a chapter by Sass (1988). It is forcibly argued by Sass that phenomenology leads to a subjectivism that denies the social nature of human being, particularly the grounding of experience in language. Both Sass (1988) and Crotty (1996) consider the contemporary use of phenomenology in psychology and psychotherapy to have become fused with the assumptions and rhetoric of North American humanistic psychology. For Crotty there is a radical, revelatory edge to Husserlian phenomenology which can be retrieved once the influence of humanistic psychology has been stripped out. For Sass, however, the approach taken by Husserl is fundamentally inadequate.

It is difficult to locate a published defence of the phenomenological position, in relation to hermeneutics, that approaches the cogency and power of Sass (1988). The most convincing argument in support of phenomenology is probably that, used alone, an interpretive hermeneutic analysis of a phenomenon does no more than incorporate the understanding of that phenomenon into a model or theory that already exists. There would appear to be no process here through which the interpretive framework itself can ever change. This is a telling criticism of hermeneutics, because it is clear that interpretive frameworks *do* change over time. The phenomenological position is that the 'natural attitude' always applies within a set of horizons or boundaries. Toward or beyond the edge of that horizon there may be vaguely sensed or poorly articulated meanings that can only be brought within the domain of understanding (the 'clearing') by careful description of the phenomenon itself. Even within the horizon there may be interpretive concepts whose meaning is ambiguous or unclear, and where careful description of the phenomenon can be helpful.

In psychology, phenomenologial studies of constructs such as anxiety, depression and schizophrenia have proved useful in clarifying meanings in ways that can then lead to more satisfactory interpretation or theorising. The argument from phenomenology, therefore, is that it may not be sufficient in itself as a way of knowing, because we live in an interpreted world and act most of the time on the basis of taken-for-granted understandings. However, although not sufficient, phenomenology is *necessary*, because in its absence interpretive frameworks become rigid and dogmatic.

## Bringing together phenomenology and hermeneutics: Heidegger

The philosopher who is most closely associated with the view that phenomenology and hermeneutics should both be seen as integral, complementary aspects of any satisfactory way of knowing about human existence is Martin Heidegger, in his book *Being and Time* (1962; original publication 1927). Heidegger (1896-1976) was a German Catholic who studied and taught philosophy at the University of Freiburg. Before offering an account of Heidegger's thought, it is necessary to acknowledge that his writing is generally obscure and hard to follow. The following account in no way claims to do justice to the complexities and subtleties of *Being and Time*, but merely offers a somewhat oversimplified and schematic outline of the broad contours of the integration of phenomenology and hermeneutics offered by Heidegger, and an examination of the implications of his approach for research in counselling and psychotherapy. There have been many books written on Heidegger and his work. A particularly clear and accessible account of his ideas can be found in Moran (2000).

Heidegger, who was influenced by Husserl and had been his assistant, was familiar with hermeneutics from his theological studies. The key to Heidegger's approach is the idea that the 'natural attitude', the very thing that Husserl and other phenomenologists would wish to suspend or 'bracket-off', in fact represented the *most important* focus of philosophical inquiry. In hermeneutic terms, the 'natural attitude' could be understood as the 'fore-understanding', the interpretive framework or horizon through which the world was understood. Heidegger sought to apply a phenomenological reduction to this aspect of life. Heidegger used the concept of 'everydayness' to describe what he was interested in. Husserl wished to transcend 'everydayness'; Heidegger wished to understand it, to create a 'clearing' in which the true nature of everyday life could be seen. His aim was to develop an appreciation of the 'essence' (in phenomenological terms) of everyday life and everyday understanding itself. At the heart of his work was the struggle to make sense of the essential nature of *being* itself: what does it mean to *be human*? If Heidegger were to be successful in this endeavour, he would be making an enormous contribution to our capacity to make sense of *anything*, since what he was aiming to do was to uncover the structure and qualities of the sense-making (or interpreting) being itself. It was as though Heidegger was trying to capture and describe something fundamental about the basis on which we belong in the world as human beings. He was trying to make sense of *existence*.

What did he find? *Being and Time* works painstakingly through three main characteristics of being and existence. First, as implied by the title of the book, we exist in and through time. More particularly, to be fully aware of one's existence as a human being requires acknowledging the finitude, the end of personal time, death. We live also in an awareness of future *possibility*, including the possibility of death. Second, we have an existence that is structured around action. Our relationship with the world is organised in terms of what we can *do* in that world, what we can do with the things that surround us. Heidegger employs the image of the hammer as a typical tool that is 'ready to hand'. Our hand knows what to do with a hammer. The third characteristic of everydayness is *care*: we are connected to the world through our anxiety, dread, and resoluteness.

Was Heidegger's analysis of *being-in-the-world* accurate and valid? Many people would doubt that it was. Some, like Caputo (1993), point to Heidegger's support for National Socialism, behaviour during the Nazi era, and failure to condemn the Holocaust, as evidence for the fundamental inadequacy of his philosophy. Others, such as Foucault, Levinas and Derrida, have followed Heidegger's lead but have developed their own ways of understanding the nature of existence. In a broader context, Heidegger is accepted as one of the seminal figures in twentieth-century philosophy.

The key lesson that qualitative therapy researchers can take from Heidegger concerns not the *results* of his analysis, but the basis of his *approach* to the task of understanding existence. Heidegger appropriated ideas from hermeneutics and phenomenology, and integrated them into something new. He did this by taking as his 'problematic' the task of understanding the nature of everyday existence. It is clear that a hermeneutic approach can be applied to the study of a text, such as the Bible, without any necessity to deploy Husserlian phenomenological reduction to construct a description of the 'essence' of the text. The text is 'out there' and the aim is to elucidate the meaning of that text in relation to an already existing system of meaning. Similarly, a phenomenological approach to studying a phenomenon such as 'number' can proceed on classical Husserlian lines, by bracketing-off interpretive assumptions until its 'essence' emerges. But each of these strategies, taken alone, falls short of the task of understanding *being* or *existence*. A solely hermeneutic approach to making sense of existence can be accused of lacking a creative edge, because it can only speak of what people have assumed existence to be. It would be a little more than a catalogue of beliefs and aphorisms.

Nothing 'revelatory' could appear. On the other hand, a purely phenomenological approach to existence would not be capable of dealing with the realisation that being human is to interpret the world: people are interpreting beings. Also, it is difficult, within a purely phenomenological approach, to deal with the realisation that *any* language used to describe existence carries its own assumptions about the nature of that to which it refers. Heidegger appreciated the value and limitations of both phenomenology and hermeneutics, and developed a new approach which combined them both. It is of interest that Heidegger is sometimes described as a phenomenologist (Moran, 2000) and sometimes as a hermeneuticist (Sass, 1988). Heidegger himself described his approach as phenomenological, a move which did not please Husserl.

The account offered here certainly oversimplifies the richness and complexity of Heidegger's contribution to philosophy, and the debates it has stimulated. Nevertheless, the point that it tries to make is that the relevance of Heidegger to qualitative research lies in the recognition that he was instrumental in opening up a new way of looking at previously taken-for-granted aspects of the world. Hermeneutics, before Heidegger, was primarily concerned with elucidating the meaning of 'special' texts. Phenomenology, before Heidegger, was primarily concerned with capturing the essences of abstract phenomena. No one had mounted a systematic attack on 'everydayness'. Who would have wanted to understand 'everydayness' before the twentieth century? Making sense of the everyday world had not been a problem until then. But for Heidegger and his contemporaries, who had lived through wars which devastated Europe, had observed massive social and technological change, and had struggled to reconcile themselves with the implications of an Enlightenment, rational image of the person, the characteristics and qualities of normal human existence had been brought into question in a fundamental manner.

How did Heidegger go about revealing the possible meanings of existence and everydayness? His integration of phenomenology and hermeneutics brought together several powerful analytic strategies. He began by drawing attention to the very process of *questioning* itself. As soon as we ask a question about any aspect of experience we are making some assumptions about that experience: 'every seeking gets guided beforehand by what is sought'. It is necessary, therefore, to examine the 'fore-understanding' from which the inquirer derives his or her questions. This is done by unravelling the meaning of the words that the inquirer has at his or her disposal for understanding and questioning. What are the cultural and historical origins of these words? How and why have the meanings of these words changed? This task requires engaging in a critical 'deconstruction' of the meaning of the language which constitutes everyday understanding of the topic. It is then possible to engage in a phenomenological description of the particular aspect of existence that is being examined. However, here again Heidegger departs from earlier phenomenological practice by seeking not only to describe the phenomenon, but to reveal what had previously been *hidden* in it. Phenomenological 'seeing', for Heidegger, is 'revelatory', it brings into the open new aspects of whatever is being investigated. It may be necessary to find new, or infrequently used, words in order to convey the revelatory nature of what has been found. Heidegger himself often used Greek terms to communicate meanings which he believed were not expressed in his native German. This whole process is informed by a different understanding of the purpose of the act of inquiry itself. Rather than seeking to produce an abstract, intellectual / rational representation of the world, Heidegger saw authentic knowing as connected with, and intrinsic to, the task of relating to the world within which one finds oneself. Finally, it is acknowledged that what is being attempted is an interpretation of a being that itself interprets. Once a 'discovery' is made by a philosopher or researcher, and an aspect of existence is revealed, this revelation will itself be interpreted and re-interpreted by others until it becomes part of everyday thinking.

## Implications for qualitative research in counselling and psychotherapy

The fusion of phenomenology and hermeneutics lies at the heart of Heidegger's work. His approach takes elements from phenomenology, and elements from hermeneutics, and creates something that goes beyond either. He was able to do this because he understood both phenomenology and hermeneutics well enough to see their limitations as well as their strengths, and to move easily back and forth between interpretation and description as necessary.

What are the implications of Heidegger's writings for qualitative researchers in counselling and psychotherapy? Probably the most obvious and central implication lies in the recognition that both phenomenological and hermeneutic sensibilities are necessary components of any attempt to study the dynamics of everyday life. Either approach taken on its own leaves the job 'half done'. In the chapters which follow, it can be seen that qualitative research in counselling and psychotherapy has attempted to elucidate various characteristics of the 'everyday' practice of therapy: the experience of the client, the experience of the therapist, the structure and qualities of certain kinds of moment in therapy, the construction of forms of existence in and through certain uses of language. What is very apparent is that very few contemporary therapy researchers go as far as Heidegger in uncovering the hidden and implicit meanings through which the everyday world is constructed. Any method of qualitative research involves the use of phenomenological and hermeneutic strategies for constructing meaning. In the end, qualitative research is a matter of finding the right balance, in the particular circumstances of each study, between phenomenology and hermeneutics. But, on the whole, the counselling and psychotherapy qualitative research community has not drawn on an adequate understanding of these basic underlying epistemologies. Hermeneutics has become reduced to 'interpretation'; phenomenology has been reduced to 'describing personal experience' and confused with humanistic psychology. And the need for a critically reflexive approach to language, as advocated by Heidegger, has seldom been adopted. A deeper grounding of qualitative research in these older epistemologies, which can only be achieved through engagement with philosophical writings, has the potential to enrich the work done by researchers in counselling and psychotherapy.

# 5

# Ethnographic Approaches to Research in Counselling and Psychotherapy

Ethnography can be defined as the study of the 'way of life' of a culture or group of people. Compared to other qualitative traditions, ethnographic research is all-encompassing. In seeking to develop a comprehensive description and understanding of a 'way of life', ethnographers are interested in *all* aspects of human behaviour: roles, rituals, belief systems, myths, language, religion, food, history, and the physical environment. Ethnographic research has been characterised as 'the art and science of describing a group or culture' (Fetterman, 1998: 473).

There are two important historical precursors to contemporary ethnographic research. The earliest use of ethnographic methods can be found in the work of pioneers of social anthropology such as Bronislaw Malinowski, Edward Evans-Pritchard and Margaret Mead at the beginning of the twentieth century. By the 1930s, the principle of carrying out in-depth, long-term fieldwork on members of specific cultural groups was then applied within the USA by the 'Chicago School' of sociology, led by Robert Park and W.H. Whyte. Ethnography is the longest established qualitative approach within the social sciences, since the prior origins of phenomenology and hermeneutics can be viewed as rooted in philosophy and theology. Compared to other social scientific qualitative approaches, ethnography has generated a much richer methodological literature, which has both anticipated and driven the key debates in the field.

The principal method of ethnographic research is *participant observation*. This procedure consists of spending time with people, listening to them and watching them, asking them questions, taking part in their daily routines. The research 'text' or data produced by participant observation are usually in the form of notes, transcripts of taped conversations, and may also include official or personal documents, photographs, video recordings and physical artefacts.

There exists a substantial literature on issues associated with the practice of participant observation. Clearly, it is no easy matter to join a social group from a different culture, particularly in the somewhat ambiguous role of 'researcher'. Questions arise around how the participant researcher makes contact, gets introduced, earns trust and gains access to what might normally be considered to be private matters. There are often difficult issues around the recording and collation of such data. Finally, there are yet more issues arising from the possibility that the researcher may come to over-identify with the group and be unable to leave, or unable to detach himself or herself sufficiently to be able to write a research report. The actual writing of ethnographic research presents another set of challenges. Ethnographic material is dense, voluminous and complex – how best can it be condensed into a readable and accessible form? Ethnographic material can also be highly sensitive and personal – how can the identity of informants be respected in confidence when a detailed ethnographic account is written? Finally, perhaps more than other approaches to qualitative research, ethnographic work highlights the *differences* between the researcher and the researched. In the end, this emphasis on difference and cultural distinctiveness raises the question of how far it is possible for someone to understand the experience of others.

The ethnographic tradition has not, on the whole, attempted to explain its methods in terms of sets of step-by-step procedures. The method of ethnographic research is *fieldwork*, and training appears to be achieved primarily through an apprenticeship model. The key research strategy in ethnography is the willingness of the researcher to spend long periods of time 'in the field', and the main criterion for success is the openness of the researcher to learning from this period of cultural immersion. Useful introductions to ethnographic method are available in Fetterman (1998) and Fielding (1993). Discussion of the issues involved in the application of this approach can be found in Atkinson and Hammersley (1994) and Denzin (1997). Goldstein et al. (1996) provide a usefully detailed account of the data collection and analysis procedures employed in one ethnographic study on a therapy-related topic.

Ethnographic methods have seldom been employed in research in counselling and psychotherapy. To some extent the dearth of ethnographic studies can be seen as resulting from the appropriation of counselling and psychotherapy by psychology and psychiatry: psychologists do not do ethnography. However, there are also a number of challenging issues arising from the private and confidential nature of therapy, and the difficulty for any ethnographer of gaining access to, for instance, an actual psychotherapy session.

Despite these considerable ethical and institutional barriers, there have been two significant published ethnographic studies on therapy topics. Both of these studies have looked at therapeutic communities. It makes sense that access to the life and work of a therapeutic community is easier to arrange than access to a small therapy clinic or private practice theory office. Typically, a fairly large number of people are involved in the work of a therapeutic community. Some of these people would be patients or staff, but there will always be others in less central roles, such as domestic staff, cooks, trainees and administrators. This diversity makes it possible for an ethnographic researcher to 'fit in' without being too conspicuous or intrusive.

The amount of information collected in ethnographic research, and the requirement in ethnographic writing to present detailed descriptions of people and places, means that many research studies in this tradition are published in the form of books or monographs rather than as articles. The book by Gubrium (1992) reports on a study of two family therapy centres ('treatment facilities') in the USA carried out by Jaber Gubrium and his student Maude Rittman. One of the centres ('Westside House') was an outpatient clinic mainly supported by government funding, and providing a variety of services, including family counselling, parenting skills classes and parent support groups. The other centre ('Fairview Hospital') was a private residential psychiatric clinic mainly funded through private insurance companies. The adolescent service comprised a 20-bed block, with a programme of therapeutic activities structured around a four-week treatment cycle. Both Westside and Fairview offered 'family-oriented' approaches to the treatment of disturbed young people, the focus of the Gubrium (1992) study.

In the Gubrium study, the research team negotiated access into specific activities at each centre, which they observed and around which they took notes:

> Mainly, we sat on the edge of proceedings, managing to be part of the background of ongoing talk and interaction. . . . Our aim was not to take down a tapelike facsimile of the proceedings, which would have been unrealistic for note taking, but to capture the substantive thrust of talk and interaction. . . . Some fieldnotes were reconstructions of casual conversations with individual patients, staff and family members. (Gubrium, 1992: 245)

In addition to these notes, the researchers had access to video recordings of therapy and supervision sessions, selected case materials, and educational materials. Little information is given about how this material was analysed, or whether informants had an opportunity to comment on the analysis that was generated.

What contribution does this ethnographic study make to an understanding of how family therapy operates? There are possibly three ways in which Gubrium (1992) adds to our knowledge of therapy. First, the book presents a detailed, vivid and highly readable descriptive account of what happens in these therapy centres. Unlike research articles in which the concrete details of what goes on in therapy is glossed over, Gubrium takes his reader inside these institutions. The reader gains a sense of what it would be like to be a staff member or patient in Westside or Fairview. Second, the research analyses the ways in which the experience of being a therapist or patient in these centres is constructed. This analysis is mainly built around attention to the use of language in the clinics, but routines, interaction patterns and physical surroundings are also taken into account. The construction of a therapeutic reality is largely structured around analysis of the ways in which staff in the centres use language to define domestic authority in the families they work with, and interpret the expression of feelings. Third, the book offers a conceptualisation of the meaning of therapy as a 'rationalisation of experience', or a 'discursive framework circumscribing the naming, sorting and categorisation of family troubles' (p. 220). The effectiveness of therapy is attributed to the capacity of staff to provide convincing and viable rationalisations:

> patients, clients, family members, and significant others hear troubles described in enticingly new ways. . . . Unfamilar terms are spoken by healing professionals therapists, counsellors, psychologists, psychiatrists, nurses, and consultants, among others – whose business it is to specify and treat the disorder of troubled lives. . . . Theirs is not the ordinary communication of the home. (Gubrium, 1992: 219–20)

The central explanation offered by Gubrium for the therapeutic impact of family therapy is that therapists are able to create a situation in which they have sufficient control and rhetorical persuasive credibility to bring patients to re-interpret, and then restructure, their ways of being together in families.

The value of Gubrium (1992), from the point of view of counsellors and psychotherapists, lies in its mixture of the strange and already known. The description of family therapy is recognisable, and, even for therapists who have not worked in this modality, merely expands what is already known: 'yes, this is what therapy is like'. But at the same time Gubrium's account of therapy is written by an outsider, someone with a rather unusual sociological 'take' on things. So, even if his descriptive account feels familiar, what he makes of these events and incidents is at times disconcerting. The book draws in the reader with convincing descriptive detail, then gradually subverts the reader's assumptions about the possible meaning of what is being reported.

The book by Bloor, McKeganey and Fonkert (1988) reports on a series of ethnographic studies of eight contrasting therapeutic communities in the UK and Holland. Although seldom cited by psychotherapy researchers, this book deserves to be a classic within the qualitative psychotherapy research literature. It includes a highly informative methodological Appendix, rich material drawn from the research sites, and an analysis that generates a conceptual framework that is potentially highly relevant for practice. All this is located within a thorough discussion of the historical origins of the therapeutic communities movement. Detailed aspects of findings and method have been presented by Bloor and McKeganey in a series of associated papers.

The approach taken by Bloor et al. was informed by a perspective on the nature of therapeutic work in the communities they studied which they described in these terms (1988: 5):

> we conceive of therapeutic work as a cognitive activity which can transform any mundane event in the community by *redefining* that event in the light of some therapeutic paradigm; thus an event may be redefined as showing responsibility, or seeking out a new and less pathogenic way of relating to others, or whatever, with the precise nature of that redefinition (and of the paradigm on which it is based) varying from community to community. To so redefine an everyday event as an occasion or a topic for therapy sets it apart and transforms it, much as the profane is transformed into the sacred by religious belief and ceremony: a simple act like mending a leak or cleaning the toilets is invested with new meaning and held up as relevant to the cleaner's recovery or rehabilitation. Any and every event and activity in the therapeutic community is open to such redefinition; there is no nook or cranny of residential life that is not open to scrutiny and potentially redefinable in therapeutic terms.

Their research reports comprised, in the main, richly detailed accounts of 'events and activities', interpreted in terms of the categories for understanding used by members of each therapeutic community to 'redefine' such events.

In addition to the substantial ethnographic studies by Gubrium (1992) and Bloor et al. (1988), there also exists a series of studies within the field of family therapy that are described by their authors as ethnographic (Kuehl et al., 1990; Newfield et al., 1990; Sells et al., 1994; Todd et al., 1991). However, although clearly influenced by the ethnographic tradition, these studies are all interview-based rather than reflecting the more all-encompassing participant observation approach that is characteristic of ethnographic work.


## Conclusions


Despite the small number of ethnographic studies of counselling and psychotherapy which have been carried out, the work that has been discussed in this chapter is sufficient to demonstrate the potential value of this approach. Ethnographic research is demanding and time-consuming and in the domain of therapy research is inevitably associated with ethical concerns around confidentiality. Nevertheless, the studies by Gubrium (1992) and Bloor et al. (1988) are interesting, informative, and readable. Ethnographic research is uniquely capable of capturing the quality and characteristics of the 'lived interactions' between therapists and client/patients in a way that does not seek to trivialise or over-simplify these encounters, but instead is willing to interpret them within their social context.

Ethnographic research also opens up the borderland between therapy and everyday life. Most qualitative research in counselling and psychotherapy focuses on what happens in the therapy room. Research in sociology and anthropology has looked at the everyday lives of people with illnesses and problems. But there has been little attention paid to the relationship between the therapy hour and what goes on outside that hour. Ethnographic research seems well suited to this task. There are many counselling and psychotherapy settings where the culture of the therapy room is embedded, but appears markedly different from that of the surrounding 'world'. Counsellors working in health clinics, student counselling centres and commercial companies are often aware of the 'clash of cultures' experienced by both their clients and themselves. Ethnographic research may be a useful method for exploring this type of issue. Therapeutic communities represent an obvious area for the application of ethnography. But there are many other counselling agencies and settings that could equally well be studied from an ethnographic perspective.

# 6

# Using Grounded Theory

Grounded theory analysis is a method that has been widely adopted by qualitative researchers, not only in counselling and psychotherapy but in other areas of social science and nursing studies. Grounded theory is without doubt the current 'market leader' in qualitative research. Its attractions are that there exists a set of explicit guidelines to follow, and an ever-expanding body of published articles that can function as exemplars and models. It is a method that gives the researcher a number of ways of rebutting the challenges of those hostile to qualitative research. It is a flexible approach that can be readily adapted to different circumstances.

This chapter begins with an overview of the principles of grounded theory, and then moves on to examining the application of this method in psychotherapy research. Finally, some of the critical issues associated with the method are reviewed.

## The origins of the grounded theory method

Grounded theory arose from the work of two sociologists, Barney Glaser and Anselm Strauss, in the 1960s. Their seminal text, *The Discovery of Grounded Theory*, was published in 1967. The title of this book captures the three main principles of the approach. First, the key task of the researcher is to 'discover' new ways of making sense of the social world. Second, the goal of analysis is to generate a 'theory', a formal framework for understanding the phenomenon being investigated. Third, this theory should be 'grounded' in the data rather than being imposed on it.

The Glaser and Strauss (1967) book remains a text with which anyone employing grounded theory needs to be familiar. However, the Strauss and Corbin (1990) book now represents the more widely used general introduction to the method. Other introductory accounts can be found in Charmaz (1995), O'Callaghan (1998) and Strauss and Corbin (1994). A widely cited account of the application of grounded theory in psychology and psychotherapy research can be found in Rennie, Phillips and Quartaro (1988).

Even though their work had grown out of the 'Chicago School' of ethnographic fieldwork, Glaser and Strauss had little to say about the personality and qualities of the researcher, or the relationship between researcher and informants. Grounded theory is primarily a method for analysing data, rather than a technique for data collection. A grounded theory approach can be used with different kinds of data, encompassing not only classic qualitative data such as interview transcripts, discourse and observational notes, but even arrays of quantitative data (Glaser and Strauss, 1967). The key skill of the good grounded theory researcher is that of being able to be sensitive to the potential multiple meanings of data:

> The goal of the analyst is to generate an emergent set of categories and their properties. . . . To achieve this goal the analyst begins with open coding, which is coding the data in every way possible. Another way to phrase it is 'running the data open'. The analyst codes for as many categories as might fit; he codes different incidences into as many categories as possible. . . . He may even code for what is not obviously stated. . . . The . . . rule is to *analyze the data line by line*, constantly coding each sentence. . . . As the analyst gets deep into the data, he discovers that all data can be subsumed as an indicator of some category in the analysis . . . a total saturation occurs: all data fit. (Glaser, 1978: 56–60, original emphasis)

The key to achieving a satisfactory grounded theory analysis lies in the immersion of the researcher in the data. The emphasis on researcher reflexivity that is found in other qualitative genres is not highlighted in the grounded theory approach in an explicit manner. However, it is clear that a researcher could not possess sufficient theoretical sensitivity without being able to reflect on his or her biases and assumptions.

One of the distinctive characteristics of the grounded theory tradition is a view that the work of analysis is best done alone, that only through the thorough immersion of a highly motivated individual in the material can an adequate degree of theoretical 'saturation' be achieved. This insistence on the value of individual engagement with research material has been problematic for some researchers. For example, students trained within the traditions of academic psychology have learned to take for granted criteria of methodological rigour such as inter-rater reliability and convergent validity. Neither of these criteria readily applies to grounded theory studies. Other researchers, for example those who espouse social constructionist or feminist epistemologies, may also be uncomfortable with an approach which seems to downplay collaborative working.

## Doing grounded theory

The initial Glaser and Strauss (1967) book which introduced the grounded theory approach set out a set of principles, with some suggestions regarding how these principles might be applied. Over time, as grounded theory has been taught and used by subsequent generations of researchers, it has gradually become more formalised into a specified set of procedures. The most widely used 'procedural manual' is the book by Strauss and Corbin (1990), although Glaser (1978) also includes a wealth of detailed suggestions on how to carry out a grounded theory analysis. Although there is some debate over the Strauss and Corbin (1990) approach to operationalising grounded theory (which will be discussed below), their set of procedural rules can be taken as typical of the way in which a grounded theory study would be pursued. Doing a grounded theory study consists of a series of steps:

1   The researcher identifies a research question that is broad, open-ended and action-oriented. An example of a research question given by Strauss and Corbin (1990: 38) is 'How do women manage a pregnancy complicated by a chronic illness?' They stress that the research question in a grounded theory study is 'a statement that identifies the phenomenon to be studied' (p. 30). Moreover, grounded theory questions emphasise *action* and *process*: people are seen as purposeful agents, engaged in action which results in, or is in response to, a process of change. The aim of grounded theory is to uncover the *basic social processes* that underlie behaviour.

2   A group of people or settings that exemplify different facets of this question is chosen. Typically, grounded theory research is carried out on data-sets collected from 8–20 informants. Fewer than 8 informants results in an approach which is essentially case-study based. More than 20 informants tends to produce too much data to be analysed fully, and will result in the collection of redundant (i.e. unnecessarily repetitive) data.

3   The researcher does *not* make any attempt to review the literature in advance of collecting data. The aim is to approach the phenomenon with an open mind, so that themes and categories 'emerge' from it rather than being imposed on it.

4   There is synchronisation of data collection and analysis. If possible, each interview (or set of observations) is analysed as soon as possible following its collection, with the emerging theoretical framework being used to sensitise the researcher to the types of issues and areas to be covered in the next interview.

5   The selection of informants or cases is made on the basis of *theoretical* interest ('can this person's account expand or test my emerging category system?') rather than on the basis of random or stratified sampling. Usually, the sample sizes in grounded theory studies are not large enough to make random sampling a realistic option.

6   Data collection ends when the category system or 'theory' is 'saturated', in other words when the researcher ceases to gain new ideas or insights from the interview or observational material that is being collected.

7   The researcher reads the material and engages in a process of 'open coding'. This activity has been defined as: 'the process of breaking down, examining, comparing, conceptualizing, and categorizing data' (Strauss and Corbin, 1990: 61). Open coding is in many ways the heart of the grounded theory method. The aim is to generate as many alternative categories as possible for segment or 'meaning unit' within the text. It is as though the analyst forces himself or herself continually to ask 'what *else* could this mean?'

8   Strauss and Corbin (1990) recommend that, whenever possible, categories are framed in terms of *activities* and processes (i.e. basic social processes) rather than static entities. Grounded theory categories tend to be active rather than passive terms (e.g. words or phrases such as becom*ing*, storytell*ing* and resist*ing* rather than static entities such as 'the process of . . .', 'narrative' or 'resistance').

9   The categories that are created through this process are filed, with each entry comprising the title of the category plus the interview quote or meaning unit to which it refers.

10   The file or set of categories is then examined as an entirety, to identify higher order categories (i.e. ideas that allow the clustering together of subsets of the initial categories that were created during open coding).

11   The connection between categories is then explored through the technique of 'axial coding'. This involves the identification of the conditions under which categories occur, and the consequences of their occurrence (i.e. what follows them). This method allows the fragmentation of the research text that took place during coding to be reversed; the pieces of the jigsaw are put back together to make a whole picture.

12   Throughout, a process of 'constant comparison' is used, through which the meanings of all categories are compared and contrasted with each other both within and across cases. This process encourages the constant refinement of the category system as a whole. For instance, initially different categories may be found to have the same meaning and therefore can be collapsed into a single category. Alternatively, different nuances of meaning may be found within a category, resulting in the original category code being split into two or three more tightly defined renamed codes.

13   Throughout all stages of data collection and analysis, the researcher keeps 'memos' and draws diagrams. These techniques enable ideas about the emerging theoretical framework to be recorded and stored for future reference, without interfering with the painstaking work of staying as close as possible to the material and conceptualising it in ways that stay 'grounded'.

14    A 'main category' emerges, which captures the meaning of the phenomenon of study taken as a whole. When working with the material, the researcher is seeking not only to describe or 'map' the overall set of meanings that are being discovered, but to identify one or more themes that capture the core meaning of the phenomenon being studied. While the majority of lower-level codes and categories tend to employ descriptive terms, main categories should reflect the emergent *conceptualisation* of the data. Ultimately, the main category or categories should possess sufficient theoretical resonance to function to link the results of the study to findings and theories from other studies.

15    The analysis is written up. Usually, a grounded theory analysis is presented first in terms of a representation which centres on definitions of the main category and the structure of subsidiary categories, with some examples of observations or interview quotes being given to exemplify each of the categories. Some researchers follow up this global represen-tation by writing further papers or chapters which offer a more fine-grained focus on particular individual categories. In writing grounded theory reports, it is usual for any interpretation in terms of formal theory, or comparison with previous research findings, to *follow* the presentation of the grounded theory model, thus honouring the principle that the method eschews any imposition of pre-existing assumptions on the phenomenon being studied.

This account of grounded theory analysis is necessarily over-simplified, and does not do justice to the subtle and challenging nature of this form of analysis. Doing a grounded theory analysis properly involves a constant checking and re-checking of every aspect of the data, so that every possible way of making sense of the data can be given sufficient consideration. The procedures of grounded theory analysis can be seen as a set of methodo-logical rules designed to ensure that the interpretation of qualitative material is carried out in a comprehensive and systematic manner.

A major practical problem with grounded theory analysis arises with the task of keeping track of the categories that are being generated through open coding. Traditionally, grounded theory researchers have either written their coding notes in the margins of transcripts or fieldwork notes and then manually cut and pasted these segments of text into files, or have copied meaning unit text excerpts on to file cards. Each file card then builds up a set of examples of that category. This is very laborious, but can also be satisfying, for instance through the creative use of colour and imagery to record a pre-verbal intuitive sense of the data. Recently, some grounded theory researchers have used software packages such as NU-DIST and ATLAS-TI, or even normal wordprocessing tools such as Word or Wordperfect, to store and catalogue categories electronically. This procedure saves time, but is felt by some researchers to reduce the potential for 'seeing' the data that is afforded when, for example, index cards are spread over a table or floor. The pros and cons of qualitative software packages are discussed more fully in Chapter 11.

## The basis of grounded theory analysis

In terms of the ideas introduced in earlier chapters of this book, it is possible to see that grounded theory can be understood as an effective packaging of some of the key features of earlier traditions of qualitative or human science inquiry:

The injunction to avoid reading about the topic prior to collecting data, and the emphasis on theoretical sensitivity, are similar to the phenomeno-logical notion of 'bracketing'.

The goal of arriving at an interpretation of the phenomenon (a grounded theory) reflects a fundamentally hermeneutic approach.

It can be argued that the achievement of Glaser and Strauss was to take the best of phenomenology and hermeneutics, separate the method off from its difficult and potentially confusing roots, and describe it in terms of a set of procedures that were relatively easy to learn and apparently replicable. Thus, as Denzin and Lincoln (1994b) have pointed out, grounded theory represents a form of qualitative research that is systematised and fits well within a 'modern', rational social science.

Grounded theory is highly appealing to students seeking to undertake Masters or Doctoral research, because there are clear instructions concerning what to do, and what the final product should look like. Nevertheless, many people using grounded theory for the first time, for instance applying it to the analysis of interview transcripts, find themselves asking the question: 'where do the categories come from?' For Strauss and Corbin (1990) there are three possible sources of category labels: (i) the analyst's own common-sense constructs; (ii) technical terms drawn from the theoretical or professional literature; and (iii) the language used by informants. There is an ambiguity here. The grounded theory model that is ultimately produced in a research study is partly a matter of how the researcher saw things anyway, partly a matter of the theoretical or professional community to which he or she belonged, and partly inspired by the everyday language of informants. Essentially, in grounded theory work the researcher takes categories, or meaning labels, from wherever he or she can find them. What matters, in the end (according to proponents of grounded theory), is whether these categories can be made to fit together in a coherent manner, and whether they are congruent with the data. But there is an uneasy compromise here between pragmatism (putting together a set of categories that 'work') and the desire to be clear about just what kind of 'theory' it is that is being produced. For example, a grounded theory that is constructed using concepts drawn from the professional literature is presumably a different kind of knowledge from a grounded theory derived from the language of informants. It is easy to see that the latter is 'grounded', but there may be a suspicion that the former may involve a subtle form of forcing of the data into pre-conceived models.

We will return to this important issue later in the chapter, after looking at an example of the use of grounded theory in psychotherapy research.

## The use of grounded theory in psychotherapy research: the work of David Rennie

David Rennie, based at the Department of Psychology in York University, Toronto, has been a pioneer in the use of qualitative methods in psychotherapy research. Since the early 1980s he has conducted a series of studies into aspects of the client's experience of therapy. These studies have used the method of interpersonal process recall interviews to collect clients' accounts of their experiences in therapy sessions. Essentially, clients are invited to listen to a tape recording of a recent session, and are asked to stop the tape and report on what they remember experiencing during the actual therapy session. The investigator asks open-ended questions to assist the client in talking about their experience. This procedure typically leads to the creation of a long taped interview, which is then transcribed, conveying many aspects of how and what the client thought, felt and did during the session being studied. Rennie has then submitted these transcripts to a very thorough and lengthy process of grounded theory analysis. He has described his use of grounded theory in a number of papers: Rennie, Phillips and Quartaro (1988); Rennie (1994d, 1994e, 1996). His work has produced a series of substantive papers reporting on his representation of the client's experience as a whole (Rennie, 1990, 1992) and then subsequently on specific aspects (or categories) of client experiencing, including client deference (Rennie, 1994a), storytelling (Rennie, 1994b), resistance (Rennie, 1994c), metaphor (Angus and Rennie, 1988, 1989), and specific therapeutic interventions (Watson and Rennie, 1994). Finally, the implications of this research for practice have been explored in a recent book (Rennie, 1998b). This body of work is probably unique within qualitative psychotherapy research in making it possible to track the application of an approach through a programme of research. What makes this set of studies even more significant is that Rennie has consistently sought to clarify the philosophical underpinnings of the grounded theory method, and has openly wrestled with its limitations and ambiguities (Rennie, 1995, 1998a).

The research carried out by Rennie and his students into the client's experience of therapy began in the early 1980s. Some of the early findings were disseminated in conference papers during the mid-1980s. It was not until 1988, however, that the work was first published in a journal article. This was a paper on method (Rennie, Phillips and Quartaro, 1988). Something of the flavour of the professional and scientific context within which Rennie was operating is expressed in the section of the paper in which the rationale for choosing grounded theory analysis was explained. Rennie, Phillips and Quartaro recount that, after giving due consideration to other potential qualitative methods that were then available, such as empirical phenomenology and the 'new paradigm' approach of Peter Reason, they chose grounded theory:

> . . . because it seemed relatively more systematic than any of the other approaches and because, compared to the phenomenological and new paradigm approaches, it places less emphasis on the role of the researcher in co-constructing the respondent's accounts. We viewed the reduced emphasis on co-construction as being two-edged: it meant that a grounded theory analysis would be less intense, but, as a compensation, would be a way of studying a relatively larger number of individuals. We were swayed by the last feature because of its implication for generalizability . . . in adopting this new method we have had to abandon most of the canons of the hypothetico-deductive approach (. . .) this . . . led us into what we now refer to as the 'period of darkness' wherein we were not sure that what we contemplated doing was credible, and we were tormented with a dread that, even if we felt that the returns from the new approach were credible, peers within our discipline would rule otherwise. (1988: 140)

There is a strong sense here of the risk to professional acceptance associated with undertaking qualitative research in a psychology environment dominated by measurement and experimentation. Rennie was not alone among psychotherapy researchers in feeling like this. The consequences of this pressure to conform to the 'canons of the hypothetico-deductive approach' was consistently to push qualitative psychotherapy researchers in the direction of methods that were more 'systematised' and less reliant on the creation of an intense (i.e. subjective and personal) relationship between researcher and researched. Here, qualitative psychotherapy research can be seen to perpetuate the researcher–subject split that has been central to modern psychology (Danziger, 1997a).

One of the strengths of Rennie's work is that it provides an excellent example of a grounded theory that is based on hundreds of hours of dedicated effort over several years, accompanied by an unwillingness to cut corners. It represents probably the best that can be achieved with grounded theory in the psychotherapy domain. Table 6.1 displays the categories which emerged from his main study of 16 interviews with 14 clients (Rennie, 1992). Here it can be seen how a grounded theory analysis is

Table 6.1   *Concepts and categories from a grounded theory study of client experiences of therapy*

**Main category 1   The client's relationship with personal meaning**

| | *MUs |
|---|---|
| (a) *The pursuit of personal meaning* | |
| Client scrutinises own processes | 302 |
| The client's track | 172 |
| Insight | 105 |
| Contact with feelings | 92 |
| Client narrative / storytelling | 89 |
| Digestion (coming to terms with a new awareness) | 47 |
| | |
| (b) *The avoidance of meaning* | |
| Client's defensiveness | 120 |
| Client's resistance | 46 |
| Playing for effect | 42 |
| Willingness to change | 25 |
| Lying to the therapist | 17 |

**Main category 2   The client's perception of the relationship with the therapist**

| | |
|---|---|
| (a) *'Nonspecific' relationship factors* | |
| Relationship with the therapist | 134 |
| Client's perception of the therapeutic task | 102 |
| Client's dependence–independence | 78 |
| Perception of therapist's evaluation | 71 |
| Therapist's manner | 52 |
| | |
| (b) *Client's deference* | |
| Concern about therapist's approach | 119 |
| Fear of criticising therapist | 91 |
| Understanding the therapist's frame of reference | 73 |
| Meeting perceived therapist's expectations | 51 |
| Metacommunication | 14 |

**Main category 3   The client's experience of the therapist's operations**

| | |
|---|---|
| (a) *Operations bearing upon the client-in-identity* | |
| Accuracy of therapist's responding | 86 |
| Therapist interpretation | 61 |
| Questioning | 36 |
| | |
| (b) *Operations bearing on the client-as-agent* | |
| Therapist use of artifices in directing client's processing | 106 |
| Advice by therapist | 66 |
| | |
| (c) *Operations bearing on therapist in relation with client* | |
| Therapist's active support | 53 |
| Therapist self-disclosure | 35 |

**Main category 4   The client's experience of outcomes**

| | |
|---|---|
| Impact of the therapy | 146 |
| Impact of the inquiry | 145 |

Source: Rennie (1992) (abridged) (Note: * indicates total number of Meaning Units contributing to each category)

structured into overarching and lower-level categories. The figures for 'meaning units' show how many examples of each category were collected, and give an indication of the scale of the coding and filing task that was involved.

The kind of overall representation of findings set out in Table 6.1 is a necessary stage in a grounded theory analysis, in that it allows the results to be displayed as a whole. Table 6.1 illustrates the richness of analysis that can be generated using a grounded theory approach, and also the way in which narrow, observation-based categories (such as *client storytelling/narrative*) are embedded within more general or conceptual categories (e.g., *the client's relationship with personal meaning*). The data presented in Table 6.1 are derived from 16 interviews with 14 informants. It can be seen that the most frequently generated categories are each grounded in more than 100 examples (meaning units that have been coded using that category). This approach to analysis therefore makes it possible to accumulate substantial evidence to support the category structure which emerges, even with relatively limited numbers of informants. The display in Table 6.1 also gives an indication of the time-consuming nature of grounded theory analysis. For example, 302 bits of text were accumulated that could be construed as reflecting *client scrutiny of own processes*. Each of these text segments (meaning units) needed to be compared with all the others, to ensure that they shared the same emergent meaning. The whole set of *client scrutiny* segments would need to be compared with material grouped under other categories (e.g., *client track*), to check for overlap. The physical task of keeping track of these pieces of information is highly demanding.

The value of a display like Table 6.1, or of a summary statement based on such a display, is that it allows the reader to get a sense of the analysis as a whole. However, only a very limited depth of discussion and exemplification is possible when a substantial number of categories is presented. So, while a table of categories is useful for readers or research audiences, in providing the overall conceptual 'map' that the researcher has come up with, it needs to be supplemented by further reports which focus on particular categories in a more fine-grained manner.

In these further reports, the category 'map' as a whole is viewed from the perspective of one category. In other words, categories are brought in to the discussion only if they shed light on the primary category that is being examined. David Rennie has published and presented a series of papers which examine in closer detail specific categories drawn from the initial set. These include papers on resistance, deference, storytelling and client agency.

It is instructive to look at the way in which these more focused grounded theory papers are written. The introduction to each paper 'sets the scene', by providing a rationale for the study, rather than reviewing the relevant research and theoretical literature. It is only in the final discussion section that theory is explicitly introduced as a means of interpreting the findings. This practice corresponds with the recommendation of Glaser and Strauss that in-depth reading of the relevant research and theoretical literature follows data collection rather than precedes it. However, in the case of David Rennie (as with any other psychotherapy researcher who is a therapist) there is no doubt that he was deeply familiar with much of the relevant theoretical literature before he ever interviewed a research informant. The use of grounded theory by professionals studying their own profession (e.g. nurses, teachers, psychotherapists) is possibly quite different in this respect from the experience of sociologists such as Glaser and Strauss, who would typically find themselves studying people and situations for which they had no specialist or insider professional or theoretical concept system.

Another interesting aspect of the way in which David Rennie's papers are written is that they rely on both narrative and paradigmatic ways of knowing (see Polkinghorne, 1995). For example, in discussing the category of *fear of criticising the therapist* in his paper on client deference, Rennie (1994a) writes in a way that combines abstract categorisation with narrative vignettes. At the beginning of the Results section of this paper, the category of *fear of criticising the therapist* is formally defined:

> This property represents the client's fear of criticizing or challenging the therapist. The category is broad enough to encompass the reluctance to criticize as well as the actual fear of criticizing. In a given instance, there may be any of a number of reasons for clients not wanting to criticize. Clients may feel that it is not their place to question their therapist's approach because they view themselves as naïve laypersons and the therapist as an expert who probably knows what he or she is doing. . . . Finally, they may worry that criticism would hurt the therapist's feelings, and jeopardize their relationship with the therapist. (Rennie, 1994a: 430–1)

Later in this section of the paper, a lengthy illustration is offered in the form of a story about one client/informant. The story is told first by the author (Rennie):

> In the inquiry session, the client . . . revealed that, in a therapy session prior to the one under study, she had been trying to understand why she pitied herself so much. She reported that her therapist, who was generally very supportive, was unsympathetic to this question of 'Why?' The therapist felt that this question was not useful and that, instead, the client should concentrate on simply accepting her self-pity and work from there. The client revealed in the inquiry that she had since heeded her therapist's wishes in terms of what she verbally focused on in her sessions with her therapist but that, inwardly, she was still preoccupied with the question of 'Why?' (Rennie, 1994a: 432)

The story is then continued in the words of the client/informant:

> She's telling me that I rip myself up too much. . . . I'm always left with another question that I can't pose to her because I feel like I'm just wiping out what she's trying to do. (ibid.)

The combination of a paradigmatic approach which specifies the properties of categories, alongside a narrative approach which exemplifies these categories both through the voice of the researcher *and* through the voice of the informant, represents a powerful rhetorical strategy. It is certainly a highly effective way of communicating the sense of the category. It is consistent with the recommendations of Strauss and Corbin (1990) who make it clear that writing grounded theory involves presenting categories (paradigmatic knowing) and also telling stories (narrative knowing). However, it poses problems for Polkinghorne's (1995) suggestion that qualitative research can be divided into either narrative *or* paradigmatic forms. With Rennie's work, and with the work of many other qualitative researchers, it seems as though both narrative and paradigmatic modes of knowing are employed *together* in the same report, and that much of the force of the report arises from the tension between the generalising thrust of categories and the vivid, convincing detail of stories.

If the programme of research carried out by David Rennie and his students into the client's experience of therapy is tracked through time, it can be seen that it has moved steadily in the direction of interpretation, theorising and application. This is again consistent with the grounded theory model. The close engagement with actual human experience that grounded theory insists upon leads to the emergence of a powerful and valid set of concepts through which that aspect of the world can be understood and acted upon. It is also perhaps worth noting that the concepts employed by Rennie have become more characteristically 'Glaserian', in the sense of foregrounding basic social processes, as time has gone on. The early version of the category system (Table 6.1) includes some 'state' or 'entity' labels, such as 'insight', 'contact' and 'factors'. The more recent work gives much more emphasis to the notion of the client as an agent who *does* things (Rennie, 2000b). Evidence for the applicability of this research programme can be found in Rennie's (1998b) book on doing therapy, which provides many examples of ways in which research findings have been the driving force behind the construction of his distinctive approach to person-centred experiential therapy.

There is no doubt that this set of studies affords an impeccable exemplar of what can be achieved with grounded theory. It is a jewel in the crown of qualitative psychotherapy research. Nevertheless, there are questions which can be asked about some of the social and cultural dimensions of this work. These concern the co-constructed nature of the 'data' and the relationship between the research and what hermeneuticists might call the 'tradition' within which it is located.

Recall that, at the outset, Rennie, Phillips and Quartaro (1988) wished to de-emphasise 'the role of the researcher in co-constructing the respondent's accounts'. The whole tenor of the empirical papers and chapters which followed reflected this intention. The concepts and categories which were put forward were attributed to the laborious work of identifying meaning units, being theoretically sensitive, etc. However, the findings reported by Rennie can be looked at from a quite different perspective. David Rennie is a skilled and sensitive person-centred therapist with a strongly affirming presence, who was able to set up a fairly unique situation where therapy clients were able to open up, perhaps as never before and never again, about their experience of their most recent therapy session. Could it be that the 'findings' were constructed in these interviews, rather than in the analyst's study? Could it be that what was achieved in this programme of work was a highly effective means for clients to find and have a voice? The grounded theory analysis supplied a systematic way of organising and presenting what was found, but the main contribution of the research was in collecting the material in the first place. To put the argument in such blunt terms is to polarise and exaggerate, but for a purpose. There is a strong tendency in the grounded theory methods literature to focus on the job of analysing data, and on the many ways that researchers can improve their analytic skills and sensitivity. There is little emphasis on the data-collection side of the methodological equation. This may not matter in social anthropology departments where students are trained in the skills required for fieldwork and ethnography (although I suspect it does matter there too), but it is crucially important in departments of nursing and psychology where students may be poorly equipped to make sense of the roles and processes involved in this kind of data collection. The richness and relevance of findings may depend more on the quality of the relationship between researcher and informant than it does on the rigour of the analysis of the data (Mearns and McLeod, 1984).

A second sociocultural issue involves the impact that Rennie's work has had on the field of psychotherapy. In my experience, among people who have read this research there are some who have been highly influenced by it (I am one of these) and others who regard it as irrelevant, who do not 'see the point' in it. Some of these less positive readers are colleagues who may be sympathetic to qualitative research but who for some reason do not connect with what Rennie has to say. Others are not sympathetic to qualitative research and wonder if his findings are valid or generalisable. These are impressionistic comments, but a review of the literature shows remarkably few citations of this body of work. This is surprising given the fact that most of these papers have been published in high-status North American journals (e.g. *Journal of Counseling Psychology*; *Psychotherapy*). The situation is similar to that described in Chapter 3, where it was argued that replication of phenomenological research is problematic and not often attempted. It is almost as though the injunction within both the phenom-enological and grounded theory traditions to abstain from reading the literature in advance of carrying out a study deters potential researchers from attempting to study well-known topics that they have previously read about. The absence of citations may therefore be due to the fact that there have been no attempts to replicate (or even partially replicate) Rennie's work on the client's experience of therapy. It is almost as though the very act of opening up this topic for investigation prevents other qualitative therapy researchers from investigating it. If they have read Rennie's papers they already know too much to do what he did, which was to approach these phenomena without presuppositions.

However, there is also, from a hermeneutic perspective, the criticism that grounded theory research does not sufficiently disclose the intellectual or cultural tradition within which the research is carried out. A researcher deciding to undertake a grounded theory study buys into the idea that categories and concepts are grounded in (arise or emerge from) the data as far as possible. To write up a grounded theory study along the lines of 'before embarking on this study I was deeply committed to a humanistic view of the person and this is what I found in the interview material' would come across as quite aberrant. And yet to obscure the fact that the research is being carried out for the purpose of refining and articulating a particular perspective is to make it that much harder for practitioners within that tradition to make a relationship with what is being written. The ter-minology used by David Rennie and his colleagues to construct grounded theory categories is permeated by the language of humanistic psychology and experiential psychotherapy. Terms such as 'reflexivity', 'flow', 'aware-ness', 'self-disclosure' are taken from humanistic/experiential discourse. It could well be imagined that a psychoanalytic researcher might come up with quite different terminology if faced with the same data. The reluctance to acknowledge the 'tradition-informed' nature of the research perhaps leaves some readers unsure about what they are getting, and where it fits in.

There is another, quite different way in which the relationship between a research programme that is located within a theoretical tradition or prac-tice community, and the members of that community, can constitute a barrier to the acceptability of the research. If the investigation comes up with ideas which go too far beyond the existing consensus, which stretch to far beyond the 'horizon of meaning' of the majority, then it will inevitably be criticised or ignored. It is possible that something of this kind has occurred in the case of David Rennie's research into the client's experience of therapy. What he has found in his studies is probably recognisable by most therapists, as reflecting processes with which they are familiar, but is none the less not at all easy to assimilate into existing theory or practice. A conventional therapist understanding of the client experience of therapy emphasises the importance of the therapeutic 'alliance'. While the elements of the therapeutic alliance can be found in the list of categories displayed in Table 6.1, Rennie's rigorous application of a discovery-oriented method forced him *beyond* these categories and through into a new way of looking at the client. The client has become an agent, in control. The client is the one who creates the therapy, who makes the relationship. And, even worse, most of the client's agency is hidden from the therapist. This new perspective radically deconstructs our previous understanding of the respective roles of therapist and client, and then finally reconstructs them in a quite different light. The implications of this shift in perspective are immense, glimpsed by Rennie himself but certainly not appreciated (or welcomed?) by his colleagues. If this analysis of the nature of Rennie's contribution to psychotherapy research is correct, it points toward one of the basic dilemmas of qualitative inquiry. If findings are correct but 'obvious' they can be dismissed as trivial and ignored. If findings genuinely transcend the current consensus they are ignored because they are too threatening or too difficult to do anything with. Is there a middle ground?

## The fragmentation of grounded theory

In the mid-1990s, at the point where his work had finally achieved acceptance within the psychotherapy research community, David Rennie's interests turned in the direction of philosophy. Specifically, he set himself the task of finding out how and why grounded theory could be considered capable of producing findings that could claim some kind of truth value. How can we know that a grounded theory analysis is valid? What kind of knowledge does grounded theory generate? What are the essential steps in the method? To unravel these questions required extensive reading in the philosophy of science. But why was this necessary? Why, having demonstrated in a series of seminal papers, that grounded theory could 'come up with the goods', was there any need to return to first principles and look again at the basic conceptual building blocks of the approach? To some extent the answer was that Rennie had always been interested in the philosophy of psychology. Philosophical issues had been raised in the first of the grounded theory papers (Rennie, Phillips and Quartaro, 1988). He worked in a department which included two of the most eminent and influential contemporary philosophers of psychology – David Bakan and Kurt Danziger. But there was a more pressing reason to look again at the underpinnings of grounded theory: the method was fragmenting.

One of the attractions of grounded theory, in contrast to competing qualitative approaches, was that it offered a specified, laid-down method that could be followed step by step to produce good quality results. The major early publications on the grounded theory method, Glaser and

Strauss (1967) and Glaser (1978), carried accounts of the method that were in many ways broad-brush and schematic, but nevertheless included enough procedural detail to give readers confidence that they could know how to apply the method properly. The material in these books was supplemented for many students by training workshops and seminars run by their tutors. However, even in Britain, where the system of being trained and mentored by someone who had himself or herself been trained by either Glaser or Strauss did not really exist, researchers felt able to immerse themselves in the books and published studies and get on with doing their grounded theory study.

All this started to change with the publication in 1990 of Strauss and Corbin's *Basics of Qualitative Research*. Compared to anything that had gone before, this book presented a much more systematised and concrete account of how to do grounded theory. It was in effect a manual for students, strong on practical techniques but with little reference to underlying methodological issues. The appearance of this book made it clear to Glaser that he and Strauss held quite different views of what grounded theory was about, and how a grounded theory analysis should be conducted. The contrast between their positions is complex and multi-faceted, but some of the difference in approach is captured in these quotations:

> Generating grounded theory *takes time*. It is above all a *delayed action* phenomenon. Little increments in coding, analyzing and collecting data cook and mature then to blossom later into theoretical memos. Significant theoretical realizations come with growth and maturity in the data, and much of this is outside of the analyst's awareness until it happens. Thus the analyst must pace his patience, and not just be patient, accepting nothing until something happens, as it surely does. It is therefore vital that the analyst learn to take the quality and kind of time it takes to do the discovery process. . . . (Glaser, 1978: 18)

> Coding is a systematic and precise set of procedures that can't be done haphazardly or at the whim of the researcher. In order for the emerging theory to be grounded, as well as valid and reliable, the procedures must be followed as carefully as those that govern good quantitative studies. . . . (Strauss and Corbin, 1990: 46)

For Glaser, coding is a matter of patience, of allowing for creative insights to arise. For Strauss, coding is a matter of following procedures. A key difference between the Glaserian and Straussian positions appears to be that, for Glaser, the crucial act of grounded analysis is one of *emergence* – the researcher must allow sufficient time for new concepts to emerge, and then must respect the discovery in whatever shape it takes. In Glaser's view, the Strauss and Corbin approach has, in specifying analytic procedures such as axial coding, become much more an act of *forcing* the data into pre-conceived forms. Papers by Melia (1996) and Stern (1994) provide further exegesis of the debate between Glaser and Strauss. Unfortunately, the death of Anselm Strauss in 1996 has inevitably changed the nature of this debate, perhaps leaving some issues unresolvable. However, in one sense there are perhaps issues here that are *forever* unresolvable. If, as was suggested earlier, grounded theory comprises an integration of phenomenology and hermeneutics, then perhaps Glaser is pulling in the direction of phenomenology ('back to the things themselves') while Strauss and Corbin are pulling in the direction of hermeneutics (applying a pre-existing interpretive framework).

The dispute is made even more complex by the fact that another group, taught by Leonard Schatzman (a former colleague of Glaser and Strauss), make claims for their own distinctive version of grounded theory (Kools, McCarthy, Durham and Robrecht, 1996). In addition, Rennie has suggested that his version of grounded theory (Rennie, Phillips and Quartaro, 1988) enables a more thorough analysis of data than either the Glaser or Strauss approaches. Turner (1981) has also described his own adaptation of grounded theory method. It would appear, therefore, that there are three, and possibly four or five, formally described versions of grounded theory analysis.

The existence of these alternative models of grounded theory leads to the question: what is the method? Is there an essential grounded theory manoeuvre that is, or should be, intrinsic to any form of qualitative research that calls itself grounded theory? This is one of the questions that David Rennie has set himself in his recent philosophical work. The other question he has been pursuing is an older one: how can realism and relativism be reconciled in qualitative research such as grounded theory analysis? In other words, to what extent can a qualitative researcher claim that his or her findings reflect reality (are objective) as against merely representing a 'reading' or understanding of the phenomenon that takes its place alongside a range of other plausible readings (relativism).

For Rennie, the answer to both of these questions has involved a return to the writings of Charles Sanders Peirce, a philosopher who worked within the American tradition of pragmatism associated with William James and John Dewey. Peirce proposed that there are three separate means of forming inferences (i.e. making rational connections between one statement and another). The first of these is induction, which basically consists of collecting together observations about the world that share common properties. The second form of inference is deduction, which consists of drawing out the logical implications of a statement (i.e. 'all crows are black, so if this is a crow it must be black'). Both induction and deduction occur in grounded theory analysis. Open coding generates multiple examples of the same meaning category (induction). Constant comparison and theoretical sampling require testing out deductions across cases (e.g. 'if this concept that has emerged in cases a, b, and c is a potential main category it should be present in cases x, y and z'). However, neither induction nor deduction get close to explaining the way that grounded theory analysts (or anyone else, for that matter) comes up with *new* categories. Peirce's notion of *abduction* does just this. Rennie (1998a: 111) explains that 'abduction is hypothesizing . . . it is any form of a new idea, including intuition and hunches'. He adds that:

> an interesting feature of qualitative research is that it involves the symbiosis of abduction and induction. This symbiosis is achieved by bracketing preconceptions of the phenomenon of interest and delaying the development of conceptualizations until they are derived from immersion in the data pertaining to the phenomenon. Moreover, the adherence to a conceptualization thus conceived is contingent on its being supported by the data as a whole. (ibid.)

This argument represents an important contribution to qualitative method. It represents a clear account of just *how* phenomenology and hermeneutics come together in grounded theory. What Rennie is saying is that the role of the phenomenological attitude is to delay a rush to judgement in relation to the meaning of a piece of data. The grounded theory analyst does not take the first conceptualisation that occurs to him or her, and certainly does not wish to approach the text with a pre-formed conceptual scheme. The analyst *waits*, and in this waiting the process of abduction can occur. Then, once the hypothesis or 'new idea' has emerged, it is tested against all other possible data. It is this recursive process of testing categories rigorously within the data that enables grounded theory to claim some degree of realism, while acknowledging the relativism that is an inevitable consequence of the fact that the concepts or categories (the grounded *theory*) is the product of one individual's perspective on the phenomenon.

Rennie (1998a) asserts that grounded theory is fundamentally a process of interpretation, if a particular kind of interpretation performed in a particular way. He therefore regards this approach as comprising an improvement on what he calls 'traditional hermeneutics', and has characterised grounded theory as 'methodical hermeneutics' (Rennie, 2000d). Grounded theory researchers are considered to be following a hermeneutic approach, but with the advantage of having devised a set of practical procedures for implementing the typically vague ideas of hermeneutic philosophers. There are at least two reasons for resisting this assertion. First, it downplays the phenomenological component of grounded theory analysis. Why not call it methodical phenomenology? A comparison of the Strauss and Corbin steps in grounded theory analysis (this chapter) with Colaizzi's (1978) formulation of empirical phenomenology (Chapter 3) reveals many points of convergence. Second, grounded theory can only be seen as a form of hermeneutics by adopting a restricted concept of hermeneutics, one which emphasises the act of interpretation but leaves aside notions of historical consciousness and the importance of language. It may be more accurate to characterise the grounded theory as one version of a methodical hermeneutic phenomenology. Like all qualitative researchers,

Glaser, Strauss and Rennie can be seen as having developed their own distinctive methods for (partially) exploiting the legacy of Heidegger's integration of phenomenology and hermeneutics.

## Conclusions

There are a number of conclusions that may be drawn from this exploration of the application of grounded theory methods within counselling and psychotherapy research. The primary conclusion must be that grounded theory 'works'. It is capable of enabling researchers to produce work that is rigorous, plausible and applicable. Although the research carried out by David Rennie has been the main focus of attention in this chapter, because of its scope and quality, there are several other pieces of grounded theory research that are well worth finding and reading. The British studies by Howe (1989, 1996) into the experience of clients receiving family therapy, by Dale, Allen and Measor (1998) into the experiences of clients who had been abused in childhood, and by Arthern and Madill (1999) into transition objects, are examples of grounded theory applied to issues of practical relevance. A number of North American grounded theory studies of aspects of experiential psychotherapy have also been reviewed by Rennie (2000a). Other useful examples of grounded theory research in counselling and psychotherapy include Bolger (1998) and Frontman and Kunkel (1994). In these studies, and in other branches of social science, education and health studies, the grounded theory approach has been associated with stimulating and important work.

However, it is also important to recognise that the claim of grounded theory to represent a uniquely rigorous and systematic approach to qualitative inquiry can be called into question. If there exist different ways of doing grounded theory (Glaser, Strauss and Corbin, Schatzman, Rennie, Turner . . .) then there cannot be a unified, 'correct' way of doing it. Rennie's (1998a) solution to this problem, which is that the essence of grounded theory can be reduced to a 'symbiosis of abduction and induction', in fact exacerbates this problem. If the core of grounded theory is accepted as being an abstract principle of this type, then surely it is possible to enact or operationalise that principle in several different ways. Maybe there are *many* grounded theory methods? If this is the case, then the history of grounded theory can be viewed as a precursor to Lincoln and Denzin's (1994) notion of qualitative researcher as *bricoleur* (see Chapter 8).

A final point that might be made about grounded theory is that it produces a particular kind of knowledge. Although it generates theory, there is an important sense in which it is atheoretical. It is difficult to conduct a grounded theory study if you are already an adherent of a 'strong' theory such as psychoanalysis – all that will 'emerge' from the grounded theory analysis will be psychoanalytic categories. Similarly, grounded theory does not lend itself at all to hermeneutic inquiry of the kind envisaged by Gadamer (1975) and exemplified in the work of Cushman (1995). In grounded theory work it can be dangerous to think too much about the tradition or intellectual community within which one operates because to do so would result in a necessity or desire to understand the historical provenance of the category labels that were arising in and through analysis. Grounded theory is an atheoretical and ahistorical method. It produces pragmatic frameworks for understanding – categories and processual models that are effective in specific contexts. It is no accident that grounded theory has been so popular in medical and nursing research. Apart from being apparently systematic and 'valid', it provides a way of conveying to busy nurses and doctors something of the private experience of their patients. Qualitative research that was too ideological and/or theoretical (Foucauldian, discourse analysis, conversational analysis, feminist research) would be less palatable to health professionals. Other methods, such as narrative analysis, are too case-based and thus regarded as not generalisable or sufficiently 'broad'. Ethnography (from which grounded theory was ultimately derived) is too time-consuming, intrusive and wordy. Grounded theory can therefore be seen as a robust method for the generation of a form of practical knowledge that is particularly well suited to making a contribution to the efficient and humane functioning of modern bureaucratic systems of health and social welfare.

And this idea leads back to a final appraisal of David Rennie's work. He has perhaps taken grounded theory further than it was ever designed to go. The pattern of activity that appeared to be associated with Glaser, Strauss and other jobbing sociologists was that they would move from contract to contract, spending perhaps two or three years on each project before moving on to something new. They would have neither the time nor perhaps the inclination to push their analysis to the point of addressing ontological questions of human agency and being. Perhaps David Rennie has done us all a great service by allowing a glimpse of the point at which the pragmatic method such as grounded theory needs to be left behind and a more philosophically informed approach, one which engages with the great traditions of hermeneutics and phenomenology, takes its place.

# 7

# The Analysis of Conversation, Discourse and Narrative

Whatever else it is about, therapy is certainly an activity that relies heavily on the use of language. Since Freud's characterisation of psychotherapy as the 'talking cure' it has been clear that at the heart of any approach to counselling and psychotherapy is the use of conversation to generate and convey new understandings. It is significant, therefore, that, until recently, counselling and psychotherapy research has not devoted much attention to the task of making sense of the use of language in therapy. In most research studies, the words used by clients and therapists have been treated as signs of something else (reports of symptoms and behaviours, expressions of unconscious processes, etc.), rather than as phenomena of interest in their own right. It has only been with the expansion of qualitative research, and the increasing influence of social constructionist ideas, that the use of language in therapy has been studied to any great extent.

Research into patterns of language in therapy has been largely based on the analysis of transcripts of therapy sessions. The central focus of this area of research has been to develop an understanding of how people *use* language in the therapy setting. This approach reflects the assumption that reality is constructed through language and is in contrast to the 'positivist' or 'foundationalist' view that language *reflects* reality. From a constructionist perspective we 'do things with words', we create relationships, 'problems' and their 'solutions' and evoke emotions through our talk. From this perspective, language is a 'performance' or an 'accomplishment'. It makes things happen. The central question for language-oriented researchers is to discover *how* language makes things happen.

A number of qualitative researchers in counselling and psychotherapy have carried out various kinds of analysis of transcripts of therapy sessions. This area of research can be divided into three broad approaches: conversation analysis, discourse analysis and narrative analysis. Although each of these approaches adopts a somewhat different stance in relation to how to interpret language use in therapy, they also share some common features. All three mainly work with transcripts of sessions, all tend to rely on interpretive analyses carried out by lone researchers, and all tend to generate research reports structured around lengthy passages of basic discourse quoted from informants. As a consequence, the dominant tradition within language-oriented qualitative studies has been to base studies on single cases or examples, or relatively small numbers of cases. Even if several cases have been included in the study, findings are often written up through detailed analysis of selected exemplar segments of text.

In this chapter, these three language-focused approaches are examined in turn. Some shared methodological issues common to all three approaches are then discussed.

## Conversation analysis

Conversation analysis has its origins in at least two important intellectual traditions. First, during the early years of the twentieth century Wittgenstein (and other philosophers) argued that the social and interpersonal reality that people experience and live in and through is primarily constructed through the use of language. It is as though life is a 'language game'. It therefore becomes interesting to explore the ways in which people employ language to make things happen. Second, a group of (mainly American) sociologists in the 1950s and 1960s decided that the way to understand social life was to analyse the micro-strategies that people used in order to manage interpersonal and group encounters. Probably the best known of these sociologists was Erving Goffman, who used a dramaturgical metaphor as a primary organising system for unpicking the minutiae of interaction. Another influential approach in this broad genre of research was *ethnomethodology*, associated with the work of Harold Garfinkel. Ethnomethodologists sought to understand micro-social processes of practical reasoning in everyday life (Garfinkel, 1967; Heritage, 1984; Turner, 1974). While Goffman and the ethnomethodologists were happy to observe what people did (as well as listening to what they said about what they did), a third sub-group decided to focus specifically on the analysis of talk, and on the ways in which relationships, experience and interaction were structured by and through talk. The key figures in the original development of conversation analysis were Emmanuel Schelgoff and Harvey Sacks (Silverman, 1998). Classic examples of early work within this research genre include Schegloff (1968), Sacks (1972) and Psathas (1979). More recently, this approach has been carried forward by David Silverman, John Heritage and others.

The use of conversation analysis in therapy research makes intuitive sense. Therapy is intrinsically a 'conversation', and the impact of therapy is supposed to occur through the achievement of the right type of conversation. Moreover, the primary data for conversation analysis (audiotapes) are relatively easy to obtain. In addition, the conventions of conversation analysis, particularly the use of detailed examination of short segments of text, tend not to produce ethical dilemmas in the sphere of confidentiality. However, there are also some ways in which conversation analysis makes no sense at all in relation to the development of a coherent body of therapy knowledge; these conceptual difficulties will be explored later.

A number of conversation analysis studies of psychotherapy have been published in recent years. These include: Edwards (1995), Gale and Newfield (1992), Miller and Silverman (1995), Perakyla and Silverman (1991) and Silverman (1997a). Following a brief account of the method of conversation analysis, two exemplar studies will be discussed to give an outline of the kind of insights that this approach can provide.

The basis of conversation analysis is the idea that institutions are organised in terms of sets of *practices*. These practices constitute the everyday means through which organisational or institutional relations of power, status and control are continually co-constructed. Analysis of the ways that people *talk*, their conversational routines, provides a powerful way to identify and analyse the practices that constitute institutional reality. In this context an 'institution' can be a large-scale social agency such as the NHS or business such as Microsoft, or it can be a small-scale micro-social institution such as a family or a therapy dyad.

In conversation analysis, it is essential to use transcripts of actual conversation as data, and to capture as much of the fine texture of the dynamics of the conversation as possible, including pauses, emphases, overlaps, interruptions, etc. Research in linguistics which examines just these para-linguistic cues has informed the work of many conversation analysts. The paper by Sacks, Schegloff and Jefferson (1974) describes a set of transcription rules that have been adopted by many researchers in this field. Alternative systems of transcript notation can be found in Atkinson and Heritage (1984) and Mishler (1986).

The process of carrying out a conversation analysis study involves collecting primary data in the form of transcripts, and then selecting excerpts from the material that will be subjected to more detailed examination. In conversation analysis research reports the convention is to provide the reader with the actual examples of transcript that are being analysed. These examples may vary in length from between four or five lines to a whole page. It is clear that in a normal journal-length article only a few such excerpts can be provided. Even in a book-length report such as Silverman (1997a) the number of excerpts is still limited in comparison to the total data set. A key task for the researcher, therefore, is to read and re-read the transcript in order to identify passages that will repay closer analysis. Then, once such an analysis has been carried out, it is necessary to go back to the transcript to search for other passages of text that either confirm or disconfirm the 'candidate hypotheses' (Silverman, 1997a: 228) that have been generated through this first phase of analysis. Like other qualitative methods, conversational analysis involves its own form of constant comparisons between analyses of different segments of the data, and a continual search for counter-examples. The goal is to ensure, as far as possible, that the analysis is *grounded* in the data.

In working with conversation material, the conversation analysis researcher employs a number of sensitising constructs or principles. These constructs suggest dimensions of conversation structure that may be revealing of the ways in which a particular 'institutional reality' is constituted. The following list of sensitising constructs is derived mainly from Heritage (1997):

*The organisation of turn-taking.* What are the 'rules' of turn-taking? What happens when a speaker departs from these 'rules'? In what ways does the structure of turn-taking practices reflect the values and goals of the institution?

*What types of conversation sequences can be observed?* There will usually be recurring patterns of interaction that flow across several conversational turns. It is possible to analyse these sequences in terms of their constituent *phases*. For example, one conversation sequence analysed by Heritage (1997) comprised an 'opening', followed by 'problem initiation', leading to 'disposal' (what was to be done about the problem) and then moving to a 'closing' or exit phase.

*Lexical choice.* Speakers choose different descriptive terms according to institutional context. For example, a psychotherapy client might use the term 'down' in everyday conversation but shift to 'depressed' in a therapy context.

*Interactional asymmetries.* Most ordinary conversations are broadly 'symmetrical' in the sense that there is an implicit rule that both (or all) participants are equal in status or knowledge. In ordinary, everyday conversations asymmetries can take many forms depending on the situation. However, in institutional discourse speakers are tied in to specific sets of roles and relationships, which are associated with consistent patterns of asymmetry. For example, in encounters between doctors and patients the doctor will ask questions and the patient will answer them. If the patient does ask a question, the doctor may avoid committing himself or herself. This kind of asymmetric conversational pattern gives a useful insight into the social reality of the 'clinic'.

These four strategies for analysing conversation, derived from Heritage (1997), represent a somewhat over-simplified account of the work of conversation analysts. Over the last 30 years, the cumulative efforts of conversation analysis researchers have generated a wide repertoire of tools for making sense of the ways in which social realities are 'talked into being'.

Within counselling and psychotherapy research, the single most important conversation analysis study has been the research carried out by David Silverman and Anssi Perakyla into the discourse of counselling provided for people diagnosed HIV positive. This research was mainly carried out in Britain and the USA in the late 1980s. In all, 93 HIV counselling sessions were transcribed (65 pre-test; 16 post-test; 12 with people living with HIV or AIDS) (Silverman, 1997a). This research has yielded several substantial publications (Miller and Silverman, 1995; Perakyla, 1995; Perakyla and Silverman, 1991; Silverman, 1997a). It would not be possible to summarise the whole of this body of work here. However, an indication of the types of findings that were produced can be given by looking at two different types of conversation structure identified in this study: *communication formats* and *concealing advice*.

The notion of *communication formats* was used by Silverman (1997a) to describe lengthy sequences of interaction that were highly typical within the HIV counselling sessions observed in this research. Two communication patterns were identified. In both, the counsellor took the role of speaker / questioner, and the client took the role of answerer / recipient. In the 'interview format' the counsellor asks a series of questions and the client provides answers. The basic structure comprises a chain of questions and answers. In the 'information delivery' format, the counsellor conveys advice and information to the client, who then at the end has an opportunity to ask questions. The counsellor may retain control during information delivery by numbering items, or by checking that information has been understood. Perakyla and Silverman (1991: 646) note that these formats 'put the professional firmly in control', and suggest that they allow the counsellor to approach 'dreaded topics' such as sex, illness and death with care and sensitivity.

Another example of conversation analysis within the research carried out by Silverman and Perakyla concerns the 'stabilisation' of advice-giving. This issue concerns the goal of the counsellor that the recipient should listen to advice and follow the course of action that is recommended, rather than ignoring what is suggested. Silverman (1997a) observed that counsellors employed an *advice-as-information* interaction sequence to overcome this problem. Counsellors appeared to be sensitive to the occurrence of two contexts within which the provision of advice was likely to be successful. These occasions were, first, when the client asked a question and, second, when questions from the counsellor elicited a problem from the client to which the counsellor could then supply a solution. There were also two contexts in which advice-giving would meet with resistance: initiating into advice prior to obtaining the client's perspective on the issue, or basing advice on a misunderstanding of the client's perspective. Silverman (1997a) suggests that the common theme in effective (or stable) advice-giving interactions was that, for the most part, the counsellor *conceals* advice in the guise of giving information. The following passage of transcript exemplifies this type of conversational sequence, and also demonstrates the way in which conversation is depicted in this type of study:

```
 1    C: 0.8)   Uh:m the other a:spect that I must cover with
 2              you as far as the fact that you're fema:le .hhh is:
 3              (.) with (.) any females wh're having the test if
 4              the test is positive .hhh we do tend to advise
 5              against becoming pregnant.
 6    0.4) P:   Mm [hm
 7    C:        [Uh::m having said that (0.8) the statistics are
 8              showing about a one in six risk to baby.=t-It
 9              depends on whether: that person is an optimist or a
10              pessimist you know as to how they look on that.
11              .hhhh So if a woman really wants a chi:ld(.) then we
12              advise her becoming pregnant sooner (.) rather
13              than leaving it.
14              (.)16
15    P:        Mm hm=
```
(Silverman, 1997a: 168–9)

This example reveals a number of important interactional strategies on the part of both counsellor and client. The counsellor invokes a key category in relation to the client – her gender ('the fact that you're *fema:le*') which is then used to warrant an appeal to what Silverman describes as 'one of the category-bound activities associated with that gender' (becoming pregnant). The notion of 'becoming pregnant' is embedded in a piece of advice ('if the test is *positive* .hhh we do tend to advise against becoming pregnant') reinforced by an appeal to factual authority ('the statistics are showing about a one in six risk . . .'). However, it does not seem as though the client, in this interaction, engages fully with the advice. After brief pauses, the client merely responds 'Mm hm', indicating a willingness to go on rather than anything that would suggest a full uptake of the advice. Nevertheless, the sequence is 'stable' in the sense that the client does not interrupt, ignore or reject the advice: the counsellor remains in control.

The research by Silverman and Perakyla is an important example of the application of conversation analysis to counselling. It is the most comprehensive study of this type, and has produced a wealth of detailed analyses of conversation sequences and patterns that open up new ways of understanding the process of HIV/AIDS counselling. Although Silverman and Perakyla attempt to address issues of theory and practice that they consider to be significant for practitioners, much of their writing is technical and assumes some familiarity with the conversation analysis approach.

The study by Gale and Newfield (1992) is more limited in scope but is possibly more accessible for readers with limited previous experience of micro-sociological methods. A more detailed, monograph-length version of this study is presented in Gale (1991). Gale and Newfield (1992) carried out a conversation analysis of one session of solution-focused marital therapy conducted by a well-known figure in this area, Bill O'Hanlon. Their aim was to 'describe how an expert therapist uses language in the therapy session to achieve particular therapeutic outcomes' (p. 153). The method section of this paper draws particular attention to the importance of producing a transcript. The authors report that 80 hours were required to produce the final transcript of the single 50-minute session which they analysed. They observed that 'the process of transcribing the session became part of the discovery process itself' (1992: 157). The analysis carried out by Gale and Newfield yielded nine categories of 'therapist procedures':

*Pursuing a response over many turns.* The therapist continues to probe for particular responses over the course of a session.

*Clarifying unclear references.* The therapist elicits further information or explanation following a brief or ambiguous statement by a client. This procedure seemed oriented toward generating accounts that could be interpreted as 'solution stories'.

*Modifying his assertion until he receives the response he is seeking.* The therapist adjusts what he is saying or requesting until the client comes up with the desired response.

*Posing questions or possible problems and answering these questions himself.* Here, the therapist produces a kind of 'anticipatory paraphrase' which allows him to anticipate and deflect possible problematic interruptions.

*Ignoring the recipient's misunderstanding or rejection and continuing as if his assertion were accepted.* In this interaction sequence, if a client objected to what was being put forward, the therapist provided an ambiguous restatement which did not properly address the client's reservations but which nevertheless enabled the therapist to pursue a suggestion or line of interpretation.

*Overlapping his talk with the husband's or wife's talk in order to get a turn.* The therapist interrupted in order to signal his wish to 'take the floor', but (usually) allowed the client to complete his or her statement.

*(Re)formulation.* The therapist takes the information offered by the client, then adds new information in order to justify a new, therapeutically intended shared understanding of the events being recounted.

*Offering a candidate answer.* The therapist asks a question but incorporates into the question a likely answer.

*Using humour to change a topic from a problematic theme to a solution theme.* For example, the therapist might imitate and exaggerate what the client has said in a comical fashion, then use this moment of shared humour to introduce a re-framing of the client's initial statement or line of argument.

Although based on only one session of the work of one therapist, this study brings into view some of the potential of conversation analysis in research into counselling and psychotherapy. Gale and Newfield (1992) produced a representation of solution-focused therapy that is recognisable, authentic and illuminating. They uncovered therapeutic conversational strategies that had not previously been described in the solution-focused therapy literature.

Significantly, Gale and Newfield (1992) generated an account of O'Hanlon's work that challenged O'Hanlon himself and to which he was invited to respond. It is instructive to reproduce his reaction to findings of the study:

> I have an elaborate explanatory model I use to describe my work, which I know has only a marginal relationship to what I actually do in therapy. Here was an opportunity to see my work through someone else's eyes and models, and to learn something new about it. I learned two major things . . . that I hadn't realised before. One is that I talk for clients. Someone once said in a preface to a question they asked during a workshop I was teaching, 'I know you don't want to put words into your clients' mouths . . .' I interrupted him to tell him that I did indeed want to put words in my clients' mouths and thoughts in my clients' heads. . . . Until I read Dr Gale's analysis, I did not realise that I did this by 'talking for' or being an alter ego for my clients. The other realisation was how much I talk over my clients' talk and ignore potentially unhelpful things they say and then attribute agreement to them. Having read that, I have shared the realisation with some clients, who have laughed and recognised the truth of the analysis. The funny thing about this is that the clients told me they hadn't realised this until I told them. After I told them, of course, they noticed it quite a bit. (O'Hanlon, 1991: x)

This passage illustrates the potential usefulness of a conversation-analytic approach to therapy process research. It also illustrates the constructed nature of social life: this kind of research changes and shapes the very thing it studies. Some useful comments on the impact of the research on the therapeutic practice of the primary researcher (Jerry Gale) can be found in Gale et al. (1996).

Readers who are not solution-focused or systemic in orientation will also find much food for thought in the Gale and Newfield (1992) study. Several of the interaction strategies described in the study would probably be considered as examples of therapeutic incompetence by practitioners trained in approaches such as psychodynamic or person-centred counselling and psychotherapy. This kind of conversation analysis introduces the possibility of becoming better able to identify both the generic or shared, and the conflicting, elements of different therapies. The shared elements may include strategies for retaining therapist control of the interaction. Although there has been little conversation analysis research into exploratory and relationship-oriented therapies, the study by Davis (1986) suggests that interactional control may be an equally important dimension of even 'client-centred' approaches.

Conversation analysis studies of psychotherapy have generally been conducted by social scientists interested in exploring the use of language in a particular social and organisational setting, rather than by therapist-researchers interested in developing applicable, practical knowledge. Gale and Newfield (1992) represents an isolated example of practitioner-oriented research within this genre. One of the main proponents of conversation analysis, David Silverman (1997a), acknowledged in his study of AIDS counselling that 'as a sociologist rather than a counsellor, it is not for me to take a position on the therapeutic . . . implications of the practices I have identified' (Silverman, 1997a: 212). However, despite distancing himself from applicability in this way, Silverman also claims that his work has been used to help AIDS counsellors acquire an awareness of conversation strategies and patterns in their practice. The positioning of a conversation analysis researcher such as Silverman as someone who is explicitly outside the professional discourse he is studying, and yet is capable of producing insights into that discourse that could be of value to professional prac-titioners, gives this kind of research a quality that can be both stimulating and frustrating to readers who are themselves counsellors or psychothera-pists. This kind of research is stimulating because it analyses and interprets the process of therapy in ways that are new, different and thought-provoking. But at the same time the research can be frustrating because it avoids addressing just those issues that are of most concern to practitioners (for example: what *are* the therapeutic implications of the practices that have been identified?).

In relation to research findings, there does not appear to be any evidence that conversation analysis researchers in the field of counselling and psychotherapy have attempted to move beyond the kind of awareness-promoting role that Silverman has described. Possibly this is because so few conversation analysis studies have been completed. Also, conversation analysis research into therapy has been dominated by the Silverman–Perkyla work on AIDS counselling, which represents a form of practice that is unusually prescriptive and information-oriented (at least in the majority of the examples which they include in their publications) and is therefore as a result perhaps somewhat difficult to generalise to other therapy settings. In principle, though, there are a number of important research questions that could usefully be illuminated through conversation analysis. For example, therapy researchers such as Elliott, Hill and Mahrer have attempted to identify the sequences of linguistic strategies employed in different approaches to therapy (see Eliott et al., 1987). Their research has tended to place therapist strategies in categories drawn from therapy models, such as 'interpretation' and 'reflection'. It could well be that the introduction of a conversation analysis perspective might help to move this work on to a more conceptually fertile level. Another area in which it might prove useful to apply conversation analysis methods might be in the analysis of patterns of talk in cross-cultural therapy interactions. For instance, Thompson and Jenal (1994) have shown that in some white counsellor–black client situations the counsellor avoids talking about race, with the outcome that the session quickly becomes superficial. By contrast, Moodley (1998) recommends the use of 'frank talking' to bring racial and cultural experiences and differences to the fore. What is poorly understood is how either 'avoidant talking' or 'frank talking' are co-constructed by therapists and clients. Here, conversation analysis has the potential to generate a much more fine-grained, critical account of what is happening in the therapist–client dialogue.

There are other potential applications of conversation analysis, related to the notion of therapist *skill*, that are worth mention. The kind of complex client-initiated conversation patterns described in, for instance, Edwards (1995) are probably difficult for many therapists to deal with. It would seem likely that this type of talk might well be associated with feelings of stuckness and impasse in therapy. Training in the skill of conversation analysis could help therapists to detect and overcome these linguistic 'traps'. There is also, certainly, a pattern of conversation 'flow' that is characteristic of 'good moments' in therapy. Therapists might benefit from increasing their awareness of the more or less facilitative aspects of their own conversational 'apparatus'. And how are these conversation frameworks or communication formats induced and maintained through training and supervision?

The point here is that it is not difficult to imagine several ways in which the concepts and findings of a conversation analysis approach might be integrated into therapeutic practice. The fact that this has not happened is indicative, I would suggest, of the primarily psychological nature of therapeutic thinking: conversation analysis is 'sociology' and sociologists don't do therapy. But from a postpsychological perspective (McLeod, 1999b), the conversation analysis studies that have been reviewed in this section therefore represent a small but significant movement in the direction of a postpsychological basis for practice. Conversation analysis deconstructs the psychological mode of 'seeing' therapy. It offers another way of seeing what is happening, and opens up the possibility of action based on what is thereby seen.

## Discourse analysis

Discourse analysis is an approach to the study of meaning that has become pivotal in recent years within social psychology in Britain. The key figures within the discourse analysis movement have been Jonathan Potter, Margaret Wetherell, Michael Billig, Ian Parker and Derek Edwards. Discourse analysis can be viewed as a form of social psychology that has taken some of the basic ideas and methods of conversation analysis but extended them into new areas while at the same time drawing on other sources of influence such as semiotics (Barthes, 1972) and (in some instances) psychoanalysis. Some of the areas of convergence and tension between conversation analysis and discourse analysis have been aired in an illuminating debate between Schegloff, Wetherell and Billig (Schegloff, 1997, 1999; Wetherell, 1998; Billig, 1999).

It is important to recognise that discourse analysis does not represent a single, unified position. There is a sense in which discourse analysis has grown up in opposition to mainstream positivist experimental social psychology. Those active within discourse analysis identify with a broadly social constructionist opposition to the dominant tradition in social psychology, and to some extent find most coherence in terms of their shared vision of what they are *against*. Within the discourse analysis tradition there are significant differences in emphasis and approach. Potter, Wetherell and Edwards have tended to concentrate on micro-analyses of naturally occurring talk (Potter and Wetherell, 1987, 1995). Billig (1987) has developed an approach which draws on notions of *rhetoric* in understanding the ways in which individuals position themselves in relation to alternative discourses. Parker's (1997, 1999) work is more overtly political, and also psychoanalytic and largely focused on critical deconstruction of large-scale social phenomena, with less attention being devoted to specific samples of language use. The location of these ideas in the context of a broader 'discursive psychology' is discussed by Harré (1995).

Discourse analysis is an *approach* or a stance rather than a method. In terms of specifying or recommending procedures for conducting research studies, discourse analysts place most weight on the capacity of the researcher to understand the *idea* of discourse analysis, rather than on his or her willingness to master particular research techniques. Nowhere have discourse analysts codified or manualised their research procedures. Indeed, they appear to have consciously decided against any such strategy. For example, in an introduction to discourse analysis written as a chapter of a methods textbook, Potter (1997) asserts that:

> There is a wide range of different ways of analysing discourse (p. 150).

> Developing skills in [discourse] analysis is best characterized as developing a particular mentality rather than following a preformed recipe (p. 158).

> Conversation analysts sometimes talk of developing an *analytic mentality*, which captures what is involved rather nicely (p. 148).

> A large part of doing discourse analysis is a craft skill, more like bike riding or chicken sexing than following the recipe for a mild chicken rogan josh (p. 147).

There are perhaps some aspects of these statements open to further interpretation. The way that Potter (1997) writes about method exemplifies the oppositional stance that discourse analysts have adopted in relation to psychology. If psychology is a discipline which places 'method' at the top of the agenda, then discourse analysts seek to subvert such 'methodolatry' by describing what they do as similar to a 'craft skill'. There is also a degree of irony for Potter in using terms such as 'mentality': one of the primary themes within discourse analysis has been the deconstruction of the mentalistic, cognitivist language of contemporary psychology. But, ultimately, there is a serious point implied in what Potter has to say. The implication is that, like bike riding and chicken sexing, discourse analysis can only really be learned through being passed on from one person to another. It is a human 'knack' that is transmitted by coaching, personal teaching, watching someone else do it, 'getting the message', and so on. There is undoubtedly a truth in this view. For most qualitative researchers, the complexities of their 'art' or 'tricks of the trade' are passed on from supervisors or colleagues rather than being gleaned from textbooks. However, the idea that method is not reducible to procedural, written-down rules, that there is an 'implicit' dimension to knowing *how* to do qualitative research, is a threat to assumptions about rationality and the nature of science that are central within modern culture. There can also be a fear that open dialogue and debate can be stifled if proponents of particular approaches take recourse in the position that other researchers cannot fully understand, or critique, their findings because they have not been initiated into an 'inner circle' of those who *know*.

The introductions to discourse analytic method offered by Potter (1997) and Potter and Wetherell (1994, 1995) are probably the best place to start for those new to this approach. These chapters provide a representation of discourse analysis in action, rather than giving a set of step-by-step procedures. The sense that is conveyed is that a competent discourse analyst will have at his or her disposal an overall appreciation of the nature of qualitative inquiry, and, in addition, a repertoire of potential ways of making sense of discourse. Some of the ways of sense-making will be derived from conversation analysis. The actual process of carrying out a discourse analysis then appears to be driven as much by an intuitive feel for what might work, rather than any pre-determined analytic rules.

The contribution of discourse analysis to research in counselling and psychotherapy can be exemplified through an examination of two recent studies: Madill and Barkham (1997), and Brown (1999).

The Madill and Barkham (1997) study comprises an analysis of a discourse theme within a single case. The client was a woman who completed eight sessions of psychodynamic-interpersonal psychotherapy in the context of the Second Sheffield Psychotherapy Project (Shapiro et al, 1990). The case was selected because of its successful outcome. The aim of the study was to develop a discourse-analytic understanding of the process of therapeutic change. Madill and Barkham (1997) pursued this aim by first identifying then analysing samples of therapeutic 'talk' associated with the main topic explored in therapy, the client's difficulties in her relationship with her mother. The main discourse-analytic tool employed in the study was the concept of 'subject position' (Davis and Harré, 1990). This concept proposes that personal identity can be understood in terms of the way that a person 'constructs' that identity in language and conversation: 'identity is . . . conceptualized as a contextually variable description within traditional cultural meanings' (Madill and Barkham, 1997: 232).

In the case analysis, the language and conversation interactions between therapist and client were examined to identify shifts in the way in which the client positioned herself in relation to 'traditional cultural meanings'. In early sessions, the client presented herself as 'the dutiful daughter'. In later sessions, a new 'subject position' emerged: the client as 'damaged child' in relation to a 'bad mother'. The tension between presenting herself as 'dutiful daughter' to a 'bad mother' is then resolved in dialogue with the therapist. For Madill and Barkham (1997), the value of this analysis lies in its ability to offer 'an understanding of therapeutic process based in a view of language use and cultural meanings rather than viewing mechanisms of change hidden within the client's head' (p. 243).

Another application of discourse analysis that has examined a topic relevant to counselling and psychotherapy is the study by Brown (1999) into self-help literature. This study exemplifies the use of discourse analysis to investigate written texts rather than to explore the type of naturally occurring talk studied by Madill and Barkham (1997). In investigating self-help books from a discourse-analytic perspective, Brown (1999) took 22 popular self-help texts and analysed them along the lines suggested by the rhetorical psychology of Billig et al. (1988), as well as drawing on other discourse theorists. Brown found that self-help discourse was organised around a set of central narrative themes and metaphors. These self-help texts predominantly characterised stress as 'the twentieth-century disease', and as attributable to 'the fast pace of modern life' and the existence of a 'primitive response syndrome'. There were a number of recurring metaphor themes running through these books: becoming 'hotter' or 'cooler'; stress as a 'battle' or 'war'; the body as a 'machine' or 'computer' that has gone wrong. Brown suggests that these metaphors serve a number of rhetorical purposes. For example:

> [these metaphors] regularly occur though a particular piece of advice is given (often formulated analogically, in the manner of 'think of it like this . . .' or 'your body is like . . .'). This positioning means that the device comes to serve as the formal grounds upon which the often bizarre advice subsequently suggested comes to appear perfectly rational and efficacious. (Brown, 1999: 31)

Brown concludes that self-help books convey an image of the self as a 'product' to be engineered (the 'serviceable self') that requires regular maintenance in order to be sufficiently robust and flexible to cope with the demands of the modern world.

It is probable that the number of discourse-analytic studies of counselling and psychotherapy will grow over the next few years, reflecting the increasing prominence of this approach within social and applied psychology. The studies that have been reviewed illustrate the limitations as well as the potential of this method. In principle, understanding the discourses surrounding and constituting counselling and psychotherapy is vitally important for practitioners. There is a sense in which therapy *is* talk (in the therapy room) and text (in case notes, books, etc.). Discourse analysis provides a variety of ways in which the operation of these 'language games' can be explored. However, there are aspects of discourse analysis that do not sit easily within the world of therapy. For instance, the notion of the individual self, and the reality of inner experiencing, are difficult to reconcile with a strict interpretation of a discourse analysis approach (Madill and Docherty, 1994). There are also aspects of discourse analysis that are problematic from a qualitative inquiry standpoint. The location of discourse analysis as an approach within *psychology* means that there can be a tendency to limit the analysis of discourse to immediate social relations, and thereby fail to track its origins back to more wide-ranging cultural and historical forces. For example, if the discourse-analytic study of the self-help literature carried out by Brown (1999) is compared with a hermeneutically informed study by Greenberg (1994) on the same topic, it can be seen that the latter was able to draw much more wide-ranging conclusions, and, arguably, produce an analysis which yielded a greater depth of understanding. In addition, the reluctance of discourse analysts to be specific about their methods makes it difficult to know whether they are, in fact, carrying out work that is distinctively different from other qualitative traditions. Might a phenomenological or grounded theory researcher have arrived at similar conclusions to Madill and Barkham (1997) or Brown (1999)? Finally, there are severe problems involved in making sense of reflexivity from a rigorous discourse-analytic perspective. Although discourse analysts such as Potter, Madill and others do make reference to their own social identities in their writing, this kind of self-referencing is typically brief and not very revealing. The difficulty for discourse analysts here is the status of any statements they might make about themselves. Presumably, any such statement would not be taken to refer to an external reality ('who I really am'; 'how I really felt when analysing this material'), but would itself need to be viewed as discourse to be analysed. Somehow this does not seem quite right. In conversation analysis, there are in operation a number of technical conventions and sociological considerations that make the non-presence of the researcher more acceptable. In discourse analysis, by contrast, the work is so personal, and so influenced by a sense that all discourse is a construction or a version that the reader continually looks for cues as to 'whose version this is', as if the identity of the author might be the place where the endless circle of relativism might stop. The rhetoric of much discourse-analytic writing indeed often hints at the position of the researcher on the topic being studied. For example, no reader could come away from Brown

(1999) under any illusion about his opinion of self-help books. For therapists accustomed to a more authentic stance, this kind of ironic semi-reflexive teasing is again a feature of discourse analysis that can be hard to take.

## Narrative analysis

Conversation analysis and discourse analysis can be seen as approaches to inquiry that seek to develop new understandings of the ways in which language constructs personal and collective realities in counselling and psychotherapy. These approaches are 'discursive' in the broad sense of that term (Harré, 1995). A third research method that also adopts a discursive perspective is *narrative analysis*. The key idea in narrative analysis is that people largely make sense of their experience, and communicate their experience to others, in the form of *stories*. It can be argued, however, that psychologists and social scientists, in their struggle to create abstract scientific theories built around 'variables', have long neglected the study of narrative and storytelling. Only from the 1970s has there been a 'narrative turn' within psychology and social science, characterised by an increasing interest in narrative as a form of knowing. One of the key figures in the making of a narrative psychology has been Jerome Bruner (1986, 1990). A summary of theories of narrative and their application in psychotherapy can be found in McLeod (1997).

The central idea in narrative analysis is that the stories told by inform-ants or research participants can be treated as a primary source of data. A 'story' can be tentatively defined as an account of a concrete, specific event, with a beginning, middle and end, active protagonist and some kind of dramatic climax. This definition can only be tentative because a great deal of theoretical debate has surrounded the issue of what comprises a 'good' story. For example, story structures and conventions can be quite different within different cultural groups.

As in other branches of qualitative inquiry, there exist competing ideas about how to analyse stories for research purposes. However, two general approaches have been developed in recent years. The first is concerned with analysis of the 'life-stories' told by people being interviewed. This work can be regarded as a form of life-history research. The second approach to narrative analysis has concentrated on the task of understanding the process of storytelling in therapy, through an analysis of session transcript material.

The development of a distinctively narrative approach to the analysis of interview data can be attributed to Elliot Mishler (1986) and Catherine Riessman (1993). Mishler suggested that often, in qualitative interviews, the most useful and interesting material was generated when informants told stories about specific episodes in their lives relevant to the inquiry theme. However, much of the time interviewers would forestall the telling of such stories, because at these points in the interview the respondent was perceived as straying 'off the point'. Moreover, even if stories were recorded in interviews, they would typically be analysed in ways that would pull apart the structure and coherence of the narrative as a unitary vehicle for communicating meaning. For instance, in grounded theory or phenomenological studies (see Chapters 6 and 3), stories told by informants would be analysed in terms of constituent themes, meaning units or categories. Such an approach might be very effective in capturing the fragmentary meanings embedded within the story, but would miss the additional meanings conveyed by the story-as-a-whole. Mishler (1986) argued that the ways in which stories were structured, and the interplay and contrast between different meaning elements *within* a story, generated a level of meaning that would rarely be reflected within non-narrative research. Mishler (1986) made available for qualitative social researchers the narrative theory and research carried out within other disciplines, for example the sociolinguistic research on oral narratives carried out by Labov and Waletzky (1967).

In practice, the use of narrative analysis has been brought to wider audiences through the writings of Catherine Riessman, a former student of Mishler. Her book, *Narrative Analysis* (Riessman, 1993) represents a clear, succinct and accessible introduction to this method. Although this book also covers narrative methods carried out by other researchers, it most usefully provides a detailed account of Riessman's own narrative approach. Her method is built around a set of basic principles:

1  An interview schedule is used that encourages informants to tell stories.
2  Interview data are collected from a number of informants to enable an understanding of different experiences and themes.
3  A few key informants are selected whose stories can be viewed as 'typical' of broader themes in the data.
4  The interview material from these key informants is subjected to detailed transcription and closer reading.
5  Exemplar narratives from within these interviews are selected for use in a paper or report.
6  The paper or report is written *around* the intact narrative text, which is reproduced in full.
7  The goal of the analysis is to assist the reader to understand the meaning of the informant's experience.

This approach shares a number of features with conversation analysis and some forms of discourse analysis: the display of an intact text; the analyst drawing on a repertoire of analytic possibilities rather than rigidly following a pre-determined set of procedures. However, there are important differences too. There is no hesitation on the part of Riessman (1993) in attributing reflexive personhood and inner experience to her informants. For example, with reference to the story of a woman survivor of marital violence (reproduced below), Riessman (1994a: 115) observes that: 'The narrative is both an individual and a social product; she goes into memory to reexperience the violence and to try, once again, to make sense of it.' Narrative analysis is therefore an approach which combines a discursive emphasis on the construction of meaning through talk and language, alongside a humanistic image of the person as a self-aware agent striving to achieve meaning, control and fulfilment in life.

The contrast between narrative analysis and the other discursive approaches discussed earlier in this chapter can be brought into focus by considering an example of the kind of material used by Riessman (1994a). The following passage is taken from a paper entitled 'Making sense of marital violence: one woman's narrative' (Riessman, 1994a). This particular narrative was selected by Riessman for detailed analysis because it 'displays many of the features common to battering situations in general' (p. 115).

## A case analysis

Tessa is a 23-year-old white woman who has been living apart from her husband for 2½ years. She looks much older than she is. It was her decision to separate; he 'was completely against it,' she says. Though she lives in a dilapidated housing project, her apartment is clean and colorful. Her son from her marriage, a preschooler, lives with her, and an older child from a previous marriage is in foster care. Tessa had held a variety of unskilled jobs, mostly in the fast-food industry; is on welfare; and has just begun to attend community college part-time. She has always loved music; and her ambition is to be a music teacher some day.

Here is the full text of the first of three episodes of Tessa's narrative account of why she divorced. (Brief pauses are indicated by (p) and longer pauses of more than 3 seconds by (P)).

## Transcript 1

1    I (Interviewer): Would you state in your own words what
2    were the main causes of your separation, as you see it?
3    N (Narrator): (p) um the biggest thing in my mind was the
4    fact that I had been raped three times by him (I: mm-hmm)
5    but at that time it didn't, it wasn't *legal* in a probate
6    court (I: mm-hmm)
7    you you couldn't get a divorce on those grounds
8    but that was my biggest (p) (I: uh-huh) complaint (I: uh-
9    huh)
10   total disrespect for me (I: uh-huh) (P) (I: mm-hmm)
11   I: Can you tell me a little more about that? I know its
12   hard to talk about
13   N: (laugh / shudder) Well, um (p) when it was time to go to

14 bed it was really rough cause (p)
15 it was like we had to go to bed together (p) (I: uh-huh)
16 and (p) if I wanted to go to bed while he was watching TV
17 he'd say 'No, stay up with me' (I: uh-huh), you know
18 and um sometimes I just wanted to stay up
19 but he would insist that I go in with him (I: mm-hmm)
20 so it was like we had to do it together (p) (I: uh-huh)
21 um when I, you know, when I finally *was* in bed I'd just
22 roll over and I just wanted to go to sleep
23 I mean scrubbing the floor every day is kinda rough, you
24 know, you're pretty tired (laugh) (I: uh-huh)
25 I guess I'm a little sarcastic about it (I: uh-huh)
26 I: Uh-huh, I know what you mean
27 N: He'd just grab my shoulder and roll me over
28 and I knew what he was I knew what it was he was doing
29 I said, 'I just don't want it tonight.' You know,
30 'don't you understand, I just don't want anything
31 tonight'
32 'No, you're my wife and in the Bible it says you've got
33 to do this' (I: uh-huh)
34 and ah, I'd say, 'I just don't want it,' you know (I:
35 uh-huh)
36 And after debating for fifteen or twenty minutes
37 I'm not getting any less tired
38 I'd grab a pillow
39 I'd I'd say, 'I'm going to sleep on the couch, you're
40 not going to leave me alone'
41 I'd get the pillow and a blanket (I: uh-huh)
42 and I went and laid on the couch.
43 Two minutes later he was up out of bed
44 (P) and one particular time he had bought me a dozen
45 roses that day (I: mm-hmm)
46 and they were sitting on top of the television which was
47 at the foot of the couch (p)
48 and he, he picked up the vase of roses
49 threw the roses at me
50 poured the water on me (I: mm-hmm)
51 and dragged me by the arm from the couch (I: mm-hmm)
52 to the bedroom
53 and then proceeded to (P)
54 to make love to me. (I: uh-huh) (p)
55 And uh (P) I didn't know what to do (I: mm-hmm)
56 I tried to push him off me
57 and I tried to roll away (I: uh-huh)
58 ah I tried to cross (laugh) my legs (laugh)
59 and it didn't (p) work (I: uh-huh)
60 He's six foot seven (p) and I'm five eight. (p)
61 and uh (P) I just had I just closed off my head (I: mm-
62 hmm)

63   all I could do was shut off my brain (p)
64   and uh (p) I got very hostile, I (p)
65   there was no outlet for those feelings. (p)
66   You know that even my neighbors as far as they were
67   concerned
68   you know, they *they* figured that, you know, when people
69   are married
70   that they love each other
71   I think, was the assumption.
72   That wasn't so.
(Riessman, 1994a: 116–17)

The contrast between narrative analysis and other forms of discursive inquiry are evident through consideration of the way that this transcript is prepared and constructed. The informant is introduced sympathetically in the opening paragraph, and placed within a social and cultural context. The use of 'present tense' writing here also invites the reader closer to the informant and to her account of this episode in her life. The narrative passage itself is clearly chosen because it provides an account of a significant slice of social reality, not because it is being used to exemplify processes of conversational interaction: the discourse is *about* something. The length and dramatic quality of the story being told not only draw the reader in to the informant's experience, but also operate to convince the reader of its significance. Yet there is enough transcription detail provided to make it possible to get a sense of how the narrative was co-constructed.

In the lengthy analysis (more than 2,500 words) that follows this passage, Riessman (1994a) uses a variety of narrative constructs to expand the meaning of Tessa's story. Some of the narrative analytic strategies employed in this section of the report are:

- examination of the overall structure of Tessa's story;
- interpretation of the co-constructive impact of interviewer responses;
- analysis of the various 'voices' in the story;
- consideration of the effect of juxtapositions between competing voices and themes within the story;
- thematic similarities between Tessa's story and wider cultural narratives regarding marriage and domestic violence;
- analysis of the effects of pauses in the storytelling performance on the meaning that is conveyed;
- analysis of the meaning of shift in clause length: towards the end of the story the narrative employs 'short, terse clauses in the simple past tense' (p. 121).

These analytic strategies are typical of this approach, and can be found in other studies carried out by Riessman, Mishler and their co-workers. Other examples of this type of research can be found in the *Narrative Study of Lives* monograph series edited by Ruthellen Josselson and Amia Lieblich (Josselson and Lieblich, 1993, 1995, 1999; Lieblich and Josselson, 1994; Josselson, 1996a). The strength of this approach lies in its systematic approach to the study of single cases (or small numbers of cases), and its capacity to combine vivid storytelling (by allowing the informant's story to be heard) with theoretical analysis.

Turning to research which has employed a narrative approach to analysing transcripts of counselling and psychotherapy sessions, it is possible to identify two contrasting narrative approaches which have been developed. The first is the method of *narrative analysis of therapy transcripts* constructed by McLeod and Balamoutsou (2000). The second approach is the JAKOB method devised by Brigitte Boothe and her colleagues at the University of Zurich (Boothe, von Wyl and Wepfer, 1999).

Narrative analysis of therapy transcripts is in many respects an application of the methods of Mishler and Riessman to the analysis of therapy transcript material, with the aim of generating new understandings of the therapeutic process, in particular the process of narrative change over the course of therapy. The approach is explicitly hermeneutic in orientation (see Chapter 2), and seeks to facilitate the construction of plausible interpretations of what might be happening within the cases being analysed. To date, the method has been applied solely to cases of person-centred/experiential therapy, with the goal of exploring the following questions:

- How and why do people tell stories in experiential therapy?
- What types of stories are told? How do these stories change?
- Are there specific types of storytelling event? How can experiential interventions (e.g. empathic responding, two-chair work) be understood in narrative terms?
- What is the role of the therapist in relation to the client's story? How is the story co-constructed?
- How do stories locate the person in a cultural context?

The method comprises three discrete inquiry stages. First, the transcript is read and discussed by different readers in order to develop a preliminary formulation of the case as a whole, and to map out the stories and topics identifiable within the text. This preliminary descriptive account of the material is then used to generate hypotheses concerning which segments of the text might repay more detailed analysis and explication. The task of micro-analysis of stories is so time-consuming and produces so much material that it is necessary to be selective in highlighting passages that are significant on theoretical grounds. In the studies that have been carried out using this method, the first session of therapy has consistently proved a worthwhile ground for micro-analysis. Other analyses have examined

**Phase 1**   *Preliminary analysis: finding structure and meaning in the text as a whole*
Reading and immersion
Identification of stories
Identification of topics
Summarising stories and sequences
Constructing a representation of the case/session as a whole

**Phase 2**   *Micro-analysis: developing an understanding of specific therapeutic events and processes*
Selecting text segments for micro-analysis
Transformation of text into stanzas
Separation of client and therapist narratives
Identification of voices
Identifying figurative use of language
Story structure analysis
Identifying cultural narratives

**Phase 3**   *Communicating what has been found*
Construction of summary representation
Theoretical interpretation
Writing
**Throughout:**   Use of reflexivity; use of other readers

*Source*: McLeod and Balamoutsou, 2000

Figure 7.1   Procedures used in qualitative narrative analysis of psychotherapy transcripts

specific events within sessions rated by clients, therapists and researchers to constitute moments of change. Once the passages for micro-analysis have been identified, a number of analytic strategies are then applied in order to 'pull out' or 'retrieve' possible meanings, and identify processes of client and therapist co-construction of meaning, in similar fashion to the work of Riessman discussed earlier, Finally, there is a writing stage in which the different elements of analysis and description are collated into a report. The key steps are summarised in Figure 7.1.

Within this approach, one of the most useful analytic strategies has proved to be the technique of *stanza analysis* invented by Gee (1986, 1991). In effect, stanza analysis comprises a creative approach to transcription. Gee argues that most conventional forms of transcription conceal the rhythmic and poetic quality of spoken language. By presenting oral story-telling in the form of a poem, the meaning and emotional impact of the story, and its narrative structure, become more readily apparent. In qualitative narrative analysis, segments of storytelling chosen for micro-analysis are reconfigured in stanza form before any subsequent analyses are carried out. An example of the difference between a 'smoothed' prosodic segment of transcript, and the same words presented in stanza form, is provided in Figure 7.2. For most readers, the stanza version is easier to understand, and more evocative of potential meaning.

*Version 1: Prosodic*

Like a typical example was last night. I uh went down to see; my husband has an aunt in the hospital right now and she's really in bad shape. And he looks after things – she doesn't have a family and so I went downtown and I met him because he was working downtown yesterday. So I met him and said 'well look because of the time we should maybe we should go have a bite to eat'. You know. And he said 'okay'. Well I just sort of thought of something fast, you know. He knows I don't particularly like Restaurant X. I'll go in there for a make-do meal but you know. Well he said 'well okay we'll go up to Lakeside there's Restaurant Y'. You know this was on the way home. And I said 'no I thought we just wanted a fast supper?' and I automatically found myself getting mad, you know. And I mean he was only trying to do something nice by saying 'I know you don't like Restaurant X or Restaurant Z', (you know, I mean), 'so we'll go to Restaurant Y'. He was trying to be nice and yet I was – its almost like I'm constantly trying to punish him.

*Version 2: Stanza form*

Like a typical example was last night
I
We went down to see

   My husband has an aunt in the hospital right now
   And she's really in bad shape
   And he looks after things
   She doesn't have a family

And so I went downtown
And I met him
Because he was working downtown yesterday
So I met him

And I said
'Well look
Because of the time
We should maybe
We should go have a bite to eat'
   You know

And he said 'okay'

Well I just thought of something fast
   You know
He knows I don't particularly like Restaurant X
I'll go in there for a make-do meal
But
   You know

Well he said
'Well okay we'll go up to Lakeside there's Restaurant Y'

   You know this was on the way home

And I said
'No I thought we just wanted a fast supper?'

And I automatically found myself getting mad
   You know

**Figure 7.2**   Prosodic and stanza versions of a client story (*continued overleaf*)

And I mean
He was only trying to do something nice
By saying 'I know you don't like Restaurant X or Restaurant Z
    You know I mean
'So we'll go to Restaurant Y'
He was trying to be nice
And yet I was
Its almost like I'm constantly trying to punish him

Figure 7.2   (*continued*)

Although various narrative analysis studies have been completed using this approach, in the form of conference papers and Doctoral theses, at present there is only one published paper which demonstrates the use of this method. McLeod and Balamoutsou (1996) used narrative analysis to identify the narrative events and processes occurring in a single session of person-centred counselling. Among the main findings of this study were: the client presented a series of stories during the session, each one an extension of previous stories; the empathic responses of the counsellor had an important role in co-constructing the client narrative; contrasts between different stories conveyed a sense of a 'storyworld' which was not expressed fully in any single story; the re-telling of a story represented a form of personal problem-solving for the client. These conclusions were regarded by McLeod and Balamoutsou (1996) as tentative and requiring further elaboration and testing over a series of cases.

The method of qualitative narrative analysis of therapy transcripts must be considered to be at a preliminary stage of development, since it has produced a relatively small number of completed studies. Nevertheless, it constitutes a systematic and pragmatic approach to exploring the process of narrative co-construction and change in therapy.

The work of Boothe, von Wyl and Wepfer (1999) is unusual in reflecting a qualitative method built on a psychoanalytic theoretical framework. The title of the method (JAKOB) is an acronym which refers (in the original German) to the 'dramaturgical analysis of objects and actions'. The core idea underpinning JAKOB is that stories told by clients in therapy can be understood *both* as dramatisations of the dynamics of unconscious object relations *and* as a form of communication with another person (the therapist). JAKOB therefore offers clinicians and researchers a method for uncovering processes that (from a psychoanalytic perspective) lie at the heart of productive therapy.

Boothe et al. (1999) suggest that narratives serve four crucial psycho-social functions:

1   *Updating.* The 'there and then' event which is the topic of the story becomes 'revitalized dramatically'. This process is only possible with

events that are bearable (i.e., not too emotionally destabilising) and enables the speaker (the patient) to develop continuity of personal experience.

2   *Social integration*. The story is told to an audience (the therapist) whose 'attentiveness, acceptance and emotional participation are demanded by the narrator. Telling a story produces nearness' (p. 261).

3   *Coping with anxiety*. The stories told in therapy are driven by the client's unconscious drive to discharge his or her feelings of anxiety and achieve some degree of control over them. The stories encapsulate the main themes in the unconscious emotional life of the client.

4   *Wish fulfilment*. Each story is structured around the central emotional conflict of the teller, and the resolution of the story can be interpreted as representing the (usually concealed) wish the client holds about how this conflict might be resolved.

The goal of the JAKOB system is to allow the analyst to discover how the client or patient 'dramatises an emotional issue'. To do this, the researcher first identifies the narratives occurring within the tape recording of a therapy session. These narratives are carefully transcribed. The reader or readers then work through a list of analytic questions in relation to each narrative:

- What is the structure of the narrative?
- Who does what in what fashion, when, where, and under what conditions?
- What does the protagonist of the story (the 'I' figure or 'actor') do, and what happens to them (their 'fate')?
- What relationships are exhibited between the actor and other figures in the story?
- What are the social rules that the actor and other figures are expected to follow?
- How does the narrative serve the narrator in terms of the four psychosocial functions described above? (updating, social integration, coping and wish fulfilment)?
- Taking the answers to all the earlier questions together, how does the narrative express the narrator's main anxiety and wish and the dynamic compromise between them?

The application of these constructs to the analysis of a therapy narrative can be illustrated through the first story told by Helga in her initial assessment interview (Boothe et al., 1999). The story is fairly brief:

1   the crucial moment was a scene
2   which made me think

3    no
4    I'm too young for this
5    I was working as a waitress at the time
6    and I had to iron a blouse for work the next day
7    and I said
8    I'll go and do that now
9    and he said
10   okay
11   then I'll watch TV
12   and I thought to myself
13   hmm . . .
14   something isn't right anymore
15   and then we fought about that
16   and I said
17   I didn't want
18   things to go on that way
(Boothe et al., 1999: 266)

The results of a JAKOB analysis of this story are necessarily lengthy and detailed, but some of the main themes can be summarised. The 'I-figure', Helga, depicts herself as having an obligation to fulfil. Only one other figure is placed in the story, the boyfriend, and he does not join Helga in striving to fulfil the obligation. This leads to a fight and the decision by the I-figure that she does not want him. Her attitude to him has an 'imperative' quality, as she seeks to control him. He retreats, toward the TV. The 'rules of the game' appear to be that 'the partner should be available to the "I" even when she is involved in her own responsibilities' (p. 267). Helga invites the listener to identify with her point of view (social integration) in a style that is itself imposing. The *wish fulfilment* that is expressed in the narrative is that the other should be submissive and available. In relation to *coping with anxiety*, the narrative operates to regulate fear of embarrassment and shame:

> the issue here is whether or not the narrator has the qualities that guarantee unconditional availability of the object. The appeal to the listener to agree is seeing the I-figure as energetic, critical, and belligerent serves anxiety reduction. (p. 267)

The *conflict* exhibited in the story between the wish for the other to be available and controlled, against the shame of not having the qualities necessary to achieve that wish, is resolved through 'protest'. The narrative begins with a proud 'no' and concludes with a proud and defiant 'I didn't want things to go on that way.' Nevertheless, as Boothe et al. (1999) observe, the narrative conveys an impression that any reality-based confrontation with the other might result in a 'virulent' attack of self-doubt and fear of shame.

The development of JAKOB is at an early stage, with few English-language publications available at this time. However, the material presented in Boothe et al. (1999) makes it clear that this method has a great deal to offer in facilitating micro-analysis of client stories in therapy. The generativity of the JAKOB method can be exemplified through further consideration of the Helga narrative. This was the first story told by the client in a first assessment interview. Nevertheless, the implicit narrative themes uncovered by JAKOB ran through all the other stories told by Helga in her therapy, and even predicted the outcome of treatment – she terminated because her (male) therapist had been 'indifferent and shown no understanding'. JAKOB has the potential to uncover (or discover) not only the meaning-systems by which individual therapy clients construct their worlds, but also to open up new understandings of the process of change in therapy itself, by allowing the 're-authoring' of these core narratives to be tracked over time. Although the JAKOB system has been described by its creators as psychoanalytic in orientation, it is important to understand that the use of the psychoanalytic concept of 'wish fulfilment' represents only one element of the system. At a more fundamental level JAKOB can be viewed as a system for opening up the meanings of the social and relational world of the storyteller, and then for mapping the trajectory of the individual through this world. JAKOB appears very much to be concerned with developing an understanding of the drama of the narrative. With adaptation (in the spirit of the *bricoleur*), versions of JAKOB could well be employed in qualitative studies of therapy narrative undertaken from different theoretical standpoints.

Although the methods of narrative analysis reviewed in this section display marked differences in emphasis, the common ground shared by each of them lies in the fact that the *story* or narrative, defined as a discrete account of an event, is taken as the starting-point for analysis and exploration. A story is regarded as a coherent 'package' of meaningful information. While the co-construction of the story might be of primary importance in discourse analysis and certainly in conversation analysis, in narrative work the activity of co-construction merely represents one dimension (if none the less a crucial dimension) of analytic interest. The focus on narrative allows entry into this form of 'discursive' inquiry for not only cultural analyses of narrative meaning but also for an image of the person as an active, reflexive agent. There would appear to be at least two ways in which human agency is inescapable in narrative analysis. First, most stories convey the actions of a live, purposeful protagonist. An assumption of human agency is therefore firmly embedded within the content of the discourse. Second, the performance of a story, as a telling to an audience, implies that the story might have been told differently, that there is a narrator who possesses some measure of aware control over his or her performance. By contrast, studies of 'discourse' and 'talk' are more heavily concerned with social context and social rules than with individual agency. While there is no doubt that there is a significant role for studies of discourse and talk in social science, a discursive approach which embraces agency is more in tune with the world-view and assumptions of most forms of psychotherapy.

## Conclusions: issues in discursive approaches to research in counselling and psychotherapy

It will be evident from the research approaches discussed in this chapter that there are different ways of pursuing qualitative research into the ways in which therapeutic realities are constructed through talk and language. It will also be evident that relatively few studies have been published within this domain. There are many aspects of therapy talk that remain unexamined. Given the importance of language usage and forms for both cognitive-constructivist and social constructionist approaches to therapy, it seems probable that much more 'discursive' research will be carried out in the future.

One of the interesting possibilities associated with discursive research lies in the fact that there have been many studies of everyday linguistic or discursive phenomena that have the potential to be applied to an under-standing of what happens in therapy. For example, the method of quali-tative narrative analysis devised by McLeod and Balamoutsou (2000) makes use of concepts and analytic strategies originally developed by sociolinguistic researchers such as Labov and Gee. It is possible to see the conversation, discourse and narrative literature as an enormous interdis-ciplinary resource that therapists and therapy researchers have hardly even started to explore. This literature represents a kind of 'pure', theory-driven research knowledge base that can be used to inform therapy research and practice, perhaps in unexpected directions. For example, Billig (1997), a prominent discourse and rhetorical psychologist, has argued that a more complete understanding of the psychoanalytic phenomenon of *repression* (and, by implication, of the psychoanalytic concept of the unconscious) could be achieved through conversation analysis. Billig (1997) suggests a discursive conception of a 'dialogic unconscious':

> [Freud] did not take seriously . . . the possibility that conversations – including those between the psychoanalyst and patient – repressed through their expression. As conversationalists talk about one set of topics, they are keeping others from discussion. How possible topics routinely remain undiscussed – and how possible questions remain unasked – requires the sort of microanalysis pioneered by conversation analysts, applied to discursive absences as well as presences. (Billig, 1997: 153)

Billig develops this notion through consideration of the famous case of Dora, presented in Freud's 'Fragments of an Analysis of a Case of

Hysteria'. Dora was a young woman of 19 caught in the centre of a web of deception surrounding the affair being conducted by her father with Frau K, the attempts of Herr K to seduce her, and the denial by her father of both sets of events. Freud interpreted the distress and confusion experienced by Dora as arising from her repression of her own sexual longings for Herr K. For Billig, however, the mentalistic, unconscious dynamic of repression as a psychic defence must have its parallel in a social, unconscious dynamic around a discourse of topics that remain undiscussed. Apparently, Herr K sent Dora flowers every day for a whole year, bought her presents and spent his spare time in her company. Yet, Freud proposes, all this occurred 'without her parents noticing anything in his behaviour that was characteristic of love-making'. Billig suggests a number of questions and directions that the discursive researcher might wish to follow in this situation:

> What was said by Dora's parents when the flowers were delivered yet again, or when Herr K arrived with another wrapped present for the adolescent? As he stood in the hallway, with all the conventional demeanour of a lover, what routines of greeting were developed? Did they make jokes about his being a suitor? (Billig, 1997: 154)

Close analysis of these domestic conversational interactions would surely generate new and useful ways of making sense of repression. In principle, there are many therapy concepts that might repay investigation along these lines: self-esteem, boundaries, resistance, depression. All of these phenomena can be viewed as being brought into being by particular uses of talk in particular contexts.

One of the most significant, and welcome, contributions of a discursive approach to research into counselling and psychotherapy is that it inevitably draws attention to issues of power and control. It is almost as though the methods of micro-analysis of texts used in conversation analysis, some forms of discourse analysis, and narrative analysis, function as a kind of social microscope that brings into view structures and processes that are all but invisible in everyday life (and in therapy).

The final point that needs to be made about analysis of discourse, conversation and narrative in relation to counselling and psychotherapy is that, like all qualitative genres, it has its limitations as a way of knowing. All discursive approaches originate in social constructionism, and adopt the stance that reality is socially, historically and culturally constructed through the use of language. It can be, and has been, argued that a strict reading of social constructionism does not allow a reality beyond language, beyond the text, and leads to a position of ultimate relativism. This kind of stance is wide open to criticism. How can we make moral choices from a position of relativism? If language is all-important, what are we to make of our bodies, our emotions, our inner fantasy life? If our subjectivity is constructed through social discourse, where is the possibility for agency and choice? These, and other, objections to social constructionism are comprehensively discussed in a collection of essays edited by Nightingale and Cromby (1999). It is important, also, to appreciate that there exist different versions of social constructionism (Danziger, 1997b). In the end, though, it may well be that the philosophical and conceptual issues explored by Nightingale and Cromby (1999) and Danziger (1997b) have more force in the academy than they do in the counselling room. Counselling and psychotherapy are forms of practical action, and not modes of theoretical reflection. For therapy practitioners, what is important in a piece of research is its pragmatic value – does it say something that might make a difference? Therapists must, in principle, be able to engage with any world-view presented by a client or patient. There is no reason for a therapist to seek to maintain a rigorous and consistent social constructionism. Practitioners of counselling and psychotherapy cannot escape from their own, and their clients', bodies, choices and emotions. If discursive studies can critically elucidate at least some aspects of all this, which they can, then that is enough to be going on with.

# 8

# Qualitative Inquiry as *Bricolage*

As may have been apparent in earlier chapters, even well-established and well-defined methods such as empirical phenomenology and grounded theory appear to have a kind of instability about them. What may at first sight seem to be a certainty about method and its application does not always work in practice. The method needs to be adapted to circumstances, the method differs according to who uses it, the researcher needs to be flexible. In addition, as Denzin and Lincoln (1994b) have pointed out, contemporary social science has seen a *blurring of genres*, with successful and influential social science writers, such as Clifford Geertz, Erving Goffman, Donna Haraway, Arthur Kleinman and Ann Oakley producing books and papers that stray into the border between science and art. These writers and researchers have done whatever they believe to be necessary to capture and express their understanding of the topic or phenomenon that they have been investigating. In doing so, they have found it necessary to transcend the confines of any one specific method or genre.

The notion that the demands of qualitative research require the researcher to improvise and create his or her own techniques for collecting and analysing material is captured in the concept of the *researcher-as-bricoleur*. The image of the *bricoleur* derives from French cultural usage:

> The meaning of the *bricoleur* in French popular speech is 'someone who works with his [or her] hands and uses devious means compared to those of the craftsman'. . . the *bricoleur* is practical and gets the job done. (Weinstein and Weinstein, 1991: 161)

What is meant here, in relation to qualitative research, is that the method emerges in response to the task of conducting a study. Rather than imposing a pre-determined method on the topic, the researcher is well-informed about a range of alternative approaches, and selects from these to 'get the job done'.

The image of the *bricoleur* is extensively used by Denzin and Lincoln (1994b) as a means of explaining how researchers can come to terms with the confusing array of methodological genres that exist. The challenge for qualitative researchers, they suggest, is to negotiate their own personal route through this methodological terrain:

> The qualitative researcher-as-*bricoleur* uses the tools of his or her methodo-
> logical trade, deploying whatever strategies, methods or empirical materials as
> are at hand. . . . If new tools have to be invented, or pieced together, then the
> researcher will do this. The choice of which tools to use, which research practices
> to employ, is not set in advance . . . [but depends upon] what is available in the
> context, and what the researcher can do in that setting. . . . The *bricoleur* is adept
> at performing a large number of methodological tasks. . . . The *bricoleur* reads
> widely and is knowledgeable about the many interpretive paradigms . . . that can
> be brought to bear on any particular problem. . . . The *bricoleur* understands
> that research is an interactive process shaped by his or her personal history,
> biography, gender, social class, race, and ethnicity, and those of the people in the
> setting. (Denzin and Lincoln, 1994b: 2–3)

It can be seen that the *bricoleur* represents a powerful and ambitious
image, with far-reaching implications. There is almost a sense in which the
*bricoleur* resembles a return to something like the role of the 'lone ethnographer' (see Chapter 1) with its implication of being able to adopt a
privileged position outside, or on the edge of, mainstream culture. A key
difference, however, lies in the kinds of knowledge claims made by
*bricoleurs*, who 'cobble together stories' (Lincoln and Denzin, 1994) rather
than claiming to produce monumental 'grand theories'.

Many accounts have been written of the experience of carrying out
qualitative research. A particularly well-written and compelling research
story is offered by Hyde (1994), in her description of her PhD study of
feminist organisations in the USA in the 1980s. Two points emerge from
her story. The first concerns the way that she found that the neat,
systematic research method with which she started – grounded theory –
just was not adequate to allow her to handle the kind of data she was
collecting, or to answer the questions she had. So, although her work was
influenced by grounded theory methods, in the end she employed a variety
of research tools and strategies in order to get the job done. The second
point concerns just how much her *personal* experiences during the research
affected her. One of the big challenges of the research was learning how to
manage the emotions that it triggered off. Towards the end of her
description of her research experiences, Hyde uses the following quotation:

> accident and happenstance shapes fieldworkers' studies as much as planning or
> foresight; numbing routine as much as living theatre; impulse as much as rational
> choice; mistaken judgements as much as accurate ones. This may not be the way
> fieldwork is reported, but it is the way it is done. (Van Maanen, 1988: 2)

The implication here is that the reality of doing qualitative research
requires flexibility. Research is in itself a process and a learning experience.
In recognition of these factors, Denzin and Lincoln have promoted the
image of the qualitative researcher as *bricoleur*, a multi-skilled individual
who assembles the tools and materials necessary to get the job done.

Wolcott (1992) is essentially referring to the same idea when he uses the concept of *posturing*: researchers need to work out their own 'strategic positions' (or posture) in relation to a number of key philosophical and technical questions. Wolcott argues that we operate in a 'marketplace of ideas' in which we invent traditions. These are very postmodern notions.

## *Bricolage* **within therapy research**

Within counselling and psychotherapy research, there remains some pressure to define and conform to methodological rules, with the result that those who have followed the path of the *bricoleur* have tended to characterise their approaches as representing a particular, named method. However, there have been two approaches which have distinctively sought to bring together elements of method from different schools of method. These are Robert Elliott's *Comprehensive Process Analysis* (CPA), and the *human inquiry* or *co-operative inquiry* approach associated with Peter Reason, Judi Marshall and John Heron. These two method genres are distinctive not only because they combine ideas from 'core' qualitative methodologies such as phenomenology, grounded theory and conversational analysis, but also because they rely (in somewhat different ways) on collaborative working between members of a research team.

In McLeod (1999a), I described these approaches as types of *practitioner inquiry groups*, because it seemed to me that they are uniquely well suited to small groups of practitioners working together on shared research tasks with the goal of producing knowledge-for-practice. In the present chapter, the emphasis will be on the ways in which these approaches represent an integrationist strand in qualitative research in counselling and psychotherapy.

## **The human inquiry method**

The 1960s and 1970s saw what some people have called a 'crisis' in social psychology. The over-reliance in social psychology on laboratory experiments, deception and attitude surveys led to a widely held view that the discipline had lost touch with actual everyday experience, and had become increasingly irrelevant and reactionary. One of the most significant publications to emerge from this 'crisis' was *Human Inquiry: A Sourcebook of New Paradigm Research* edited by Peter Reason and John Rowan (1981). Although it is clear that the core idea of a 'new paradigm' is attributable to Reason, Rowan and Heron, each of whom writes several sections of the book, there is an attempt to weave in the contributions of many people from different disciplines who share an opposition to the positivist-empiricist image of science: Rom Harré, Gordon Allport, Abraham Maslow, Aaron Esterson and so forth. However, it is probably fair to say that the 'new paradigm' approach has never blossomed into the hoped-for revolution in social science. Instead, its main outcome has been the existence of a thriving, international, but relatively small group of researchers connected and networked in Britain through the Centre for the Study of Organisational Change and Development at the University of Bath.

The method which has come to be associated with this group has been variously known as *human, collaborative, participative* or *co-operative* inquiry. The approach is based on a set of key epistemological principles:

- True knowing involves embracing the subjective dimension of experience. The goal is to cultivate an 'objective subjectivity' or disciplined reflexivity.
- Knowledge is irrevocably linked with action. The approach has been strongly influenced by the action research tradition in education and community work. Researchers seek to generate understanding in and through their practical activities and to produce outcomes that make a difference in the real world.
- Knowledge is intrinsically collective and relational. Human inquiry researchers rarely work on their own, but instead operate as members of inquiry groups in which each person is viewed as a 'co-researcher'.
- Creating knowledge is a cyclical process. An inquiry group will progress through stages of reflecting on experience, generating hypotheses, testing hypotheses in action, reflecting on the experience produced by this practical action, challenging these new insights in the group, etc.
- Knowledge which does not respect the whole person is destructive of the world. The human inquiry tradition has placed particular emphasis on the spiritual, emotional, relational and embodied dimensions of experience.
- The most useful end-point of research or inquiry may not necessarily be in the form of a research paper or book. Drama, poetry, art and social action may all be legitimate research 'outputs'.

These principles provide a kind of integrative meta-perspective which can encompass any of the methods discussed in other chapters of this book. For example, members of an inquiry group may decide to engage in phenomenological description of their experience, may carry out interviews and analyse them using grounded theory, or conduct discourse analysis of recordings. A fundamental underlying assumption of human inquiry is the humanistic trust in the creativity, integrity and truth-seeking capacity of the person, and in the 'sense-making' capacity of individuals and groups. The structure of the human inquiry experience can be viewed as an invitation for each member of the group to become an effective *bricoleur*, drawing on the sense-making skills and prior experience that they possess.

For a human inquiry or collaborative inquiry group, following a previously laid-down set of research procedures would be seen as a denial of these humanistic values, and in all likelihood as an avoidance of the challenge of engaging authentically with the discovery process.

The use of the human inquiry method in research in counselling and psychotherapy appears to have been largely confined to studies involving professional counsellors and psychotherapists, rather than clients or patients. An exemplar study has been William West's (1996, 1997) investigation of the experiences of therapists who were also spiritual healers. Here, a group of therapists with parallel interests and practice in healing methods found their participation in an inquiry group to be highly rewarding and meaningful. The study yielded a level of understanding of the topic, in terms of conventionally publishable material, that might not have been achievable using interview methods or a focus group. However, for the people actually involved in the group there was an added factor of acquiring an enhanced experiential and personal knowledge of the topic. In Stiles's (1993) terminology, this form of inquiry has a great deal of *catalytic validity*; it has the potential to empower participants in ways that would never occur in more conventional research.

The applicability of the human inquiry method to aspects of client experiences of therapy appears to be more problematic. I personally do not know of any published studies which have used this approach with clients. My experience with my own students who have attempted this kind of study is that it is difficult to draw a line between therapy and inquiry in an inquiry group comprising clients and facilitated by a professional therapist who has initiated the research. The inquiry group becomes a therapy group. In itself this may not be a bad thing, if a therapy-type experience is what participants want, but from a research point of view it leads into difficult territory regarding ethics, confidentiality and safety. It may be that human inquiry studies set up and operated by clients or service users to fulfil their own inquiry goals would create a much more clear-cut and manageable situation. Such studies would make a welcome and valuable contribution to a literature that remains overly dominated by professional interests.

Further information on the theory and practice of human inquiry methods can be found in Reason (1988a, b, c, 1994a, b), Reason and Heron (1986), Reason et al. (1992) and Heron (1996). The approach is popular with many therapists, who find that it resonates with their position in relation to therapy. It is probable that many more examples of human inquiry research into topics in counselling and psychotherapy will be published over the next few years. Human inquiry is essentially a dialogical approach to research, and it may be that the recent expansion within the social sciences of notions of what constitute acceptable forms of writing and rhetoric (see, for example, Hertz, 1997; Gergen, 1997) will create the conditions for human inquiry investigations to come into their own.

## Comprehensive Process Analysis (CPA)

Comprehensive Process Analysis (CPA) is a method that has been devised by one of the leading American figures in psychotherapy research: Robert Elliott. The body of work associated with Elliott (1984, 1993) has been described as the 'events paradigm', because it aims to develop new understandings of significant change events in therapy. There are four key principles which inform this 'events-focused' approach. First, it is assumed that there exist within therapy sessions significant moments or events during which clients experience positive, meaningful and lasting shifts in their awareness, understanding or sense of self. In principle, the study of significant change events also encompasses the identification and analysis of negative and damaging events, but the study of unhelpful events has received much less attention within this approach. The second key assumption underlying CPA is that the important processes that occur during therapy as a whole are more *visible* or salient during significant events. In other words, it is easier to observe those aspects of therapy that make a difference by selecting key moments than by trying to record or observe everything that happens. Third, the complexity of the therapeutic process is best captured through micro-analysis of fairly brief segments of interaction. Over longer sequences, the potential complexity of what is happening makes meaningful analysis and interpretation extremely difficult. Fourth, the best possible understanding of an event is achieved by eliciting and combining the accounts of all participants: the client, the therapist and any external observers (the researcher or research team).

In most CPA studies, a therapy session is recorded using audio or video taping. At the end of the session both client and therapist are asked to use the Helpful Aspects of Therapy (HAT: Llewelyn et al., 1988) to identify the most helpful event in the session and the least helpful event. This technique comprises a short questionnaire which invites the informant to write a brief description of the event, explain when it occurred during the session, how long it lasted, and rate its helpfulness on a nine-point scale. The purpose of HAT is to enable the later stage of comprehensive process analysis to be carried out on events that are clearly clinically significant. However, in principle other methods could be used to identify significant events. For example, if a researcher was interested in the meaning and effects of long silences, he or she could choose to focus CPA on 'silence events', regardless of whether the client or therapist perceived these as being significant.

The next step in most CPA research is to conduct an Interpersonal Process Recall (IPR) interview with the client, then with the therapist, around their experience of the target event or events. Essentially, the informant is asked to listen to the segment of tape which includes the event, and the minute preceding and minute following the event. A set of open-ended questions is employed in order to elicit as full an account of the experience as possible. For example, the person is asked what made the event (or aspects of it) significant, what their intentions were at each moment within the event, what they believed the intentions of the other person were, and what their overt and covert reactions were to the actions of the other person. Although the informant may be asked to make quantitative ratings of aspects of the event if appropriate rating scales are available, to provide an alternative data on the structure of the event, the main aim of this phase of the inquiry is to generate a rich and detailed descriptive narrative account which represents as completely as possible the experiences of client and therapist. The IPR interview, and the relevant segment of the actual therapy tape, are recorded and transcribed, and comprise the basic qualitative text which is then subjected to compre-hensive process analysis. However, members of the research team also listen to, and make notes on, any other therapy sessions that have been recorded, and on the sections of the current session that are not included within the IPR procedure. The event itself becomes the vivid and densely analysed central focus of the study, while other material is used to provide an understanding of the background context and consequences of the event. A somewhat more focused version of these procedures, known as *Brief Structured Recall* has also been developed (Elliott and Shapiro, 1988).

The aims of CPA are to understand:

(a)  the *context* out of which significant events arise (e.g., client coping style, therapeutic alliance),
(b)  the important features of the *event* itself (e.g., therapist interpretation, client expression of interpersonal fears), and
(c)  the *impacts* of the event (e.g., insight, decreased depression). (Elliott and Shapiro, 1992: 164–5)

The goal is to develop models of different types of change event. These models can be based on single-case analyses (e.g., Elliott, 1993a,  1993b; Elliott and Shapiro, 1992; Hardy et al., 1998; Labott, Elliott and Eason, 1992) or derived from thematic analysis of change sequences observed over sets of similar events (e.g. Elliott et al., 1994).

It is in the actual analysis stage of CPA that the extent to which this method represents a *bricolage* becomes most fully apparent. The analytic procedures used within CPA are drawn from a wide variety of methodo-logical genres, including:

1  *Conversation analysis.* The text of the therapy session is transcribed using the protocol of Sacks, Schegloff and Jefferson (1974), which allows the complexity of the linguistic performance (in-breaths and out-breaths, backchannel utterances, tongue clicks, etc.) to be displayed.

The analysis also proceeds by treating each 'speaking turn' as a separate unit, and by building up models of 'conversational sequences' – techniques that are central to conversation analysis and linguistics.

2  *Identification of client and therapist intentions and response modes.* This aspect of CPA draws on previous work by Elliott, Goodman and Dooley, Hill, and Stiles, each of whom have devised taxonomies of intentions or response types (see Elliott et al., 1987).

3  *Analysis of the content or meaning of utterances.* In this section of the analysis, the researchers take each statement made by therapist and client and seek to summarise its core meaning, including what is said explicitly and what is implied 'between the lines'. This dimension of the analysis draws on the ideas of Searle (1969) and Labov and Fanshel (1977).

4  *Analysis of client and therapist style and emotional states.* Descriptions and ratings of *how* client and therapist talked or acted are carried out.

The basis of CPA is both phenomenological (describing the experience) and interpretive (drawing on a range of pre-existing interpretive schemes in conducting the analysis).

It is important to note that the method of Comprehensive Process Analysis reflects different strands of experience within Robert Elliott's life. In his early research career, he studied with Schegloff, one of the main figures in conversation analysis. He then carried out research into response modes. His practice as a psychotherapist is experiential/humanistic, which is reflected in the collaborative style of CPA and its emphasis on the centrality of individual experiencing. He has worked with, and been influenced by, Les Greenberg, who has developed a somewhat similar method of event-oriented research, known as *task analysis* (Greenberg, 1984a, b, 1992; Rice and Greenberg, 1984b). The process-experiential approach to therapy, created by Greenberg, Rice and Elliott (1993), has influenced and been influenced by the development of CPA. Finally, as a qualitative researcher operating within the domain of academic North American psychology Elliott has been faced throughout his career with the challenge of justifying the methodological legitimacy and rigour of his approach.

The unpublished CPA Manual (Elliott, 1993) is an example of *bricolage* in action. It contains philosophy, linguistics, psychology, psychotherapy theory, personal reflexivity and poetry. It brings together a dazzling inventiveness in terms of analytic technique and suggestions on how to 'get the job done'. Elliott himself writes in the Manual that:

> The methods and categories presented here are intended as a 'set of tools' meant as helpful guidelines and suggestions; they are not intended as definitive or restrictive precepts. The researcher should feel free to 'create new methods' as the need arises; or to extract particular parts of the CPA method which he or she finds useful. (Elliott, 1993: 91)

However, it is perhaps indicative of the current state of qualitative research in counselling and psychotherapy that virtually no one appears to have responded to Elliott's invitation to treat CPA as a *bricolage* which could be disassembled. Possibly the only study which has taken this direction has been the research reported in Grafanaki (1996) and Grafanaki and McLeod (1999), which has used and adapted several of the elements of CPA in an investigation of client and therapist experiences of moments of experiential congruence/incongruence, and how these experiences relate to the process of storytelling and narrative reconstruction. As one of the participants in this research, I can confirm the sense that CPA can function effectively as a 'set of tools' which can be deployed in a variety of different ways depending on the purpose of the investigation.

## Some implications of the image of researcher-as-*bricoleur*

The idea of researcher-as-*bricoleur* is, and was surely intended by Denzin and Lincoln (1994a) to be, subversive. Adopting the posture of the *bricoleur* throws into question the purpose and status of mainstream, rigorous and codified qualitative methods such as grounded theory and empirical phenomenology. What is highlighted through the metaphor of the *bricoleur* is the view that knowledge is not produced by method. There is no methodological 'sausage machine' that allows the researcher to crank the handle and produce 'findings'. The *bricoleur* is not a machine operator of this kind, but is conceived as someone whose work is informed by a broad philosophical and interdisciplinary perspective. Recall that the initial stage of the creation of the human inquiry method involved a massive review of humanistic approaches to knowing (Reason and Rowan, 1981). Comprehensive Process Analysis, too, emerged from an in-depth understanding of relevant aspects of philosophy, psychology and sociolinguistics. The *bricoleur* is someone who both fully understands and 'owns' his or her perspective on research.

But how many qualitative researchers have the time or inclination to develop the kind of overview that would enable them to become effective *bricoleurs*? In any case, does not the achievement of a satisfactory *bricolage* depend on the prior mastery of previously existing qualitative concepts and methods? In practice, the majority of qualitative researchers are postgraduate students undertaking Masters or Doctoral research. It may be unhelpful to suggest the role of *bricoleur* to novice researchers who could be in danger of becoming confused or unable to complete their studies. For that matter, what suitable training might there be for those seeking to become *bricoleurs*? These issues are familiar to counsellors and psychotherapists. They are basically the same issues that are associated with debates over integration and eclecticism in counselling and psychotherapy, and trigger the same kinds of strong emotion. Hammersley (1999), a leading qualitative researcher has urged caution in relation to the notion of the 'bricoleur', and argues in favour of more traditional modes of qualitative research.

There is another critical perspective on the notion of research-as-*bricolage* – that of the reader or consumer of research. In Chapter 1, it was argued that it is necessary to be aware of the *rhetorical* nature of research writing. The way that an article or monograph is written has a persuasive function in convincing readers of the truth-value of the knowledge claims being made. Readers become socialised in ways of decoding and evaluating different types of rhetorical device. In Chapter 11, the relevance of an understanding of rhetoric in making sense of the issue of 'validity' in qualitative research is discussed. The notion of the *bricolage* undermines the operation of rhetorical conventions. After all, we learn to expect what a grounded theory or phenomenological paper will look like. We become sensitive to what should be there, and have access to a critical discourse to help us make sense of absences of what should be there. But presumably a *bricoleur* extends her or his creativity into the writing process itself; there are many different ways to write up the findings of a study. The rhetorical eclecticism of the researcher / author introduces the necessity for the *reader* also to become a *bricoleur*, and to develop his or her skill in assembling meaning from what is offered. Where does this lead? Lincoln and Denzin (1994: 583) invoke a cyberworld in which:

> New forms of the text, building on hypertext, will appear. This will change the traditional relationship between the reader and the writer. In the electronic spaces of hypertext, readers become writers, *bricoleurs* who construct the text out of the bits and pieces and chunks of materials left for them by the writer. The writer now disappears, receding into the background, his or her traces found only in the new hypertext that has been created by the reader.

This image may appear strange and unlikely. But just as an earlier generation of social scientists such as the anthropologist Clifford Geertz blurred the genres of research and literature, perhaps the next generation, or this one, will find ways of productively blurring the genres of research and website.

The notion of the researcher-as-*bricoleur* has so far had little impact on the world of qualitative researchers in the field of counselling and psycho-therapy. The researchers discussed in this chapter can be viewed as implicit rather than explicit *bricoleurs*. The image of the *bricoleur* is influenced by both postmodern thinking (the erosion of 'grand narratives' and privileged perspectives) and the experience of conducting ethnographic research. There are many ways in which ethnographic inquiry demands that the researcher deploys 'whatever strategies, methods or empirical materials as are at hand' to get the job done. As postmodern and ethnographic ideas permeate qualitative research in counselling and psychotherapy, therapy researchers will be forced to engage more fully with the concept of the *bricolage*.

# 9

# How to do Qualitative Research

The perspective on qualitative inquiry presented in this chapter differs from the focus of earlier chapters. Previous chapters introduced and discussed the major 'schools' or 'genres' of qualitative research, for example phenomenology, hermeneutics, ethnography and grounded theory. The intention now is to propose that all of these approaches are variations on what is basically a single way of knowing. This chapter suggests that there may exist a *generic* qualitative method. By considering the practicalities and pragmatic decision-making involved in such activities as creating a qualitative text, and developing a position in relation to the phenomenon of interest, it can be seen that the different 'brand name' approaches to qualitative research in fact share a common set of procedures and inquiry strategies. It may be helpful to regard qualitative research as comprising a basic common or generic method out of which different traditions (such as phenomenology, hermeneutics, ethnography and grounded theory) have emphasised particular aspects for their own purposes. This position is consistent with the idea that qualitative research *as a whole* represents a significant movement within the social construction of knowledge in contemporary society (see Chapter 1).

The idea of a generic method is likely to be more popular with students than with expert researchers. Those who have spent years developing expertise in approaches such as grounded theory or phenomenology tend to be highly aware of the differences between what they do and the ways in which other qualitative researchers operate (even researchers who might claim to use the same approach). Most experienced qualitative researchers are either academics or affiliated to academic institutions. There is a strong 'argument culture' within the academic world, characterised by attacking and defending positions, building allegiances and so on. The 'argument culture' is driven by the economic and social rewards associated with 'distinctive' or 'original' ideas (yet what is original in human science?), by the competitive habits of men, and probably by many other factors. The point, in relation to qualitative research, is that it is much more interesting for academics to debate difference than it is to work toward consensus. Indeed, it would be argued by many academics that it is only through critical debate that knowledge can advance.

However, students undertaking qualitative research for the first time are in a quite different situation. For the most part, students carrying out research studies function within strict time limits. In the space of perhaps one academic year, a student may need to select a research topic, design and carry out a study, and write up the findings. Usually, students are more interested in the topic than the method. But if a student decides to use a qualitative method, then he or she is faced with some very hard decisions. Which method to use? Grounded theory? Phenomenology? Discourse analysis? And then – how to choose between them? To read enough about grounded theory, phenomenology or discourse analysis in order to get to the point of being able to make an informed choice would in all likelihood take longer than the whole time available to complete the research project. In practice, most students end up using the method that their supervisor has used in his or her research. Often, this arrangement works well enough, resulting in an acceptable dissertation or thesis, but it forestalls the spirit of inquiry of students in relation to method. The issue of methodological choice does not arise.

For both students and experts, there are a number of advantages associated with the idea of a 'generic qualitative method':

- It makes it easier for new researchers to get started.
- It de-mystifies qualitative research, and thus encourages more people to use qualitative methods.
- Researchers are more able to be flexible in relation to the challenges arising from their engagement with a topic – there is more freedom to adopt the role of *bricoleur*.
- It makes explicit the skills, personal qualities and support structures necessary for effective qualitative work.
- Researchers are forced to think about, and justify, *everything* they do – it will not be possible to claim validity and rigour merely through following a pre-determined 'package' of procedures.
- Qualitative researchers will be required to become familiar with the overarching philosophical and political factors that shape methodological choices.
- Increasing rapprochement and dialogue between existing qualitative genres is developed.

These advantages are particularly significant in relation to qualitative research in counselling and psychotherapy. There are few active qualitative researchers within the therapy research arena, and (one would hope) it is in everyone's interest to find ways of working more closely together.

The account of a generic method presented in the following section depicts qualitative research in three sections. First, there is a list of the main researcher activities and strategies associated with qualitative work, presented in terms of a series of steps. The aim is to convey a sense of what people *do* when they do qualitative research. The second section reviews the *repertoire* of ways of collecting and analysing qualitative data, and writing up findings, that a competent qualitative researcher might seek to acquire. Third, there is a discussion of some of the core images or organising principles that can be employed to give coherence to a research study.

## The elements of a generic qualitative method

Some of the main features of the structure of a generic approach to qualitative research are summarised below. The set of procedures that is described is not intended to be exhaustive, but rather to map out in general terms what is involved in doing a qualitative study. Also, the procedures are described as if for someone contemplating undertaking qualitative research for the first time. Experienced researchers tend to have developed their own style and do not usually spend time considering methodological choices, or engaging in background reading on the philosophy of science, to any great extent.

1   *Choosing the topic.* The researcher or research team selects a topic or area of inquiry which is perceived as personally meaningful and engaging. If the study is to be successful, the topic must be capable of stimulating the imagination, energies and 'need to know' of the researcher or research team.

2   *Identifying the audience.* It is also helpful to commence research with some idea of the intended *audience* for the eventual study. There are probably five primary audiences for research:

- **the researcher.** Some research is carried out to answer 'burning questions' that have emerged for the researcher himself or herself in the course of his or her life and work. The criteria for success in 'personal' research are based around personal development, fulfilment, the enhancement of a personal sense of understanding, or a catalyst for action.
- **colleagues.** Much research in counselling and psychotherapy is stimulated by questions arising within therapy agencies or organisations, or peer networks. This kind of research aims to provide information and insights that will make a practical difference to co-workers.
- **academics.** Many research studies are carried out in universities by people taking Masters or Doctoral qualifications, and so the requirements and expectations of an academic audience may be salient. Research aimed at academic readers needs to be methodologically rigorous, and well-informed by the theory and previous research. The practical and personal criteria that are relevant to personal and peer audiences (usually) carry much less weight with an academic audience.
- **managers and policy-makers.** Research which seeks to influence either

local or national policy-making must be sensitive to the policy 'agenda' of this particular audience, and have a good sense of the kinds of evidence that this constituency would find credible and convincing.

- **clients and service users.** Research that aims to communicate directly with users of therapy services needs to be designed around the requirements of publications that users would read, and the types of question that users would find relevant.

Each of these audiences or research consumers has a slightly different set of interests, and a different set of requirements around communication formats, use of technical language, tolerance for methodological detail, etc. The 'fitness-for-purpose' of a piece of research depends largely on having a clear idea at the outset of the nature of the eventual audience (or audiences) for the final product.

3  *Developing a greater awareness of the topic.* An initial phase of informal, personal research, reading and consultation to sensitise the researcher to the contours of the phenomenon and the available possibilities for access to appropriate informants or sources of information.

4  *Formulating a research question.* The formulation of an initial, open-ended research question. Qualitative research does not aim to 'test' hypotheses, but to describe, analyse and interpret the construction of aspects of the social world.

5  *Keeping a personal research journal.* Maintaining some kind of personal research journal or 'memo' system designed to capture personal and intuitive dimensions of the process of 'meaning-making' as they occur. It is usual to begin this log with an account of the researcher's presuppositions and expectations, written *before* beginning systematic fieldwork or data collection.

6  *Developing awareness of method.* Reading and consultation designed to sensitise the researcher to different qualitative approaches that might be taken in relation to the particular topic of interest. Inevitably, this process will include looking at specific methods texts such as Strauss and Corbin (1990) or others cited in earlier chapters of this book. But what is more useful is to spend some time reading philosophy, and reading research papers. Personal investment in reading about philosophical issues and perspectives relevant to the pursuit of qualitative inquiry allows the researcher to develop an overview or 'conceptual map' which makes it possible to evaluate the claims of competing qualitative genres. A recommended core 'philosophy of qualitative research' reading list would comprise Crotty (1996), Hammersley (1993), Polkinghorne (1988, 1995), Rennie (1998a, 1999, 2000c, 2000d) and Sass (1988). A useful book which offers a review of contemporary debates in the philosophy of social science

is Fay (1996). The edited collection by Hoshmand and Martin (1994) provides a series of accounts by well-known qualitative psychotherapy researchers of the philosophical, pragmatic, and personal considerations that shaped their choice of method. The papers in a Special Issue of *British Journal of Guidance and Counselling* by Etherington (1996), Grafanaki (1996), Riches and Dawson (1996) and Walsh (1996) are useful in terms of getting 'inside' the experience of doing qualitative research in counselling. It is also essential to read actual qualitative research articles, to gain a sense of the type of research 'product' that would be appropriate, attractive or exciting for you as a researcher. In reading research papers for this purpose it is important to keep the focus less on the substantive content and more on the method, keeping in mind the three questions outlined in Chapter 1 – How was the research done? What is the social context of the study? How relevant are the findings for practice? It is worth keeping in mind that there is a much wider choice of interesting qualitative research papers in social science and health journals than in psychology, counselling and psycho-therapy journals. The ideal is to find a paper that can function as a 'model' or 'image' for the research that is being planned. The topic of the 'model' paper may be irrelevant, but its approach to participants, methods of analysis, and style of presenting findings can usefully act as a preliminary guide. Finally, this phase of background reading on method should encompass material on *ethics* and *validity* (see Chapter 11).

7   *Choosing an approach.* Following the process of reading and consul-tation described in the previous section, the researcher is ready to espouse a 'posture' or orientation in relation to the inquiry process. This will either comprise a decision to orient the research within a mainstream research 'genre' (e.g. grounded theory, discourse analysis) or a choice to develop an approach which reflects an individual '*bricolage*'.

8   *Deciding on techniques of data collection and analysis.* The choice or creation of a method for collecting material relevant to this question. There are many different ways of collecting qualitative data or 'text', and many different approaches to analysis. An outline of the existing repertoire of available data collection and analysis strategies is provided below.

9   *Finalising the research plan.* Although a preliminary research plan may have been formulated at the beginning of the project, it is only at this point that the researcher can have a detailed specification of how he or she will collect, record and store data, negotiate informed consent and safeguard confidentiality, and analyse findings. In many research settings, a detailed plan needs to be submitted for external approval, for example to an ethics committee or doctoral supervision committee.

10   *A period of immersion in the phenomenon.* Making a space within the researcher's life that will allow thorough immersion in the project for a

period of time sufficient for processes of incubation, uncertainty and chaos, discovery and critical appraisal to take place. In other words, the researcher must be able to *concentrate* on the research task. This is the stage where 'data' is collected, through interviews or other methods, and then analysed. The importance of the researcher's immersion in, and commitment to, the research process is given special emphasis by Moustakas (1967, 1990a, b; Douglass and Moustakas, 1985) in his writing on the topic of *heuristic* research methods. Moustakas argues that it is essential that researchers engage in the equivalent of a personal 'journey of discovery', which draws upon all their resources and capacity to know and learn. A similar conception of the degree of personal focus that is required in good qualitative research can be found in Glaser (1978). Both writers point out that qualitative discoveries cannot be forced: there is always a degree of waiting and patience, and a requirement for a readiness to be surprised. When planning qualitative research, it is necessary to be realistic about the amount of time that it may take to arrive at a satisfactory end-point. Typically, a descriptive study can be carried out in around six months. However, achieving a convincing conceptualisation of the material may take much longer, perhaps as long as two years.

11   *Compiling the research text*. Collecting qualitative data through interviewing or other techniques (see below), and then bringing this research material (interview transcripts, observational notes, memo entries, etc.) together into a research text.

12   *Refining the method of analysis*. Developing a set of rules and procedures that will prevent premature closure on the process of analysis and interpretation, and ensure that all sections of the text are sufficiently included in the analysis.

13   *'Condensing' the research text*. Constructing a descriptive summary of what has been 'found' in the text to provide an initial overall sense of what seems to be 'there'.

14   *Analysing: comprehensive and exhaustive analysis of the research text*. Carrying out a more detailed analysis of the text, or selected portions of it, in order to develop a more fine-grained understanding and to generate, if possible, new insights or 'discoveries'. Ideas and hypotheses generated during the course of the study, and recorded in memos or in a learning journal, provide one of the sources of analytic categories at this point.

15   *Checking*. Continuing the analysis beyond the point of boredom by continually checking the adequacy of the framework of understanding that has emerged, for example by seeking counter-examples, checking construc-tions with informants or colleagues, reflecting on findings in relation to the

'quality criteria' associated with the posture or genre that has been adopted, etc.

16    *Writing*. Collating, condensing and authoring the several pieces of writing that have accumulated during the research process (e.g., memo and journal entries, sections of transcript, lists of themes and categories, etc.) into a report, paper or thesis. An important task within this stage is that of constructing a 'summary representation' of the new understanding of the phenomenon that has been achieved, to make it easier for future researchers to build on the findings of the study.

17    *Theorising*. Depending on the nature of the report or paper, the process of writing may also include an interpretive discussion of the theoretical implications of the study, and a review of how the findings confirm or bring into question the results of previous studies of the topic or phenomenon.

*Throughout* these steps, a qualitative researcher will normally seek opportunities to test out parts of the work (the interview schedule, the analysis of the first interview, the emerging analytic framework, etc.) with a range of audiences, such as supervisors, research support group members, strangers on trains, informants, their nearest and dearest, and so on. Researchers working in teams or research groups may be continually engaged in this kind of support, validation and co-construction. Also, throughout the research the inquirer needs to be ready to deal with a range of emotional reactions associated with the work. Qualitative researchers report a variety of difficult feelings. There can be feelings of *dependency* arising from the experience of largely relying on others (informants, contacts, gatekeepers) for the successful completion of a task that has great personal significance. Many researchers encounter almost unbearable *anxiety* around being in 'impossible' situations where the normal everyday rules of interaction do not appear to apply. Most researchers dip in and out of feelings of *depression, despair* and *confusion* triggered by the anticipation and fear that nothing will be found, and that the research (and the researcher) are worthless and incompetent. Finally, qualitative researchers often feel *anguish* and *guilt* at the prospect of betraying the trust of informants (Josselson, 1996b). It is important to recognise these emotions (along with more welcome feelings of elation following discovery) as being intrinsic to *good* practice, rather than as indicative of personal shortcomings. A research journal, colleagues, supervisors and personal therapy can be effective vehicles for working through such emotions. The point, of course, is not to get rid of the feelings, but to learn from them. Just as the therapist's countertransference operates as a rich source of information about the client and the state of the therapeutic relationship, the researcher's feelings give clues to what is *most important* in the research situation. It is also essential to understand the potential connections between these emotions and the conduct and analysis of the research. For example, have some informants been avoided and others sought out because they, respectively, are anxiety-provoking or welcoming? How do the feelings evoked by an interviewee shape the categorisation and analysis of the interview transcript material?

## Acquiring a repertoire of qualitative research skills

Perhaps the principal distinguishing feature that marks off 'research' from other types of writing about the experience of counselling and psychotherapy is that research always makes reference to a body of 'data'. These data are the primary evidence upon which conclusions are supposedly based. In principle, the 'data' are publicly available. For example, occasionally a student submitting research for a PhD or Masters may be asked to show the examiners their fieldnotes or interview transcripts. Very occasionally, researchers re-analyse data collected by others. Forms of writing that are not based on a publicly accessible set of data are not normally considered to constitute 'research'. So, for instance, psychoanalytic and other clinical case studies that are based on the therapist's selective recall of sessions, would not normally be viewed as 'research'. On the other hand, hermeneutic historical studies, such as Cushman (1995), where the original sources are open to re-analysis by others, *are* viewed as 'research'. The collection of data following rational, publicly verifiable principles is a cornerstone of the liberal democratic ethos that informs work in the social sciences. In the absence of 'data', truth claims are inevitably based on authority. Only when the 'books' are open and 'above board' can free debate take place (Gergen, 1997).

However, the concept of 'data' does not sit comfortably within qualitative research. Data are 'the things that are given', and the use of the term within science probably originates in the Enlightenment empiricist philosophers such as John Locke and David Hume, who talked about a 'sense datum' – the raw information that impinges on sense organs such as vision or touch. The basic idea appears to be that a sense datum contains uninterpreted (and therefore unprejudiced) information about a reality that is 'out there'. In contemporary usage, 'data' has come to mean an array of information, as in 'data set' or 'data bank'. Data are 'bits' of information that can be collected and stored. In both the empiricist and contemporary meanings of data there is an assumption of neutrality: data are intrinsically valid and it is up to us to draw the correct conclusions from them.

In qualitative inquiry there are no 'data' of this type. The information or 'material' that we collect comprises different kinds of accounts of experience and events. The process of collecting this material is inevitably personal and collaborative to a greater or lesser extent. For example, the process of participating in a qualitative interview involves a meeting of two people and the formation of a relationship. It is a conversation in which 'understanding or its failure is like an event that happens to us'. The stuff we piece together is not 'given' but is 'constructed'. Qualitative researchers construct representations of aspects of social life. These constructions usually take the form of written texts. Note the difference between a 'text' and a 'data set'. The former is multi-voiced and narratively structured. The latter is logically and numerically structured.

The influence of psychology on counselling and psychotherapy research has meant that even qualitative researchers can often fall into the trap of regarding their work as *data collection* (like picking apples from a tree) rather than text construction (like writing a story).

In this section, a number of different strategies for constructing qualitative texts are reviewed. The phenomena of counselling and psychotherapy are complex, elusive and sensitive; it is important to recognise that there are many ways in which these phenomena can be approached. Each of these approaches highlights and emphasises certain aspects of the phenomenon in question, and downplays others. The notion of researcher as *'bricoleur'* (see Chapter 8) can be seen as an attempt to create assemblages of methods that are both practicable and do justice to the topic. Whatever method is used it operates in a subtle fashion to *position* the researcher in relation to the field of inquiry. Wolcott (1992) has suggested that research is an act of *posturing*; the investigator adopts a particular posture or attitude concerning his or her assumptions about people and knowledge.

There are many ways of gathering qualitative accounts. In qualitative social science and psychotherapy research, at the moment, there is a tendency to operate as though semi-structured interviews and open-ended written accounts were the only feasible methods of inquiry, applicable to all circumstances. An (incomplete) list of methods is given in Table 9.1. Here it can be seen that there are many ways of collecting 'data' about the process and outcome of therapy.

The majority of published qualitative studies of counselling and psychotherapy are based on the analysis of texts collected through interviews or open-ended questionnaires. It is important to be aware that there are many other techniques that can be employed. Even within the area of interviewing there are a number of alternative creative strategies that are worthy of consideration. For some purposes, it can be effective to collect informants together into a 'focus group'. The use of focus groups allows a group of research informants to interact with each other, and generate useful qualitative data not only in response to the researcher's questions, but through spontaneous dialogue with each other. There are a number of books around that offer guidelines on how to do carry out focus group interviews Greenbaum, 1998; Krueger, 1994; Stewart and Shamdasani, 1998; Vaughn et al., 1996). There is also an expanding literature on the

Table 9.1   *Methods for creating qualitative texts*

Interviews
  open-ended
  semi-structured
  individual vs. group
  recall interviews
  think-aloud protocols
Questionnaires
Observation
  participant observation (ethnographic)
  non-participant
Transcripts of naturally occurring talk
Personal documents
Public documents
Projective techniques
Experiential/personal methods

application of focus groups in research on therapy-related topics (Bristol and Fern, 1996; Herman et al., 1996; Powell et al., 1996; Rodriguez et al., 1998). A useful variant of the focus-group method is *Nominal Group Technique* (Delbecq, Van de Ven and Gustafson, 1975), which combines focus-group and brainstorming strategies. A method that is being increasingly widely used to enable larger samples of participants to comment on themes identified in focus groups is the *Delphi* technique (Fish and Busby, 1996; Delbecq et al., 1975). This method involves sending out by mail lists of key statements derived from interviews or group sessions, and asking participants for their comments, amendments and ratings. Examples of therapy studies using the Delphi technique are Heath et al. (1988) and Neimeyer and Norcross (1997). In other research situations, rather than the mere asking of questions, it can be productive to use various props and devices to facilitate the interview. The method of Interpersonal Process Recall (IPR) has been described in the context of the work of David Rennie (Chapter 6) and Robert Elliott (Chapter 8). With IPR, the client or therapist listens to an audiotape or watches a videotape of the therapy session and is invited to stop the tape whenever they recall what they had been experiencing during the actual therapy session. This approach, which derives from the work of Kagan (1980, 1984), is an excellent method for generating rich accounts of the moment-by-moment experience of therapy process (Barker, 1985). Another method for augmenting interviews is to use the *think-aloud protocol* technique (Ericsson and Simon, 1984; Fonteyn et al., 1993; Smagorinsky, 1994). Here, rather than asking an informant to report on their memory of how they carry out a task, the researcher sets up a simulation of the task itself and invites the person to give a 'running commentary' while they are performing. For example, Sandell and Fredelius (1997) were interested in the ways in which both therapists and policy-makers prioritised patients for psychotherapy, and asked their research participants to 'think aloud' while reading case material and deciding which cases should receive subsidised therapy. Their data was analysed through ratings and statistics, but in principle could have been approached using a qualitative method such as grounded theory or ideal type methodology. The use of *projective techniques* is currently unfashionable in psychology, despite strong evidence for the value of this method (McClelland, 1980). A projective technique invites the participant to respond to an ambiguous stimulus. The assumption is that the person's response functions as a 'projection' of their deepest attitudes and motives (Hingley, 1995). Compared to questionnaires, there are two advantages to projective methods. First, the person is not as aware of the meaning of their response, and is more likely to respond freely rather than offer a socially desirable answer. Second, the projective approach stimulates creativity and playfulness, and brings an additional dimension to the research being undertaken. A useful account of the application of projective techniques in qualitative research can be found in Branthwaite and Lunn (1983). A further method that has a long history within qualitative research is the use of *personal and official documents*, such as diaries, letters, memos, case notes, leaflets, etc. (Allport, 1942; Macdonald and Tipton, 1993). An advantage of these sources is that they have not been created for research purposes, and are therefore free from any influence from the investigator. Counselling and psychotherapy are activities that generate significant amounts of personal and official documentation. Until now, this source of qualitative text has been largely ignored by researchers. Another important method for collecting data that has been neglected in therapy research has been *participant observation* (see Chapter 5). In recent years, some social scientists have developed an approach in which, in effect, researchers observe, record and reflect on their own involvement in a situation. This method of *experiential research* has not been applied within the field of counselling and psychotherapy, but clearly has a huge potential contribution to make. Examples of experiential research can be found in the writings of Carolyn Ellis and her colleagues (Ellis and Bochner, 1996; Ellis and Flaherty, 1992; Ellis et al., 1997; Kiesinger, 1998). A powerful example of the use of experiential research in counselling can be found in Etherington (2000).

## Analysing qualitative texts: a repertoire of methods

The aim of this section is to consider the different ways in which qualitative text can be analysed. Just as there exists a repertoire of techniques for generating qualitative text, there also exists a repertoire of techniques and strategies for facilitating the process of finding meaning. However, it is essential to recognise that analytic procedures do not, in themselves, generate themes and categories. Meaning emerges from qualitative text from the active engagement of the researcher with that text, from his or her drive to know and understand. Methods of analysis can provide a structure and a framework that ensures, as far as possible, that all aspects of the text are given due weight. Following a set of analytic procedures can be useful in avoiding premature closure, forcing oneself to look as closely as possible at the text, and as a reminder of the goals of the inquiry. But 'findings' can only be 'found' by someone who is actively searching.

The notion that the process of analysis begins only when all the data is collected and securely stored in a computer arises from the quantitative research tradition. In quantitative research, there is little point in analysing statistical data until all the numbers are in, because the whole analysis would need to be carried out all over again with the whole data set. Also, the goal of objectivity in, for example, experimental research would demand that the researcher resists analysing data until the experiment has been completed, to avoid the danger that his or her knowledge of early trends in the data might introduce an unconscious bias over the remainder of the experiment, through seeking to 'pull' the results in a particular direction. However, these considerations do not apply in qualitative research. In qualitative work, the main tool of inquiry is the researcher. If it is accepted that the researcher is a person continually engaged in sense-making and finding meaning, then it follows that the process of analysis and interpretation of qualitative material (notes, transcripts, documents) takes place all the time. Some qualitative researchers set aside a period of time for 'analysis', following the phase of 'data collection', and assume that this is when analysis happens. It is better to regard such a period as an opportunity to pull together the various strands of analytic understanding that have emerged during the course of the study, and then to check them as systematically as possible against the material, in a search for counter-examples, deviant cases and new or more aptly phrased categories.

It is not possible in the space available here to provide an exhaustive list of all the different analytic procedures that have been devised by qualitative researchers over the years. The aim instead is to offer examples of some contrasting techniques, to illustrate the range of alternatives that can be considered when planning or conducting a research study.

## Writing memos and jotting down ideas throughout the course of the research

Many insights seem almost just to 'arrive' at odd times, for example when walking along a road. Other ideas can arrive when interviewing, or when transcribing. Sometimes these ideas turn out to be of little value, because they do not apply to other informants, or because they are triggered by a book the researcher has recently read, or a movie that he or she has seen, rather than by the actual research. But there are other times when fleeting ideas may turn out to be vital elements of the subsequent analytic framework.

## Constructing a preliminary descriptive summary of the material as a whole

One of the primary tasks of qualitative research is to *describe* the phenomenon or social process that is the focus of the research. The other tasks, according to Wolcott (1994), are *analysis* and *interpretation*. A key idea in hermeneutic approaches to inquiry is that of moving back and forth between the whole text and detailed parts of the text. An understanding of detailed parts is always informed by the context provided by the text as a whole. At the same time, the detailed analysis of sections of the text may result in new ways of seeing the meaning of the whole text. It can be useful to anchor this process of moving back and forth by writing a tentative, preliminary statement which seeks to capture the initial sense of *all* the material that has been collected (or that has been collected up to that point). For example, in a study which comprises a series of interviews, it can be helpful to compose a 500-word narrative summary of each interview, covering the main themes and the overall impression gained by the interviewer.

## Organising / segmenting the text into discrete meaning units

Although it is important to develop a sense of the meaning of the text as a whole, good qualitative work always depends on being able to open out the meanings associated with small segments of the text. It is only by forcing oneself to get beyond the initial 'common-sense' reading of a text that the qualitative analyst can generate the type of new insights that make this work worthwhile. While it is quite possible to 'expand' the meaning of text through a process of intuitive immersion and reflection, most researchers find it both helpful and necessary to decide in advance on the 'meaning units' around which they intend to build their analysis. In earlier chapters, it could be seen that, for instance, empirical phenomenologists examined the meaning of short statements, while, by contrast, narrative-analytic researchers focused on the meaning of whole stories as units. Grounded theory is an approach that embodies considerable flexibility around the length and structure of meaning units (words, phrases, sentences, paragraphs). Conversation analysis typically takes a short sequence of conversational turns as the principal unit of analysis. The intention in all of these approaches is the same, which is to apply a systematic method of 'segmenting' the text, of dividing it into workable bits whose meaning and properties can be closely examined.

## Labelling, coding and categorising meanings

Once the text has been segmented into some kind of 'meaning units', the researcher is faced with the crucial task of making some statement about what these units might actually *mean*. All qualitative research involves attributing meaning to segments of text. It is here that the tension between phenomenology and hermeneutics is most acute. Qualitative researchers influenced by phenomenology seek to describe meaning in terms of what the statement or piece of observed behaviour might mean *to the informant*. Interpretive approaches to qualitative research mainly seek to give meaning in terms of the cultural meaning systems (or theory) of the researcher / inquirer, rather than that of the informant. Grounded theory has largely adopted a stance that integrates both of these strategies, in being open to meanings arising from informants *and* those generated by the analyst. In practice, the tension between hermeneutic and phenomenological meaning-making strategies is more a matter of emphasis than an absolute dichotomy. Within the hermeneutic research tradition, the notion of 'fusion of horizons' (see Chapter 2) implies that the horizon of understanding of the researcher should be expanded and changed by contact and engagement with the horizons encompassed by the text. Similarly, few phenomenological researchers would argue that research which focuses on the experience of another person can ever be wholly free from being shaped by the pre-suppositions and language of the inquirer. One of the central arguments of this book is that qualitative research *always* involves a synthesis of phenomenological and hermeneutic 'ways of knowing'. It is significant that Comprehensive Process Analysis (Chapter 8), a qualitative model that reflects a sophisticated appreciation of these issues, purposefully opens a space for parallel consideration of the texts produced by both 'participants' (the client and therapist) and researchers. The practicalities of meaning categorisation represent another set of choices for qualitative researchers. Some researchers write their category notes on double-spaced, wide-margin copies of the text. Others prefer to copy these notes on to file cards that can be sorted within boxes. There are also several software packages that facilitate the coding of qualitative text. Examples of the strategies adopted by qualitative researchers during coding and categorising can be found in the methods texts introduced in previous chapters. Whatever system is adopted, it is essential that the researcher should be not only painstaking and thorough in recording categories, but should also be as playful, imaginative, creative and sensitive as they can in generating all the *possible* meanings implicit in segments of text.

## Sifting and ordering: identifying themes and patterns

In most research studies, the consequence of engaging in categorising or coding meaning units is a massive expansion of the text. Where before there might have been 200 pages of interview transcript, there is now a confusion of annotated transcript, computer files, file cards or post-it notes containing category phrases along with information about the segments of text to which they refer. It is probably important for qualitative researchers to allow this process of expansion to continue to a point of frustrated, overwhelmed despair. When the previous 'fore-understanding' or structure of meaning of the researcher dissolves or 'unfreezes' in the face of the complexity of the text, the opportunity for discovery opens up. However, the moments of discovery that a researcher records in his or her memos or personal journal, or which arrive during data analysis, require to be documented, checked and explained so that they can be communicated to other people. The grounded theory notion of 'constant comparisons' captures well the experience of taking each interpretive category and checking it against as many other segments of the text, and other categories, as possible. The key questions include: Does this category apply in all cases? In what ways do counter-examples change the meaning of the category? Does the way that the category is phrased accurately capture the meaning that is being conveyed? Are there other categories with similar meanings – when these similar categories are placed side by side does another, overarching category emerge? What happens when the meaning of the category is 'imaginatively varied' – is it possible to imagine its limits or its opposite? For many qualitative researchers, the stage of sifting and ordering is made easier by finding ways to display the categories in some kind of visual form. Patterns in the material can often be 'seen' more clearly by laying out file cards on a table, pegging them to washing lines, mapping them on large pieces of paper or whiteboards, or moving them around a PC screen. A very useful source of ideas in relation to this aspect of analysis is Miles and Huberman (1994).

## Deciding on the main theme or storyline

Qualitative analysis is fundamentally holistic in nature. Good qualitative analysis looks at the text from all possible angles, and seeks to capture a sense of what the *whole* of it might mean. Some qualitative research writing aims to capture and convey this sense of an overall, holistic, understanding of a topic. Phenomenological research and, to some extent, ethnographic research, usually attempts to lay before the reader a comprehensive descriptive account of whatever aspect of the social world has been studied. By contrast, other qualitative approaches (grounded theory, the discursive approaches, hermeneutic research, some ethnographic work) adopt a strategy of illuminating the topic by exploring it from one specific vantage point. It is common in qualitative research to generate a research text and analysis that can then be 'mined' or written up in terms of different themes. The work of David Rennie into the client's experience of therapy exemplifies this strategy. Rennie (1990) started with a report which conveyed an overall sense of his analysis as a whole. However, this overview was followed by a series of papers reporting on specific themes within the material, for example client deference (Rennie, 1994a), the client's experience of resistance (Rennie, 1994c) and so on (see Chapter 6 for details of this body of work). There are several advantages in writing up qualitative research from a series of thematic perspectives or following different 'storylines'. The first advantage is that it is easier to do justice to the data, because there is more space available to include quotes and examples relating to particular aspects of the data, rather than the data-set as a whole. Second, it is easier to develop a theoretical discussion of the material, and link it up to previous research, when there is a narrower focus for discussion. Third, concentrating on discrete themes within the material is more likely to yield papers which practitioners will experience as offering them specific, applicable knowledge.

### 'Ideal type' or vignette analysis

Qualitative research has been dominated by methods, such as grounded theory and phenomenology, that seek to extract common or general categories across all informants or sources. In counselling and psychotherapy, on the other hand, practitioners are faced on an everyday basis with the task of responding to individuals, or developing strategies or policies appropriate to sub-groups of clients. Qualitative research that is case-study based is clearly relevant to an understanding of processes and dynamics occurring in individual clients, but says little about properties of aggregates of clients. An analytic approach which combines the sensitivity of the case study method with the possibility of generalisation involves using the notion of *ideal types*. The proposal that social life could be understood through the analysis of 'ideal types' is attributed to the sociologist Max Weber, and appears to have been mainly employed by German psychotherapy researchers (Frommer et al., 1996; Kuhnlein, 1999; Tress et al., 1997; Wachholz and Stuhr, 1999). The approach relies on a process of comparing and combining case descriptions until an irreducible set of distinct case patterns emerges. This procedure is in effect a qualitative version of cluster analysis. These studies are all based on a method of ideal-type analysis devised by the German qualitative researcher Uta Gerhardt, whose work does not seem to have been translated into English. Brief introductory accounts of the method can be found in Flick (1998: 234–5), in Wachholz and Stuhr (1999: 331–2) and in Stuhr and Wachholz (2000). Similar approaches to working with combinations of individual case configurations have been reported by Cummings et al. (1994) and Miller et al. (1997). The Miller et al. research group describe their method as structured around the construction of representative case *vignettes*.

## Writing

The final stage of any qualitative study involves compiling a written report in the form of an article, book or dissertation. Although some qualitative researchers have experimented with alternative forms of dissemination, including drama, performance art, video and poetry, these vehicles have up until now not been received particularly well. The work of writing qualitative research is difficult. All qualitative researchers struggle with what has been called the 'crisis of representation', the challenge of conveying on paper the richness of understanding that the researcher has developed, and the various 'voices' of informants. Qualitative research does not lend itself easily to publication in the standardised formats (Introduction–Method–Results–Discussion) and scientific rhetoric-systems employed by most journals in counselling and psychotherapy. The task of writing for scientific publication is even more difficult when the researcher wishes to include reflexive first-person writing. The outcome of these various difficulties is that the majority of qualitative research papers in counselling and psychotherapy are not at all easy to read, particularly for practitioners. This is problematic given the aspiration and belief of most qualitative psychotherapy researchers that their work has the potential to become more relevant for practice than statistical research has ever been (Morrow-Bradley and Elliott, 1986). In writing qualitative research, there are some basic rules to be followed:

- The research should be written in a form that will communicate with practitioners.
- The report should include enough qualitative research text to allow readers to develop their own interpretation of the material.
- The procedures through which the researcher collected and analysed the material should be clearly explained.
- It is helpful to describe the context of the study, including not only the 'pre-understandings' of the researcher but also the social and institutional environment in which the research took place.

- At the end of the Analysis or beginning of the Discussion sections of the report it is useful to include a 'summary representation' of what has been found. The presence of a summary representation gives future researchers into the topic a set of preliminary hypotheses or under-standings against which they can compare their own findings, thus allowing a cumulative, 'joined-up' body of understanding of the topic to be constructed.

Issues associated with writing qualitative research have been discussed by Ellis and Bochner (1996), Wolcott (1990) and McLeod (1999a). This question is also explored further in Chapter 11.

## Consensual Qualitative Research as a generic method

One of the most significant evolutions in qualitative research in counselling and psychotherapy during the 1990s was the development by Clara Hill and her research group at the University of Maryland of a guide for conducting qualitative research (Hill, Thompson and Nutt-Williams, 1997). This group has been one of the most productive research teams in the world; their method of *Consensual Qualitative Research* (CQR) has generated several papers in prestigious journals (Hayes et al., 1998; Hill, Nutt-Williams et al., 1997; Knox et al., 1997; Ladany et al., 1997; Rhodes et al., 1994).

CQR is explicitly based on ideas and principles drawn from grounded theory, Comprehensive Process Analysis, Giorgi's empirical phenomenol-ogy, and feminist values concerning open collaboration and respect. It is probably fair to describe CQR as an integrative approach rather than a *bricolage* (Chapter 8), since it is not intended that it should be adapted to the circumstances of specific studies. The method is a team-based approach, in which a small group of four or five researchers collect and analyse data. Their analyses are checked by an independent external *auditor*, who has the task of challenging collusive interpretations and avoidances. There are three broad stages of data collection and analysis:

1 Responses to open-ended questions from questionnaires or interviews for each individual case are divided into domains (i.e., topic areas).
2 Core ideas (i.e., abstracts or brief summaries) are constructed for all the material within each domain for each individual case.
3 A cross analysis, which involves developing categories to describe consistencies in the core ideas within domains across cases, is con-ducted. (Hill, Thompson and Nutt-Williams, 1997: 523)

These stages are described in detail, with examples and practical hints, in the 'Guide' (ibid., 1997). It is suggested that, as well as its research applications, the experience of using the method functions as a useful addition to the training of counsellors and psychotherapists.

One of the areas in which CQR diverges from classic grounded theory and phenomenological approaches is in the pre-selection of domain categories, on the basis of a review of the literature, *in advance* of engaging with the actual data. Hill, Thompson and Nutt-Williams (1997) describe their initial set of domain categories as a 'start list' (Miles and Huberman (1994), and consider that its use is necessary as a means of managing the 'overwhelming amounts of data typically collected in qualitative research' (Hill et al., 1997: 543). This aspect of the method, together with the built-in requirement to achieve group consensus on category descriptions and labels, has the effect of perhaps restricting the 'discovery-oriented' potential of the method. It is probably fair to suggest that papers using CQR are strong on comprehensive, convincing description, and weak on the generation of exciting new conceptual frameworks. Nevertheless, the method represents a robust and highly practical addition to the range of qualitative methods of therapy research currently in use. The thoughtful integration of ideas from 'brand name' methodologies such as grounded theory and phenomenology mean that CQR can be viewed as a truly generic approach.

A significant feature of CQR is that, unlike other qualitative approaches, it has spawned its own critical literature. The 'Guide' was first published as a 'major contribution' in *Counseling Psychologist*. This is a journal in which each issue includes a major article followed by a series of brief commentary papers. The lengthy Hill, Thompson and Nutt-Williams (1997) paper was therefore published alongside commentaries from Hoshmand (1997) and Stiles (1997), with a concluding rejoinder from Hill, Nutt-Williams and Thompson (1997).

The input of Stiles (1997) to this debate is well worth reading in its own right, as an exploration of some of the basic methodological issues in qualitative inquiry. Stiles points to a number of ways in which the pro-cedures outlined by Hill, Thompson and Nutt-Williams (1997) import the assumptions of quantitative methods around sampling criteria, role of theory, nature of consensus and the goal of objectivity. At the heart of Stiles's critique is the view that:

> truths about human experience are not fixed and known (or not known) by individuals but rather emerge and evolve in dialogue. A corollary is that the sort of interviews proposed by Hill et al. (1997) – seeking responses in standard categories – runs a risk of eliciting mainly conventional understandings. (Stiles, 1997: 589)

The tension between 'dialogical' and 'conventional' understandings cuts through the whole field of qualitative inquiry. Good work inevitably possesses a dialogical character, and, to use another phrase of Stiles (1997), offers a kind of *permeable* knowing that is flexible and receptive.

The critical reception offered to the 'Guide to conducting consensual qualitative research' was no more hostile than the response would be if a grounded theory, discourse analysis, or phenomenology research team had published a set of guidelines to their approach in a journal which invited commentaries from adherents of alternative approaches. The methodology of qualitative research is inevitably contested. It is always a matter of negotiating the best path in the circumstances. While other researchers can identify different emphases, these positions may be right for them, but not necessarily congruent with the overall aims of the researcher or research group being criticised. The value of CQR is evident in the many successful research studies that have been completed using this perspective. The existence of at least the beginnings of a critical debate over the implications of adopting certain analytic procedures and not others is one of the positive spin-offs of the development of generic approaches.

## The achievements of a generic approach to qualitative research

If it were true that the best qualitative research resulted only from the application of well-established methodologies such as grounded theory or phenomenology, then it would be hard to find good examples of research conducted in accordance with the set of general principles outlined in this chapter. This is not the case. The body of work produced by Clara Hill and her group using CQR, discussed in the previous section, can be viewed as a product of a generic method. However, it may be that these researchers regard their approach as a contender for a new 'brand name' methodology, rather than as describing a set of principles. There are also many examples of studies which do not make any claim to follow a specific, named method, but have made substantial contributions to the field of qualitative research in counselling and psychotherapy. Three such studies are summarised next.

The first of these studies is a research monograph by O'Neill (1998). This research comprises an analysis of interviews carried out with over 90 therapists and clients around the issue of 'negotiating consent'. O'Neill's particular interest was in the ways in which therapists told clients about alternative treatments, and how clients received this information. The Methods section of this monograph is elegantly written and argued, and touches on a variety of methodological sources in psychology, social science and cultural studies. However, O'Neill resists any pull to locate his work within a specific approach, referring to his analysis merely as 'thematic'. He suggests that 'qualitative analysis is a somewhat more self-conscious version of the meaning-making in which we all engage throughout our lives' (1998: 45). The O'Neill study is notable for the effective manner in which the author allows the voices of informants to be heard, and yet at the same time abstracts from these voices a more general set of themes which are then examined in terms of their implications for practice.

Another piece of research that can be viewed as following a generic approach is a book by Lott (1999). This study concerns the emotional bond that can develop between women and their therapists. Lott, with her co-worker Marie Cohen, received 274 open-ended questionnaires back from female therapy clients, and carried out 120 interviews. The findings are presented in a style which makes effective use of personal, reflexive material, and are discussed in relation to relevant theoretical and research literature. This book opens up new understandings of the intensity of client experiences, and has important practical implications for both therapists and users of therapy. One of the most interesting aspects of the book arises from the fact that its author is *not a researcher*. Deborah Lott is a writer on medical issues who had been in therapy and was driven to find out more about her (and her friends') experiences in therapy. She comments on her research role in these terms:

> I felt certain that I could write a book that no therapist could write because as a journalist I would be freer to ask the hard questions, freer to question the basic assumptions that underlay the field, freer to explore the disagreements between the various schools of thought. (Lott, 1999: 9)

From the point of view of academic researchers there are a number of limitations of the Lott (1999) study that concern the level of detailed information supplied, sample characteristics, analytic procedures, validity checks, etc. On the other hand, it cannot be denied that her work makes a significant contribution to the literature on the client's experience of therapy, and generates a variety of insights that could be pursued in further research. The quality of the study lies not in its formal adherence to a 'method', but in the commitment and integrity of the investigator, her positioning outside of the therapy establishment ('free to ask the hard questions'), and her capacity to write in such a way as to allow her informants to 'speak for themselves'.

A third example of the use of a 'generic' approach to qualitative research in psychotherapy is a paper by Roberts (1996). In this study, interviews were carried out with eight partners/spouses of clients undergoing psycho-dynamic therapy. Roberts was interested in the 'perceived repercussions' on the partner of their spouse/partner being in therapy. Although this paper was published in a leading research journal (*British Journal of Psychiatry*), no details of how the interview data were analysed were given. Findings were presented in terms of 'common themes'. There is also an interesting discussion of the impact of the research on participants. Despite (or because of?) the absence of methodological detail, this paper is a fine piece of work, which opens out new understandings of a neglected area of inquiry.

It may be significant that the studies by O'Neill (1998) and Lott (1999) were published as books rather than in the form of research articles. The space afforded by a book or research monograph allows the author room to describe his or her method in detail without the need to give it a summary description such as 'grounded theory'. Book-length accounts also allow sufficient examples and quotes to be provided, so that the reader can be convinced of the validity of both the argument and the evidence on the basis of what he or she can actually read, rather than on the basis that the author followed a particular method. Finally, journal reviewers and editors may have perhaps fallen into a habit of expecting all qualitative papers to cite a 'named' method. At the present time the best (or only) way to publish a 'generic' qualitative paper in a research journal may be to give the method a name.

## Images of qualitative inquiry: some organising principles

The final section of the chapter moves away from discussion of specific steps and strategies involved in doing qualitative research, to a consideration of the overall understanding that a qualitative researcher might possess concerning what they are doing. There exist a number of different *images* of qualitative research. The work of any individual qualitative researcher tends to be intelligible in terms of the image or images he or she has espoused in relation to their research role. For anyone beginning qualitative research for the first time, it can be helpful to adopt one of these core images, as a means of giving coherence to their investigative style.

### The scientist

The dominant image that informs the practice of qualitative researcher in counselling and psychotherapy is that of the scientist. Few qualitative researchers, nowadays, explicitly refer to the notion of objectivity, in the sense of claiming to produce knowledge that is 'factual' or 'objectively true'. However, the language of 'consensuality' and 'convergence', emphasis on the 'rigour' of methods and procedures, or a lack of acknowledgement that 'findings' are co-constructed (between researcher and informants), all indicate that the researcher believes that there exists a single knowable 'truth', and that he or she possesses the means of securing that truth. The absence of any apparent interest in discovery, as opposed to the confirmation of already known truths, is another reflection of the scientist image. The image of the scientist is deeply embedded in the fabric of western modern cultures, and conveys to many people a person whose work is honest, dispassionate, balanced, rational and makes a significant contribution to social well-being and progress. There are, however, other meanings of 'science', which apply in particular to the rationale for qualitative research:

> Shortly after the turn of this century . . . two distinct perspectives on social inquiry were in competition. The quantitative tradition, with its realist orientation, was based on the idea of an independently existing social reality that could be described as it really was. Truth was defined as the correspondence between our words and that independently existing reality. Common to this perspective, which allowed that facts were separate from values, was . . . a 'God's Eye' point of view. The interpretive tradition, based on an idealist temperament, took the position that social reality was mind-dependent in the sense of mind-constructed. Truth was ultimately a matter of socially and historically conditioned agreement. Social inquiry could not be value-free, and there could not be a 'God's Eye' point of view – there could only be various people's points of view based on their particular interests, values and purposes. (Smith and Heshusius, 1986: 5)

This passage highlights the implications for qualitative researchers of embracing the image of the scientist. As qualitative researchers, do we accept that, within our field of inquiry, facts can be 'separate from values'? Do we aspire to a 'God's Eye' perspective?

### The embodied witness

God might be believed to possess an all-seeing, all-knowing view of things. A quite different view of things is obtained from the perspective of ordinary mortals, who feel their way around a physical, ground-level world. An alternative to a 'God's Eye' image of the position of the researcher can be found in a wonderful essay by the feminist social scientist Donna Haraway (1988), which argues that researchers should be aiming to develop *situated knowledges*. Rather than 'the god trick of seeing everything from nowhere' (p. 581), which represents an attempt to create a 'total' or 'totalizing' knowledge, 'I am arguing for the view from a body, always a complex, contradictory, structuring and structured body, versus the view from above, from nowhere . . .' (p. 589). This 'view from below' is always from a specific, embodied person and place. It contributes to the science and politics of 'interpretation, translation, stuttering, and the partly understood'. Haraway makes the point that situated knowledge makes it possible to steer a middle course between objectivity and relativism. The objectivity of the 'view from above' is, for Haraway and many other researchers and scholars in the social sciences, at best an illusion and at worst a form of control. On the other hand, the relativism, the 'view from nowhere', associated with some forms of radical social constructionism, is equally misleading and dangerous:

> Relativism is a way of being nowhere while claiming to be everywhere equally. The 'equality' of positioning is a denial of responsibility and critical inquiry. Relativism is the perfect mirror twin of totalization . . . both deny . . . location, embodiment, and partial perspective; both make it impossible to see well. Relativism and totalization are both 'god tricks' promising vision from every-where and nowhere equally and fully, common myths in rhetorics surrounding Science. But it is precisely in the politics and epistemology of partial perspectives that the possibility of sustained, rational, objective inquiry rests. (Haraway, 1988: 584)

Only from a 'partial perspective' is it possible to 'see well': 'vision is better from below the brilliant space platforms of the powerful' (p. 583).

## Art as a metaphor for qualitative research

Gaining an overall sense of what qualitative researchers do, and what they produce, can be facilitated by considering debates and developments in a different area of endeavour – art. It is possible to look at a qualitative research paper or monograph as a form of *representation* of the world. Visual art, similarly, offers representations of the world. In both cases, someone (the researcher or the artist) has *constructed* the representation that is being presented, even though (at least usually) the audience is invited to ignore the 'frame' around the work and somehow 'enter' it as if it were a region of reality. The different genres of qualitative inquiry can be likened to various genres of visual art. Traditional ethnographic research produces a big-canvas picture which seeks definitely to capture the complexity of a social group. A painting by Brueghel, such as *The Wedding Feast* renders visible the way of life of a community. A grounded theory study is along the same lines, but on a smaller scale. A grounded theory paper presents a highly realistic picture of people *doing something*. Phenomenological research, on the other hand, resembles a hyper-real slice of reality, a highly distilled and densely detailed single image, perhaps similar to the approach taken by artists such as Van Gogh or Manet. Narrative analysis seeks to produce a richly textured canvas in which more general human meaning is conveyed through the depiction of an image from a single life, as in a Rembrandt portrait. A hermeneutic study may appear, at first glance, as if it portrays a scene from everyday life, but on closer examination the depiction of figures in the scene can be understood as evoking and symbolising mythic themes. Other forms of qualitative research increasingly depart from the realm of representational art, and appear to have affinities with trends in modern art. For example,

Comprehensive Process Analysis comes over as a kind of dismantling, a sculpture which looks like a piece of engineering, in which an everyday object is taken apart, but given an evocative and poetic title. Conversation analysis is almost like works of art in which a mundane object, such as a soup can, is blown up to the point where the texture of the image becomes visible. Discourse analysis goes further in this direction, by seeking to subvert the viewer's perception of everyday events and images, by stripping them of meaning. The new experiential research (e.g., the work of Carolyn Ellis) is similar to some contemporary art (Tracy Emin, Gilbert and George) in which the artist's life becomes the work of art. The relationship between psychoanalysis and modern art is well known, and there are many artists whose work give visual form to the kind of effect Freud and others achieved through psychoanalytic case studies. The art of Francis Bacon is an example. Here, a seeming portrait of an individual is distorted by forces of desire and animalism.

These examples of ways in which art might be taken as a metaphor for qualitative research in counselling and psychotherapy are not based on any deep scholarly knowledge of art history. Interested readers may find some satisfaction and pleasure in selecting other pieces of art that, for them, operate more appropriately as metaphors for pieces of qualitative research with which they are familiar.

There have been two trends within the history of art which appear particularly relevant for those pursuing qualitative research. The first trend can be characterised as a fracturing of genres. Continually, groups of artists find new ways of making art. Genres that have emerged in recent times include: pop art, minimalism, performance art, installation art and many others (Archer, 1997). There is an acceptance of pluralism and diversity within the art world that social scientists might do well to follow. Although there may be continual cries of public outrage at the latest 'nonsense' that artists produce, the category and meaning of 'art' appears to be broad enough to incorporate whatever artists do. Successful art does not seem to depend on following the procedures of a pre-existing genre, but of continuing to find new ways of 'making art', however that might be achieved. The second major trend has been in relation to notions of what is 'real'. Anyone viewing a Constable landscape would take it for granted that this is what the landscape being represented did actually look like. Anyone viewing Kandinsky's *Sea Battle* (1913) would not assume that the picture was attempting to record what a battle actually looked like, but was instead seeking to convey something of the meaning or 'essence' of the experience of battle. There are genres of art, such as Surrealism, which play around with the notion of what is real. Letting go of the idea that visual art is either a painting or sculpture that is supposed to represent what something really looks like appears to have enriched art, and has opened up possibilities for aesthetic knowing. Here, again, is an idea that has resonance in qualitative social science, particularly in qualitative psychotherapy research. The conventions of scientific method have resulted in an emphasis in much qualitative research on various forms of convergent validity. Researchers have sought to demonstrate that what they are writing faithfully represents a set of real events or experiences 'out there' in the world. Artists have shown that there are truths and knowings that do not depend on realism.

The metaphor of research-as-art allows qualitative research to be understood as *ways of seeing* (Berger, 1972). An understanding of art involves appreciating that any form of art constructs what it represents; it is one among many alternative ways of seeing. For Berger, the meaning of a piece of art depends on the relationship between the viewer and the artwork. For example, the European tradition of painting nude women must be understood not only as a way of expressing timeless values such as 'beauty', but of reinforcing gender relations: *'men act* and *women appear'* (Berger, 1972: 47). This relationship changes over time. For example, viewers of art works may hold ideas about gender that are different from those which prevailed in the era in which a painting was originally produced. Also, the social location of art has shifted significantly over time (Benjamin, 1970). Art-works previously existed as single copies, as almost sacred objects found in churches or the homes of the rich. To see a painting, one would need to travel to visit it. Now, of course, images are easily reproduced, and art has become a commodity. The experience of 'seeing' the *Mona Lisa* is quite different today from how it would have been in the seventeenth century. As Benjamin puts it: 'the uniqueness of a work of art is inseparable from its being imbedded in the fabric of tradition' (1970: 217). The 'imbeddedness' of qualitative research in tradition, and the effects of changes in that tradition, can be observed in the case of psychoanalytic case studies. The early case studies written by Freud and his followers were largely read by those who participated in psychoanalytic culture. These studies enjoyed limited circulation, and the majority of people who read them were those who had been analysed, or had heard Freud and other psychoanalysts talk at international congresses. One can imagine that these case studies would have had a quite different meaning for such readers than they might have for the much wider contemporary audience exposed to critiques of psychoanalysis, ideas about method, other forms of therapy, and so on. When qualitative research papers are published in books and journals they become a commodity, to be understood and used in a myriad of ways. These understandings can sometimes be quite different from the meanings that the research holds for the circle of people who worked together to produce it in the first place. The implicit, oral knowing that develops in the process of research may not transfer to the printed page. Alternatively, the reader of the printed page may find meanings denied or overlooked by the researcher.

Finally, one of the basic differences between art and qualitative research is that in art there exists a community of critics and art historians who function to comment on, and review, the meaning and significance of art-works. These people exist because there is a public willing to pay for their services. Ordinary people consume art by purchasing work, visiting exhibitions, reading books. Quite often, the views of art critics and historians are reported in newspapers and on television – this is not wholly an elite academic specialism. The presence of the art criticism industry produces a shared language for talking about art. It also contributes to the existence of a group of informed consumers, who form a supportive audience for artistic productions. This exists in qualitative research in the social sciences, never mind within the much smaller domain of qualitative studies of therapy. The effect is that we are denied opportunities to learn how to read well, and to reflect on how to write better. Some of the implications of this fact are discussed by Czarniawska (1998).

## Qualitative inquiry as relationship

Different approaches to qualitative research can be distinguished through the way they represent the relationship between self and other, knower and known. The grounded theory approach primarily acts as a vehicle for the other's experience. The aim is to help the reader to understand a previously unmet other. The stance of researcher is that of facilitator of communi-cation from silenced/unknown group to dominant group. Phenomenology looks instead at categories of experience that all of us participate in – anger, loneliness, learning, being understood. The goal seems to be to see oneself in others, to understand self through understanding others. There is, following Husserl, an implied universalism in phenomenology, whereas grounded theory is implicitly local. A hermeneutic approach is much more a way of exploring or negotiating the relationship between self and other. It can involve a questioning of the self, as the experience of difference is allowed to challenge previously held assumptions (the 'fusion of horizons'). Discourse analysis places the knower in a very privileged position of seeming to 'know better' than anyone else, to the extent of being able to tell the rest of us how we do what we do. It reveals the basis of our tricks and magic. The 'other' in discourse analysis is not a specific named other, but comprises 'people in general', who are playing the same old games of gender and social class domination. The self is one of a group of insiders who have the ability to see through all of this, but do not disclose their own preferred positions (Haraway's 'view from nowhere'). Narrative analysis seems to adopt a relationship of celebrating and affirming the story of the other, but in a somewhat one-sided manner, with little or no space for the active engagement of the 'other'. These are just some of the 'images of relationship' that exist within different genres of qualitative research. The issue of the relationship between researcher and research participant/informant is of special significance to researchers in the area of counselling and psychotherapy, because it mirrors debates surrounding the preferred relationship between therapist and client. In the research domain, the relationship between researcher and audience/reader provides an additional source of alternative 'images of inquiry' (see Gergen, 1997).

## Qualitative inquiry as conversation

In thinking about what it is like to do qualitative research, it may be helpful to look at it as something like a *conversation*. Anyone who is a counsellor or psychotherapist is a participant in a slow, endless conversation about how best to understand relationships, how to help, what we mean by 'change', what the good life consists of, and so on. These are big topics for conversation. Research feeds into these conversations. When we carry out research interviews we are engaging in a particular type of conversation. Reporting findings at a conference is another type of conversation. The great thing about good qualitative research is that it can shift the ground of the conversation. It allows something to emerge.

> We say that we 'conduct' a conversation, but the more genuine a conversation is, the less its conduct lies within the will of either partner. Thus a genuine conversation is never the one that we wanted to conduct. Rather, it is generally more correct to say that we fall into conversation, or even that we become involved in it. The way one word follows another, with the conversation taking its own twists and reaching its own conclusion, may well be conducted in some way, but the partners conversing are far less the leaders than the led. No one knows in advance what will 'come out' of a conversation. Understanding or its failure is like an event that happens to us. Thus we can say that something was a good conversation or that it was ill fated. All this shows that a conversation has a spirit of its own, and that the language in which it is conducted bears its own truth within it – i.e., that it allows something to 'emerge' which henceforth exists. (Gadamer, 1975: 383)

The philosopher Richard Rorty (1980) argues that scientific knowledge, in the human sciences, is not a matter of holding up a 'mirror to nature', but is better understood as being like participating in a conversation. The choice of qualitative method is a conversation, taking place not only between individuals but between the traditions and value systems within which people live. There is a 'big', overarching conversation going on between the proponents of qualitative research styles associated with the stages/phases identified by Denzin and Lincoln: the 'authoritative voice' of the traditional era; the 'rational, systematic voice' of the modernist era;

and the 'multiple voices' of the postmodern era. But then at the same time there are local conversations taking place between colleagues, or between students and supervisors.

## Researcher as journalist

The idea of being described as a producer of *journalism* would be abhorrent to the majority of qualitative researchers. Journalists have a poor image for many people: intrusive, selective in the use of information, interested more in boosting circulation than in the pursuit of truth. Nevertheless, journalism plays an important role in a democratic society, in facilitating public debate over issues, and providing members of the public with information through which they can make decisions. Denzin (1997), one of the leading figures in qualitative social science, has written persuasively about 'merging ethnography with journalism', drawing on the concept of 'public journalism' developed by Charity (1995). The image of the qualitative researcher-as-journalist brings into the foreground the role of research in raising public awareness, and promoting a form of textuality that turns citizens into readers and readers into persons who take democratic action in the world' (Charity, 1995: 83). Making the link between research and journalism also encourages a willingness to take seriously what journalists have to say about therapy. For example, important contributions to the understanding of the experience of clients in therapy have been made by Dinnage (1988) and Lott (1999), both journalists. The image of researcher-as-journalist also introduces the question of what journalists do well, which is to write in such a way as to reach substantially larger audiences than those who read qualitative research. There is a great deal that researchers can learn from journalists about effective writing.

## Researcher as storyteller

Some people describe qualitative research as 'narrative' research, because it produces narrative accounts of the world, rather than statistical / quantitative accounts. This use of the term 'narrative' has not been employed within this book, because it involves too broad a sense of what might be considered as narrative. There is much to be gained from sticking to a more specific concept of narrative, which equates with the act of storytelling. The psychologist Jerome Bruner (1986) has offered a distinction between 'narrative' and 'paradigmatic' ways of knowing. Narrative ways of knowing are based on storytelling. Stories organise and convey our experience of the world in a manner that integrates action over time, characterisation, emotion, morality and social context (McLeod, 1997). Stories are concrete, located in an actual time and place, and specific. Paradigmatic knowing, on the other hand, consists of abstract conceptualisation, the construction of systems of thought built out of 'factors', 'variables, 'laws' and 'rules'. Paradigmatic knowing does not refer directly to specific instances, but makes generalised statements. Bruner (1986) argues that, although both narrative and paradigmatic ways of knowing are essential elements of human intelligence, conventional science, including psychology and social science, has in the past tended to concentrate more on the development of paradigmatic generalisation than on the construction of 'good stories'. The rise of qualitative research can be viewed as part of what has been termed the 'narrative turn' in philosophy and social science; since the 1970s, there has been an increasing acknowledgement in these fields of the importance of narrative knowing. However, as suggested earlier, to describe qualitative research as 'narrative' research is misleading. Many qualitative researchers seek to generate paradigmatic frameworks for understanding. A clear example of a paradigmatic approach in qualitative research can be found in the grounded theory use of *categories*. An essential contribution to understanding the role of stories and narrative in qualitative research has been made by Polkinghorne (1995). He makes a contrast between research which collects informants' stories, and then analyses them in terms of paradigmatic general concepts (as in grounded theory), and research which may collect stories and other forms of information from participants but uses this data to tell a story (as in case-study research or Riessman's narrative analysis). Polkinghorne (1995) perhaps draws too definite a distinction between these broad research strategies. There are some examples of qualitative research, such as the work of David Rennie (Chapter 6) where findings are presented in the form of an interplay between narrative (stories) and paradigmatic (categories) forms. Nevertheless, the underlying point to Polkinghorne's (1988, 1995) argument is that, one way or another, qualitative research involves a sensitivity to stories. Qualitative researchers can be seen as story-gatherers and storytellers.

## The multiple images of qualitative research: ways of knowing and the limits of method

In the preceding sections some recurring images that have informed the work of qualitative researchers have been discussed: all-seeing deity, embodied witness, artist, person-in-relationship, participant in a conversation, journalist, storyteller. These images help to *position* the work of qualitative researchers in relation to society (e.g., insider vs. outsider) and make it possible, I hope, to see some of the work in a fresh light.

The primary aim of this chapter has been to point out the limitations of method. Good qualitative research does not derive from following a procedural recipe-book. There is no *method* that produces interesting and useful qualitative findings. Qualitative research is a matter of applying the sense-making capabilities that we already possess in an organised and careful manner. An awareness of *methodological* issues and debates provides researchers with a necessary perspective on the work. Methodology lays out the choices and the implications of these choices, in relation to the adoption of alternative research approaches and strategies. Method locks the researcher in to one approach and one point of view from the start. Once a study has been completed, readers will want to know about the method that was used to generate findings, because this information makes it possible to understand and appreciate the meaning of a study. But this account can be assembled at the end. Good qualitative research is a matter of imagination, creativity, courage, personal integrity, empathy and commitment. Method is just the means of channelling these qualities.

# 10

# The Role of Qualitative Methods in Outcome Research

Up until now, within psychotherapy research, qualitative methods have primarily been employed to study either the cultural-historical context of therapy, or various aspects of the therapeutic process. There have been very few qualitative studies of the outcomes of therapy. This absence is perhaps even more striking when consideration is given to the large numbers of quantitative/experimental outcome studies that have been published. Huge resources have been devoted to quantitative research on outcomes, while almost no resources have been devoted to qualitative studies of the same issue. While methodological pluralism (Howard, 1983) may have permeated the world of therapy process research, it has had little impact on the world of outcome studies.

Many therapy researchers regard randomised controlled trials, or other quantitative research designs, as being obviously and self-evidently the most appropriate way to study the effects of counselling and psychotherapy on clients. Few therapy researchers consider that qualitative methods have much to offer in this arena. In this chapter it is therefore first of all necessary to develop a critique of the use of existing outcome research, before moving on to look at some of the ways in which qualitative methods might be employed.

Carving out a role in relation to therapy outcome research represents a major challenge for qualitative researchers. Counselling and psychotherapy are activities which are constantly called upon to demonstrate their legitimacy by producing evidence of effectiveness. Substantial amounts of funding are allocated to outcome studies. In an environment where health funding agencies are increasingly implementing policies around evidence-based practice and empirically validated treatments, the pressure to generate plausible outcome findings is likely to increase, despite the massive number of studies that have already been carried out. If qualitative research in counselling and psychotherapy is to be taken seriously, it must get to grips with the problem of investigating outcome.

## The rhetoric of the randomised controlled trial: power, control and silenced voices

> To neglect the implications of our rhetoric is to lose control of what we say. (Bazerman, 1988: 275)

> It is now so clear that writing is a political act . . . any act of representation of the Other is inherently political. (E.M. Bruner, 1993: 6)

One of the key differences in emphasis between qualitative and quantitative approaches to evaluating outcome concerns the questions of *power* and control. In quantitative, statistical research, the investigator exerts a high degree of control over what informants ('subjects') can say, and what is done with their words. Qualitative evaluation research takes a more collaborative stance – there is a built-in openness and possibility of dialogue. The issue of power and control therefore represents a useful starting-point for an exploration of the distinctive contribution that qualitative research might make in the field of counselling and psychotherapy outcome studies.

The authoritative guide to current trends in psychotherapy research is the *Handbook of Psychotherapy and Behavior Change*, edited by Allan Bergin and Sol Garfield (1994a). Anyone consulting the index of this book will find that there are 39 entries under the word 'power'. Most of these entries refer to the topic of statistical power, which is concerned with the capacity of statistical tests to detect differences between groups under conditions of sample size, scale reliability, and so forth. There are also some references to the interpersonal power of therapists in relation to their clients. Nowhere in the book does there appear to be any consideration of the question of political power. There is no discussion of the social and political forces or interest groups that shape the kinds of research that are carried out. There is no reflection on the power of researchers based in the academy to influence the forms of practice which are regarded as legitimate for clinicians to pursue. In the psychotherapy literature, these meanings of power may often appear to be so far in the background as to be invisible and unspeakable. This is a strange and curious state of affairs. Most practitioners of counselling, psychotherapy and allied professions are confused and suspicious about the motives of researchers. Why does this piece of research need to be done? What will it prove? What is the point? In whose interest is this? Practitioners are also well aware of the political nature of much research. How can we prove to the unit manager that therapy is cost-effective? What do we need to do to satisfy them that we are evaluating our work in a satisfactory manner? How do we persuade them not to introduce a limit of six sessions for every client?

The concept of social power threads through the social sciences and has been addressed from many different perspectives. The central meaning of social power can be defined in terms of the ability of some people to control the actions of others; most of the time power is based in social structures of authority rather than on personal qualities. Although psychotherapeutic writers such as Carl Rogers have introduced a notion of *personal power*, this idea does not seem particularly relevant to discussions of psychotherapy research. The power of research and researchers relies only partially on personal virtues, such as passion, personal integrity and possession of vision. Power in psychotherapy research depends much more on social status, institutions and ideology. The power of psychotherapy researchers is grounded in who they are, where they are, and how they speak. The concept of *voice* can be used as a means of opening up an awareness of how power, control and influence are exerted. In many ways social power hinges on the question of whose voice is heard. Who has a voice? What is the quality of the voice? What rhetorical strategies are used to persuade the listener of the truth of what is being said in that voice? How are other voices silenced?

In addition to the concept of voice, it is essential to acknowledge that the operation of power and authority can be observed in ordinary, everyday social relations. Sometimes, forms of social control are highly visible and dramatic, such as pickets at the entrance to a factory, or a row of police vans on a street. But, as Foucault and others have pointed out, it is unhelpful to restrict the study of power to such overt moments of physical control of space by or against the state. Power is all around us, all the time, in the way we speak and listen, the way we read and write, and so on. Later in this chapter, there is a discussion of how the politics of psychotherapy research is reproduced in the language and structure of articles published in psychotherapy research journals.

## The politics of psychotherapy outcome research

In Britain, the politics of psychotherapy outcome research has been brought into focus through the recent publication of a study commissioned by the (English) Department of Health, examining the effectiveness of different forms of therapy for various client groups. This report formed part of a Strategic Policy Review of Psychotherapy Services, and has been widely disseminated in the form of a book, *What Works For Whom? A Critical Review of Psychotherapy Research* by Tony Roth and Peter Fonagy (1996). The political agenda of this project was encapsulated in a question posed in the first paragraph of the text:

> is there research evidence that would help funders of health care decide on the appropriate mix of therapies for their populations? (Roth and Fonagy, 1996: 1)

Behind this statement lies the decision of the National Health Service in Britain to adopt a policy of 'evidence-based' treatment (Rowland and Goss, 2000), which in itself can be placed in the context of the major

organisational changes in the British health care system that were introduced in the 1980s and 1990s with the aim of reducing costs and encouraging the privatisation and commercialisation of sections of health care
provision. So, it would be clear to most readers of *What Works for Whom?*
that Roth and Fonagy were not producing a book for mere academic
reasons. There was more at stake. This was being paid for by the state, in a
very direct fashion.

Roth and Fonagy (1996) argue very forcefully that research findings are
seldom directly applicable to policy decision-making. They use the metaphor of 'translation' to explain their approach. They saw their task as that
of translating the results of research into a set of guidelines and recommendations for policy and practice. Chapter 3 of the book sets out in great
detail a wide range of difficult issues that must be faced if a true evidence-
based psychotherapy service is to be achieved. Throughout the book, the
experience of the authors as clinicians is apparent; they are well aware of
the dangers of an over-simplified approach to this problem.

However, despite the subtlety of Roth and Fonagy's analysis of the
difficulties involved in the kind of translation they are attempting, they are
clear about the type of research evidence which can be regarded as valid
and 'true': randomised controlled trials (RCTs). They write that: 'RCTs
provide the only valid – albeit limited – source of evidence for the efficacy
of various forms of psychological treatment' (p. 19). The research studies
that are reported and discussed in *What Works for Whom?* are predominantly RCTs. There is no mention, as far as I can detect, of any kind
of qualitative evaluative studies, or of the potential value of qualitative
approaches. Also, despite the fact that both senior authors are psychoanalytically trained, there is no credence given to evidence from clinical
case studies. There are many other sources of evidence that can be used to
evaluate the effectiveness of counselling and psychotherapy: naturalistic
studies, user satisfaction surveys, professional consensus judgements. Yet
none of these is reviewed by Roth and Fonagy (1996). The evidence which
'counts' comes from RCTs.

What are the implications of using evidence from RCTs on which to
base policy decisions into 'the appropriate mix of therapies'? Here are just
some of the consequences of the RCT as a research method:

- The voice of the client or service user is not heard. RCTs do not include
  accounts of how recipients feel about the kind of therapy they have
  received.
- The voices of the therapist and the therapy supervisor are not heard.
  RCTs do not include accounts of how practitioners feel about the kind
  of therapy they have delivered, or what they have learned from
  participating in the study.
- The research reinforces the medicalisation of therapy, for example
  through use of assessment/diagnostic measures and the use of

randomisation. These strategies are consistent with a medical model approach (the client is a passive recipient of treatment; treatment is regarded as equivalent to the administration of a 'drug'; the patient is 'ill').

- The expense and complexity of RCTs means that they are carried out in elite establishments associated with universities, and therefore rarely focus on forms of therapy that are not well represented in the academic establishment, e.g. feminist, transpersonal, gay affirmative, multicultural, telephone counselling.
- The use of methodological concepts and values drawn from experimental, laboratory science means that the social, cultural and political context of the research is rarely explicated. For example, how often in a published report on an RCT study does a researcher write that 'Three of the therapists quit because they were not paid enough and were sick of following the treatment manual', or 'We used two of the hospitals as no-treatment control conditions because the chief executives would have nothing to do with therapy'.
- The ethical problems arising from no-treatment waiting lists or placebo control groups that last beyond three months, and the financial costs and client attrition associated with longer treatment periods mean that the vast majority of RCTs subject clients to a fixed, limited number of sessions.

There are undoubtedly many other problematic features of the RCT as a research strategy that might be mentioned. The point that is being made here is not that RCTs are worthless – there is a logical compellingness and persuasiveness to the RCT that cannot be matched by any other research design. The argument, rather, concerns the political effect of constructing knowledge about therapy in this manner. What does it mean for the Department of Health to weight RCT evidence in this way when it sets about assessing the case for or against different forms of therapy?

Again, there are many issues embedded in this question, and for reasons of space they can be unpicked in only a provisional, partial and somewhat superficial manner. Nevertheless, it seems difficult to avoid the conclusion that the emphasis on RCT evidence has the effect of reinforcing the status and economic power of existing elite groups within the psychotherapy profession, and denying a voice to those with less institutional power. A properly run RCT is the most expensive form of psychotherapy research imaginable, which can only be attempted by those enjoying considerable control over resources. The increasing reluctance of governments to fund big-ticket social research means that there is every chance that the number of RCTs being carried out is already in decline. The methodology of the RCT, and the kind of conceptualisation of therapy that it assumes, supports a medical-model approach to therapy: assessment, diagnosis, specified treatment by a detached expert, measurement of results using standardised technology, lack of interest in patient preferences, individualisation and medicalisation of social problems. The easy fit between the RCT and time-limited interventions meets the needs of purchasers eager to drive down costs. Finally, an RCT is a method that does not readily allow real criticism or resistance on the part of users and practitioners to surface.

## The construction of reality in quantitative outcome research

Another approach to making sense of the nature of power and influence in psychotherapy research is to examine the way that research is written. After all, few counsellors or psychotherapists will ever actually participate in a randomised controlled trial, and may be affected by research-informed policy decisions only in an indirect fashion. On the other hand, reading a research article is an experience that is likely to be a part of the everyday world of many practitioners as well as of researchers.

In selecting a research paper for analysis, a count was made of the number of times different research journals were cited in the reference list in the Roth and Fonagy (1996) book. This exercise showed that the most widely quoted research journal was the *Journal of Consulting and Clinical Psychology*. Having identified the *Journal of Consulting and Clinical Psychology* as the single most influential publication outlet, I then chose, as an exemplar study, 'Supportive versus cognitive-behavioral intervention programs in achieving adjustment to home peritoneal kidney dialysis', by Hener, Weisenberg and Har-Even (1996). This paper was of special interest to me because I had become involved in some research into the counselling needs of home dialysis patients, and I hoped that a careful reading of it would contribute to my understanding of the role of therapy in relation to that group of people. Moreover, it is a typical example of an RCT.

The Hener et al (1996) study reports on the effectiveness of supportive and cognitive-behavioural therapy offered to couples in which one spouse had been diagnosed with end-stage renal disease and was receiving home-based peritoneal dialysis. The supportive therapy was broadly psychodynamic in orientation, focusing on the experience of loss. The cognitive-behavioural therapy focused mainly on coping strategies, stress-management and problem-solving. Therapy (eight sessions) was carried out by well-qualified, carefully supervised practitioners. Evaluation was conducted through self-report questionnaires completed by clients at the beginning of therapy, at the mid-point, and on termination. The effectiveness of therapy was compared with outcomes in a no-intervention control group, and in a healthy matched comparison group. Therapy turned out to be significantly more helpful than no therapy, and there were no appreciable differences in outcome attributable to the different forms of intervention.

The Hener et al. (1996) paper is a straightforward, conventional account of an RCT. It is clear and easy to read, with a great deal of information presented succinctly using a linear structure that makes it possible to follow the story of the research study from background literature through methods and results, and finally to conclusions. However, it is also possible to stand back from this paper and look at it as a piece of rhetoric, to question the way it is written. How does this article persuade us that what is being said is true? Through which voice or voices does the article speak? Are there silenced voices that might offer alternative accounts of this research project? *Who* is speaking or writing in this paper, what role does he or she adopt, and what role or roles are we offered as readers? And what might these rhetorical devices tell us about the nature of conventional psychotherapy outcome research? Some of the more salient rhetorical features of the paper are summarised below.

## Viewpoint and voice

The paper is written from the perspective of a detached observer, from what has been described as a 'God's-eye view' (see p. 152). The whole paper is written in a third-person style, in which the active agent is often an object or artefact rather than a person. For instance, in the first paragraph we are told that 'this article compares', that 'reports focused' and that 'studies addressed'. The literature, here, is presented as a reified object rather than as a human construction. Later, in the methods section we learn that 'students were trained as interviewers' (p. 734) and that 'senior clinicians . . . served as supervisors' (p. 735). The actions of these participants, and indeed of all other people involved in the study, including the researchers, seems to be stripped of intentionality and purpose. The literature review can be described as expressing the *voice of science*. This section of the paper is in slightly larger type, with plentiful references. It is written in the present tense, as if we, the readers, were receiving eternal truths about the psychological and medical dimensions of dialysis. At the point of transition from the literature review to the method section of the paper the writing changes to the past tense as the authors begin to give an account of what happened in this specific study. It is as though there is a switch here from the voice of science to a more local *voice of the clinic*. Being less powerful, the voice of the clinic is represented in a smaller typeface. At no point in the paper do we hear the voice of an actual person. There are no first-person statements of any kind from any of the innumerable people who contributed to this research study: researchers, interviewers, hospital staff, patients, therapists, therapy supervisors. Not only are they silenced, but the dialogue between them is also silenced. None of the many conversations which must have taken place is reported at all. The dominant voice in the paper is monologic, rather than dialogic.

## Positioning of the reader

Who is the reader of this paper expected to be? In this paper, the nature of kidney disease and dialysis is described in some detail, as is the form of therapeutic intervention. The paper could therefore be understood, in principle, by someone who had no prior knowledge of peritoneal dialysis or of either of the modes of therapy. On the other hand, the paper does assume prior knowledge of statistical techniques and psychometric test design, neither of which is explained in the text. It is almost as though the paper is most accessible to readers who are not particularly interested in either kidney patients or therapy (because neither topic is covered in enough depth to satisfy such readers) but to readers who are interested in it as a piece of research. The single longest section of the paper is the method section, and even in the concluding discussion section more than half of the space is devoted to methodological issues. Moreover, there is a sense in which the reader is viewed as a potential critic or competitor to be appeased (this is a *trial*). For example, more space is given to justifying the measures used, and providing details of their reliability and validity, than is spent describing the type of therapy that was employed. Although the paper is not rich in metaphoric language, there is a recurring root metaphor of *competition* implied by the title (supportive *versus* cognitive-behavioural) and phrases such as a 'failure to operationalize' which must be 'guarded against' (Hener et al., 1996: 739) and 'this study is somewhat unique' (ibid.).

## Passion, emotion and interest

The 'scientific' style of writing which is used in the *Journal of Consulting and Clinical Psychology* serves to conceal the emotion and drama of the events that are being recounted. Although Hener et al (1996) never tell us why they conducted this study, it is a fair guess that an important element in their motivation was to demonstrate the efficacy of cognitive-behavioural therapy. They give the alternative therapy the non-title of 'supportive therapy', and the range of measures they choose seems designed to mirror the goals of their cognitive-behavioural intervention. In addition, the ending of any story is always significant, and in this case the authors end the paper with a concluding comment on how the cognitive-behavioural therapy might be made more effective in a future study. They hold out no such hope for the supportive therapy. The passion, interest and emotion of all the other participants in the study is similarly hidden from view by the literary form of the randomised controlled trial. The emotions felt by clients in the study are operationalised and titled: Anxiety, Depression, Sleep Difficulties, Sexual Difficulties, Social Distress. The feelings of therapists and supervisors do not seem to be included at all. As a reader, one might wonder whether the participants in the study would, therefore, recognise themselves and their experience in what was written. And what might it mean if they do not recognise themselves? This study achieves high levels of validity in terms of the canons of psychological and medical science. But can it really be *true* if participants do not recognise themselves, their world, their reality, in the text?

## Certainty / ambiguity

One of the most salient features of this article, in contrast to other sorts of report that might have been written about the same research project, is the extent to which key statements are backed up by technology. While the authors offer descriptive accounts of such matters as the characteristics of participants and the nature of the treatment, their statements about the social and emotional adjustment of patients, and how these factors change over time, are always backed up by numerical indices derived from measurement instruments. The effect of this rhetorical device is to suggest a sense of certainty: the measures are as accurate and unbiased as can be – they must be correct. The extensive self-justification offered in support of the technical properties (validity, reliability) of the measures reinforces this tendency toward certainty. At the beginning of the discussion section of the paper, the results are summarised in a way that again emphasises certainty: 'both treatments were effective' (p. 738), 'improvement, or at least a lack of deterioration, was seen on all scales' (p. 739), 'improvement was obtained in the emotional, cognitive and interpersonal areas' (p. 739). In fact, the evidence presented earlier (for instance, in Table 5) shows that while the majority of patients and their spouses benefited from therapy, there were some who did not. Likewise, although the majority of those who did not receive therapy deteriorated, there appeared to be some who improved. This kind of finding is typical of RCTs. However, the genre of experimental reports to which this kind of article belongs is one in which mystery and ambiguity is not permissible. The goal is to achieve as much certainty and mastery as possible, and to ignore that which cannot be explained. Yet, it could well be argued that it is in ambiguity that new learning can occur. One might suppose that among the people who took part in this study – researchers, therapists, patients – there were a fair number of new understandings and unexpected learnings. These are interesting, but have no place in a scientific paper.

## *The exclusion of the social*

The final rhetorical strategy to be discussed – briefly – concerns the exclusion of all but the most perfunctory information about the social context in which the research was carried out. The focus of the paper is rigorously limited to those variables over which the researcher can claim to have some control (this is a randomised *controlled* trial). As a consequence, there is nothing about the complex social world in which kidney patients exist. People who use home dialysis need to have on-going relationships with doctors and nurses at their clinics, some of whom may have an awareness of psychological and emotional issues, and some not. Patients may be involved in self-help groups, or be involved in difficult negotiations with welfare benefits agencies, employers and family members. Hener et al (1996) recognise that kidney patients have social problems (they include a measure of Social Distress) but they do not provide any basis for understanding, for example, the ways in which these therapies may or may not have fitted into the different social worlds of patients attached to different hospitals.

## Power and exclusion in written knowledge

In recent years, there has been a growing body of interest in what Bazerman (1988) has called the 'shaping of written knowledge'. Using the style manual of the American Psychological Association as an example, Bazerman shows how each social science discipline develops a tradition of writing that codifies its intrinsic values and philosophical assumptions. The APA style manual, which is espoused by the *Journal of Consulting and Clinical Psychology* and most of the other journals cited by Roth and Fonagy (1996) represents the distinctive voice of behaviourism. Bazerman points out that in the early years of the behaviourist tradition, for instance as seen in the classic papers by John B. Watson, authors often wrote in the first person, offered a uninterrupted narrative account of what they had done, and used footnotes. The adoption of a third-person viewpoint, standardised sub-headings and different referencing style (name and date) were stages in a movement toward the establishment of a style which came to be regarded as the 'only proper way to write science' Bazerman (1988: 268). The new referencing system signified a science that accumulated knowledge through incremental steps rather than active debate:

> it is very convenient for listing and summarizing a series of related findings, but is awkward for extensive quotation or discussion of another text, and even more awkward for contrasting several texts in detail. The format is not designed for the close consideration of competing ideas and subtle formulations. (p. 274)

Table 10.1   *Textual traditions in the human sciences*

*The mystical tradition.* Use of metaphor and evaluative language to enter the 'presence of the unknown'. Examples are Jung, Laing and Lacan: 'Lacan writes obscurely but with a confidence that exudes first-hand knowledge of mysteries not fully clear to the reader' (Gergen, 1997: 155). There is a status difference between writer and audience; the reader is ignorant and unaware but potentially able to achieve enlightenment or grace. The reader is privileged compared to the unenlightened masses who do not hear the word.

*The prophetic tradition.* The writer creates an inspirational picture of a future not yet available to the reader, and/or warns of future catastrophes. Examples are Marx, Lasch, Bellah. There is a status difference between writer and reader but reader is not special (as in mystical tradition).

*The mythic tradition.* Creation of moral stories with a clear narrative structure. Freud, Piaget, Weber and Foucault all draw on elements of this tradition. A status difference exists between writer/teller and reader.

*The civil voice.* Use of literal language and objective evidence. Respect for the reader, whose integrity is never in question, but who is seen as a competitor in a hierarchy of truth, prestige and power.

*The autobiographer.* The experience of the writer serves as a 'lens through which to understand the world' (ibid.: 163). Autobiographical writing may often be used to disrupt the taken-for-granted assumptions and surface of the civil world. The reader is invited to identify with the writer; the writer–reader distance that typified earlier traditions is subverted.

*The fictionalist.* Experimental writing, such as novels, poetry, drama. A genre that encourages the 'expansion of vocal registers', a multivocal text. High degree of author–reader intimacy and identification, but also the possibility of *ironic distance.*

*Source*: Gergen, 1997

The use of standard sub-headings and a greatly expanded method section safeguarded the researcher against methodological critique, reflecting the importance of methodological rigour rather than theoretical understanding in behaviourist science.

The significance of the APA/RCT genre in psychotherapy research can be placed in a wider context by drawing upon Gergen's (1997) discussion of the range of differing rhetorical or discursive traditions that can be found in the human sciences. These traditions are summarised in Table 10.1. It is clear that the APA/RCT tradition is part of what Gergen characterises as the *civil voice*:

> within the vast cadres of the sciences there is little but intonation left of the moral and emotional expressiveness so central to the preceding [mystical, prophetic and mythical] traditions; the metaphors of the mystical are largely replaced by literal language; and obscurity is abandoned in favor of 'straight talk'. Divine beings now reappear in secular form as 'seminal' thinkers; the drama of prophecy is shorn in favor of experimental prediction and actuarial projection. Not only does the prevailing 'scientific style' strive for dispassionate and mundane clarity, but it manifests an unfailing concern for evidence, and serves as a model of careful restraint. (Gergen, 1997: 160)

Gergen argues that while the earlier mystical, prophetic and mythical traditions can be traced back to religious origins, the civil voice emerged in seventeenth-century England as a form of discourse that supported the development of the natural sciences within a group of upper-class gentlemen-scholars. However, in recent years in such disciplines as sociology, anthropology and cultural studies, researchers have sought to find ways of creating new genres of social science writing, such as autobiography or life history, and fiction, that reach out to different audiences, support different forms of cultural life, and, essentially, reflect and represent more fully the world in which they live.

## Writing therapy outcome research

The way we write about therapy is a political act. It has been suggested that the 'civil voice' or APA/RCT genre of writing operates to exclude many important and interesting aspects of the therapy research process by effectively silencing the voices of almost everyone concerned to the point where all that can be said is what can be made to conform to the behaviourist rhetoric of the standard research paper. This genre of producing and writing research knowledge makes huge hegemonic claims. As we have seen from an analysis of the Roth and Fonagy (1996) report commissioned by the Department of Health, it would appear as though the civil voice is the only voice to which the government will listen. In the end there is a deep, deep irony in all this. As therapists, we do our best to help our clients to express their feelings, accept their desires and their agency, and to develop constructive, dialogic relationships with the other people in their lives. As therapy researchers we seem to find it very hard to achieve any of these goals. The mainstream of research-based writing about therapy is unreflexive, distanced, permeated by a scientific ideology that is neither appropriate nor satisfying. To return to the study by Hener, Weisenberg and Har-Even (1996) one can only wonder at the energy and commitment that went into the making of that piece of research. All over the world there are therapists, nurses and doctors who are desperate to know more about how therapy or counselling can be applied to help people adjust to the experience of kidney failure. That Hener, Weisenberg and Har-Even managed to persuade their hospital service (or someone) to provide the resources for intensive therapy with these patients is nothing short of miraculous. How much they and their colleagues have to teach us. Would we have learned any less about the effectiveness of therapy for home dialysis patients if they had chosen to write in the traditions of mysticism, prophecy, myth, autobiography or fiction? Could qualitative research, which has the potential to allow different voices to emerge, make a contribution to our understanding of how much, and in what ways, counselling and psychotherapy may or may not help people?

## An alternative: qualitative outcome research

Qualitative methods represent the main alternative to the quantitative paradigm described and critiqued in earlier sections of this chapter. In principle, it would be feasible to evaluate the effects of therapy by analysing qualitative data sets generated by such techniques as: individual or focus-group interviews with clients, therapists and significant others; transcripts of therapy sessions; personal documents such as diaries and case notes; open-ended questionnaires or written accounts; narrative responses to projective techniques; ethnographic participant observation; biographies and novels. Virtually none of these methods has been employed in published therapy outcome research. It is possible that unpublished qualitative studies exist, in the form of internal reports for agencies and clinics, or student dissertations. The mind-set that prevails within the counselling and psychotherapy world, of equating evaluation with the application of 'measures', may have impeded publication of such studies.

The discussion here will focus on four studies: Howe (1989), McKenna and Todd (1997), Kuhnlein (1999) and Dale, Allen and Measor (1998). None of these studies comprises a wholly satisfactory approach to the question of qualitative evaluation of psychotherapy. They represent tentative steps toward a qualitative evaluation methodology for psychotherapy, but are nevertheless valuable in terms of showing what is *possible* in terms of qualitative outcome research.

Howe (1989) is the most detailed example of qualitative evaluation of psychotherapy currently available. This investigation examined the effectiveness of the family therapy provided in a social work agency, as experienced by the members of 34 families who had been offered therapy over a 12-month period. Twenty-three of the families (68 per cent) had entered therapy, with the remainder either declining or failing to turn up for the first session. Qualitative data was collected on 32 families, including 22 of those who had received therapy. Family members were interviewed (between two and three months after the end of therapy), and further information was obtained on the outcome and process of therapy from agency files and therapist notes. This material was analysed using an approach based on grounded theory (Glaser and Strauss, 1967). Further information on aspects of the analysis of the data has also been given in Howe (1996).

What kind of evaluative picture does this qualitative study generate? Clearly, Howe (1989) does not offer estimations of improvement assessed through changes in scores on standardised measures. Nevertheless, the study as a whole does supply a readily understandable and practicable account of the effectiveness of this form of therapy with this group of clients. Only five of the families reported that they had gained from therapy. Another five were ambivalent about their experience of therapy. The other 12 families left before the end of therapy, usually after two or three sessions, and were critical or dismissive of the treatment they had received. It is important to recognise that the effectiveness of this therapy was being judged in terms of the criteria employed by the families. What Howe was interested in was whether they saw themselves as having benefited from therapy. Unlike most outcome studies, the rich descriptive detail provided by this qualitative research allows the reader to gain a detailed appreciation of *how* the therapy operated, and to understand *why* the therapy was effective or ineffective. The study generated a number of suggestions as to what this team of therapists might do to improve their success rate.

From a qualitative research perspective, there are certainly a number of limitations to the Howe (1989) study. He focused entirely on one set of stakeholders (the families). There was an absence of 'informant checking', where findings are taken back and discussed with research participants. There was no use of an independent 'adversary' or 'auditor' (Hill, Thompson and Nutt-Williams, 1997) to review the adequacy of his inter-pretation of the data. These are some of the ways in which the plausibility of the study might have been enhanced. Other researchers conducting quali-tative evaluation studies of psychotherapy would undoubtedly be able to improve on Howe's work. But the key point is that the Howe study demonstrates that qualitative evaluation of psychotherapy is *possible*. The study shows that qualitative research could, in principle, deliver on the basic questions that therapy outcome research needs to consider: 'How much do users benefit from the intervention?' and 'How do success rates compare with other studies?' Compared to (most) quantitative outcome studies, a qualitative approach can be seen to have the advantage of *also* being able to address questions such as: 'What actually happens in this kind of therapy?' 'What aspects of practice enhance or reduce outcomes?' and 'What can be done to make this therapy more effective?'

The study by McKenna and Todd (1997) consisted of lengthy interviews (90–120 minutes) with nine clients of a university psychotherapy clinic in the USA. The main aim of the study was to examine patterns of longi-tudinal utilisation of psychotherapy services over time. However, in responding to questions about their pattern of involvement with psycho-therapy and other mental health agencies, most informants were able to articulate their personal assessments of the value of each treatment episode in relation to their needs at that point in their life. McKenna and Todd used the technique of the *time-line* to assist informants in ordering their accounts of previous therapies. Interview material was transcribed and analysed with the help of a computer qualitative analysis software programme. Findings were presented in the form of individual case vignettes and an analysis of general themes.

The results of the McKenna and Todd study illustrate one of the strengths of qualitative research – its sensitivity to categories employed by informants to make sense of their life-experience. In qualitative research, rather than the researcher imposing his or her analytic categories on experience (e.g. in the form of questionnaire items or rating codes), the aim is to be as open as possible to the ways in which informants themselves construe events. Here it emerged that the clients interviewed by McKenna and Todd differentially evaluated the effectiveness of therapy episodes depending on what they were looking for at that stage in their lives. Some therapy episodes were characterised as introductory and intended to do no more than allow the service user a preliminary *exposure* to therapy. One informant described such an experience as 'breaking the ice'. Other episodes, labelled *discrimination* therapy encounters, were seen as enabling the person to 'shop around' to find a good match between himself or herself and a therapist. There were also *formation* episodes, where the person felt that significant and lasting change had occurred; *consolidation* therapies, where the person was not seeking to change but merely to reinforce what had been gained in a previous formative experience; and finally *holding* therapies, in which the person did not feel that he or she was making much progress. These holding therapies could be perceived as useful ('kept things from getting worse') or frustrating (wanting more but not knowing how to get it).

The McKenna and Todd (1997) study is based on a small number of clients who had used one therapy centre (although in the past they had all used other therapy services too). It would not be sensible to claim that the types of episodes identified in this study could be generalised to all clinical settings or clients. All the same, their work opens up an understanding of how clients perceive the effectiveness of therapy. For one client, a brief 'exposure' to therapy may be just what they need at that point in their life. For another client, who has been exposed to different approaches and learned to discriminate between them, only a formative therapeutic experience would be regarded as effective. For some time after that experience, further transformative therapy would not be welcome, whereas opportunities to consolidate would be rated highly.

Research by Kuhnlein (1999) into the experiences of people who have completed in-patient cognitive-behavioural therapy reinforces the findings of McKenna and Todd (1997). In retrospective interviews carried out two years after the end of therapy, Kunhlein asked 49 former clients about what their therapy had meant to them, and how they made sense of it within the context of their lives as a whole. She found four contrasting types of experience. First, there were clients who saw themselves as 'overburdened'. These people viewed their emotional problems as resulting from a series of critical life events, and attributed the helpfulness of therapy to its ability to provide them with a 'retreat' from these troubles. A second category of client defined their problems in terms of 'deviation' from social norms. These clients expected their therapists to function as expert medical practitioners, diagnosing the problem and giving advice which would lead to a 'cure'. The third way of making sense of therapy was to view problems as caused by personal 'deficits' which could be overcome by acquiring appropriate interpersonal coping skills and strategies. The fourth pattern was described by Kuhnlein as the 'developmental-disturbance type'. These people saw their problems as caused by a complex interaction between personal characteristics, individual life events, and social or domestic circumstances. During therapy, they gained insight into the factors in their life which had contributed to their problems, which gave them confidence that they could overcome any similar problems should they recur in the future. Kuhnlein found that these patterns of belief were not influenced by the experience of therapy, but had remained basically unchanged over the course of several years. Like McKenna and Todd (1997), this qualitative study identifies different types of outcome. The implication for psychotherapy outcome research is summarised by Kuhnlein in the following terms:

> It is not appropriate for psychotherapy research to concentrate predominantly on objectifiable expert evaluations and on the change of isolated single spheres of life or modes of behaviour. We have to acknowledge that the adequacy of thinking, feeling and acting cannot be measured by universal standards, even within the same social and cultural context. (Kuhnlein, 1999: 285)

The discovery by McKenna and Todd (1997) and Kuhnlein (1999) of distinct patterns and meanings of change represents an important contribution of qualitative research to a more complete understanding of psychotherapy outcome. Existing quantitative approaches to outcome are based on an assumption of 'universal standards'. If groups of clients experience outcome in different ways, then a range of practically significant questions follows: Do measures based on 'universal standards' fail to reflect certain important types of change? What is the relationship between client 'change schemas' and preferred forms of therapy?

A qualitative outcome study carried out by Dale, Allen and Measor (1998) reports on interviews carried out with 40 people who had received counselling in relation to abuse they had experienced in childhood. These informants supplied information on 130 counselling experiences. As might be expected in a qualitative study, the interviews generated useful insights into the processes associated with effective and ineffective therapy. However, the researchers were also able to estimate the success rate of these counselling episodes. Although virtually all of these clients reported having had a positive overall experience of counselling, around one-quarter described counselling experiences that they felt had been harmful to them. In many of these cases they had been unable to tell their counsellors about their dissatisfaction, instead adopting a strategy of 'pretending to be better'.

The four studies described in this section demonstrate that qualitative interview data can be used to generate useful information about the effectiveness of therapy. Some of the methodological issues associated with this form of evaluation research are discussed in the following section.

## The logic of qualitative outcome research

Different evaluation 'logics' prevail within quantitative and qualitative research. In a randomised controlled trial, the causal link between intervention and outcome is established through statistical analysis of group data. For example, the anxiety scores of the group of clients who receive therapy are compared with the scores of those in a control condition. If randomisation has been successful, then it can reasonably be concluded that differential outcomes are due to the intervention. This is a powerful framework for attributing cause and effect relationships. In a qualitative study, on the other hand, the link between intervention and outcome is established through descriptive accounts given by therapy participants. Howe (1989) found that the families he interviewed were able to be explicit about whether or not their problems (usually difficulties with a teenage child) had improved over the course of treatment. Howe's report gives many examples of families reporting attitudes and behaviour that had changed or remained the same over the period of time before, during and following therapy. However, informants would sometimes attribute these changes to therapy, sometimes to their own efforts, and at other times to external or chance influences. As one mother said: 'everything's fine at home now . . . but what we did at home was ten times more use than what they did' (Howe, 1989: 77). In a qualitative interview, events are constructed into a *narrative* account. The use of the time-line technique by McKenna and Todd (1997) is an example of one of the ways in which informants can be helped to reconstruct the story of their therapy.

One way of understanding the methodological issues associated with the use of self-report measures in psychotherapy outcome research is that, here too, respondents attempt to narrativise their experience but that the linguistic constraints of the questionnaire format impede their capacity to do so. Their answers to questionnaire items are not straightforward behavioural reports, but reflect the story they tell themselves about their life and their therapy. At least in qualitative research the fact that the research is concerned with how clients (or indeed, other stakeholders) construe or 'narrativise' their experience is openly acknowledged.

One of the interesting aspects of the Howe (1989), McKenna and Todd (1997) and Dale et al. (1998) studies is that therapy clients appeared to be quite willing to be critical of their therapists in these interviews. In research that employs client-satisfaction questionnaires at the end of therapy, it is usual to observe a 'ceiling effect' in which the majority of clients give ratings at the extreme positive end of the scale. Why are clients more willing or able to give a balanced view of their therapy in the context of an in-depth interview, where they tend to give an exaggerated positive evaluation on rating scales? It may be that satisfied clients fill in satisfaction questionnaires while unsatisfied ones do not complete them, or that less satisfied clients are more willing to be interviewed. However, it may also be that the interview situation encourages a reflective stance which allows the person to give a more complete account of the meaning of an important experience in their life. The 'demand characteristics' of a brief end-of-therapy satisfaction questionnaire may contribute to answers dominated by a wish not to undermine the reputation of the therapist who has done his or her best to help. Schwartz (1996) has described some of the ways in which the language used in questionnaire items invites particular answers. By contrast, the 'demand characteristics' of an extended interview with a neutral researcher give permission for the person to express the ambiguities and complexities of their sense of whether, and how much, therapy has helped them. The logic of qualitative evaluation, therefore, must be seen as being grounded in a willingness to accept ambiguity, rather than being wedded to a 'horse race' mentality in which the therapy with the highest gain score is the winner. In terms of producing new knowledge that contributes to debates over evidence-based therapy, it would appear that qualitative evaluation is better able to explore the limits of therapeutic *ineffectiveness*. Participants in the Howe (1989) and Dale et al. (1998) studies reported somewhat lower success rates than in other published research. For example, in the Dale et al. research, some 10 per cent of counselling episodes were described by informants as being positively harmful.

Qualitative methods have traditionally been considered as most appropriate for research which seeks to uncover the *meanings* embedded within a slice of social life or piece of action. Qualitative research is seen as contributing to the growth of *understanding*, rather than to the collection of factual knowledge and construction of causal explanation. In research into the outcomes of psychotherapy, attention to the meaning of treatment and the development of an understanding of therapeutic gain are important goals. But outcome research also needs to feed in to policy debates where there is a demand for more precise statements about *who* benefits from *which* therapy and *how much*. In recent years, researchers employing quantitative methods and clinical trials have begun to estimate the comparative benefits of different types of therapy by constructing estimates of reliable clinically significant (or socially significant) change. The estimates are derived by working out for each individual client whether that person has or has not achieved enough in therapy be considered a 'success' case. In principle, there is no reason why this kind of statement about individual cases cannot just as easily be generated from qualitative data. There exist techniques within qualitative methodology, such as the use of triangulation and external auditing (Hill, Thompson and Nutt-Williams, 1997), that would allow the reliability of statements about clinically significant change to be built on inter-observer consensus. So, although there are important differences between the 'logic' or 'rhetoric' of qualitative and quantitative approaches, it is also possible to see how these approaches can converge around, for example, a requirement to make specific recommendations to external audiences. It is also possible to envisage ways in which qualitative and quantitative approaches might be combined within outcome studies (Dennis, Fetterman and Sechrest, 1994). Mixed-method strategies include: using the findings of qualitative analysis to interpret quantitative results; drawing on qualitative material when sample sizes are too small to allow statistical analyses of sufficient power to be carried out; employing qualitative methods as a heuristic device to develop hypotheses that can be tested using quantitative methhods; using change scores to identify sub-groups of clients to be studied more intensively using qualitative techniques. In future, a fundamental use of mixed methods might be to establish a greater understanding of the parameters of clinical effectiveness for different treatments. For example, it seems clear that client-satisfaction questionnaires tend to produce the most optimistic estimates of effectiveness, while open-ended in-depth interviews yield the most conservative picture, with randomised trials reporting effectiveness rates that are somewhere between. Qualitative interviews appear to be, at present, the most sensitive method for evaluating the harmful effects of therapy and also for recording its greatest individual successes. The standardised self-report methods used in randomised trials appear both to inhibit criticism of therapists and reporting of deterioration, and also give little scope for clients to describe the hugely positive transformational experiences that can sometimes take place in counselling. For example, informants in the Dale et al. (1998) study used phrases such as 'changed my life' and 'it's made such an incredible difference'.

## Conclusions

This chapter has attempted to explore the notion that qualitative evaluation methods may have something to offer in the area of outcome research. Qualitative studies of the effectiveness of interventions have been used for some time in fields such as education (see Greene, 1998, for a recent review of this work). Within the counselling and psychotherapy research community, Howard (1983) and Goss and Mearns (1997a, b) have made powerful pleas for increased methodological pluralism.

However, while pluralism (in the form of qualitative methods or mixed methods) has become acceptable in psychotherapy process research, it has had little impact on outcome methodology. Although the qualitative outcome studies reviewed in this chapter must be seen as pilot studies, as limited and tentative, they do provide a basis for moving forward. There are many other qualitative research techniques which can be applied in psychotherapy outcome research, either in isolation or in conjunction with quantitative measures. When there are 480 qualitative outcome studies (the number of controlled trials reviewed in the Smith, Glass and Miller meta-analysis published in 1980), we will be in a better position to judge the contribution of this approach.

A central theme in this chapter has been the need to make a 'clearing' within which qualitative outcome research might be pursued. The 'every-day' or 'natural' assumption of most therapists and researchers is to take for granted the validity and common-sense plausibility of existing instrument-based approaches to therapy outcome research. In the tradition of Gadamer and Heidegger, it is necessary critically to question and deconstruct this existing framework of understanding, particularly around its use of language, before a new understanding can begin to be put in its place. It is also necessary to take a phenomenological stance, in seeking to find new ways of 'seeing' old concepts such as 'outcome' and 'change' in terms of what they *really* are.

# 11

# Critical Issues in the Use of Qualitative Inquiry

In previous chapters, the nature and scope of qualitative research in counselling and psychotherapy has been reviewed. It is clear that carrying out qualitative research can be a problematic business. Something which seems on the face of it so simple and beguiling ('let's find out about this fascinating topic by interviewing a few people') gets harder as it goes along. There is an in-built reflexivity to good qualitative research. It is a matter of making something (collecting material from an informant, making an analytic or interpretive connection, writing a sentence) and then looking at what has just been made and asking a whole series of reflexive questions: Can I do that? Is it justifiable? How else could it be? What does it mean?

Behind the practice of qualitative inquiry there lies a set of key dilemmas which generate this constant flow of reflexive, self-tormenting questions. These issues are ultimately never resolvable, and are perhaps best seen as representing the qualitative researcher's engagement in a human conversation which both precedes any of us and will continue long after any of us is gone. These core issues overlap and flow into each other, but can be somewhat inadequately identified in terms of two key themes: the search for *validity and truth*, and the development of *critical reflexivity*. This chapter explores these issues and then concludes with some suggestions for future directions in qualitative research in counselling and psychotherapy.

## Validity and truth

> Of course there are always colleagues who ask, 'Why can't you just be normal social scientists?' To this, we reply, 'Better to admit what all of us really know: we're just mucking about looking for truth.' (Bochner, Ellis and Tillman-Healy, 1998: 59)

One of the major challenges for qualitative researchers has been the struggle to establish agreement over the criteria which are to be applied when making judgements over the quality of a piece of research. In the quantitative sciences, there would appear to exist a broad consensus concerning how best to interpret a range of 'quality control' procedures around constructs such as validity, reliability, sampling, statistical power and even publication citation counts. There are several aspects of quantitative studies where an external appraiser can unequivocally judge that what has been done is right or wrong. For example, statistical tests can only be applied when certain assumptions can be made about the distribution of data and the level of measurement. Although at the margins there is always some debate over these matters (how else could scientific progress be maintained?), on the whole there is a well-defined and well-known set of validity criteria which are employed on a routine basis by quantitative researchers.

The situation in qualitative research is quite different. If, as has been argued throughout this book, the 'findings' of a qualitative study are generated through the active personal engagement of the investigator with the phenomena of interest, then it is inevitable that what is produced will, to a greater or lesser extent, bear the mark of the investigator's 'approach'. The kinds of things that are said in qualitative interviews are influenced by the presence and skill of the interviewer. The kinds of categories that emerge from a grounded theory analysis depend on the language system and world-view of the analyst. How, then, can the results of a qualitative study be deemed as 'reliable', if reliability is defined in terms of the possibility of obtaining the same results on two different occasions with different researchers?

In quantitative research the notion of validity refers to the capacity of a measure accurately to capture or reflect some characteristic of objective reality. For instance, a ruler is a valid measure of length. We have no trouble in assigning 'length' as a characteristic of all objects in the everyday world. In qualitative research, two problems arise in relation to the concept of validity. First, for those researchers influenced by constructivism, social constructionism, or hermeneutics, there is no assumption that there exists a fixed, knowable external reality: all experience of reality is constructed, one way or another. Second, even if it were to be admitted that, for practical purposes, an 'objective' external reality might exist, the signs that are used to signify this reality are words, not numbers. These words are slippery. Any linguistic representation of events and experiences relies upon a language that is ambiguous, figurative, narratively structured, and so on. Quantitative researchers arrive at agreements over validity and reliability, in the end, by comparing sets of scores. Qualitative researchers can only compare sets of words.

It is clear that the specific quality criteria used in quantitative research cannot be applied in qualitative research in any straightforward manner. Nevertheless, the same issue remains: is a piece of research any good? There are many occasions on which judgements need to be made concerning the 'truth-value' of a qualitative study: 'Do the findings of this study provide a satisfactory basis for changing my therapeutic practice?' 'Should this paper be published?' 'Should this candidate be awarded a PhD?' Beyond these specific occasions or choice points, there is also a need for qualitative researchers to have access to a vocabulary and body of exemplars that allow them to articulate and reflect on good and poor practice. How else can we discuss our work in a constructive manner? In the absence of a differentiated critical language there can be a tendency for the alleged weaknesses of pieces of research to be attributed to personal shortcomings. This kind of *ad hominem* criticism merely fragments the research community, and does little or nothing to improve standards.

There appear to be three strategies for dealing with the question of quality in qualitative research. The first is to refer to epistemological principles that transcend any single methodological approach. The following statement by Howard attempts to define a set of core 'epistemic' values that can be applied to both quantitative and qualitative studies:

> Epistemic values . . . are those criteria employed by scientists to choose among competing theoretical explanations. . . . The most salient epistemic value for the working scientist would likely be *predictive accuracy*. Although some degree of inaccuracy should be tolerated in the early stages of a theory, in the long run a theory must demonstrate predictive accuracy if it is to be acceptable. A second desideratum is *internal coherence*. That is, a theory should hang together properly, having no logical inconsistencies or unexplained coincidences. A third desired value is *external consistency*. The theory must be consistent with other theories and also the general background of scientific expectation. Theories that contradict other accepted theories from the same or related disciplines are subject to a certain amount of skepticism. *Unifying power* is a fourth valued characteristic of scientific theories. The ability to bring together hitherto disparate areas of knowledge is a valued trait for theories. Another crucial criterion is *fertility*. Theories are fertile not only because they make correct, novel predictions but also because they function like a metaphor might in literature and provide the scientist with imaginative resources to overcome anomalies and to make new and powerful extensions of our knowledge base. . . . A final epistemic value might be *simplicity*. Although less widely accepted than the others among contemporary philosophers, it still possesses a certain appeal among certain scientists. (Howard, 1985: 257–8)

If qualitative research concepts such as 'interpretive framework', 'grounded theory main category' or even 'phenomenological description' are used in place of 'theory', it can be seen that Howard's (1985) formulation of epistemic values works fairly well. The findings of a qualitative study should 'hang together', and 'provide . . . imaginative resources'. Nevertheless, no matter how attractive it might seem, the strategy of relying on higher-order epistemic or scientific values as a way of resolving disputes about quality issues in qualitative research is doomed to failure. In the end, there is always a requirement to be more specific about what counts as 'accuracy', 'coherence', 'fertility', 'consistency' and 'simplicity'. How are these abstract values put into action? What are the procedures that qualitative researchers need to follow to ensure that they sufficiently respect such values? Judgements about research quality may be informed by abstract principles, but in the end rely on the application of specific criteria and standards.

A second strategy for maintaining standards in qualitative research has therefore been to define distinctive sets of criteria and procedures that are specific to qualitative research. In a sense, this approach has almost been that of writing a 'quality control manual' for qualitative researchers. There have been many attempts to identify the core criteria for evaluating qualitative research. Particularly influential, in relation to the counselling and psychotherapy research community, have been the contributions of Packer and Addison (1989) and Stiles (1993). Much of this material is summarised in McLeod (1994), but Stiles (1993) remains the definitive account, and essential reading for any qualitative researcher. The main themes in these guidelines have centred on clarity of explication of methods, presenting sufficient evidence, and establishing credibility through 'member checks' (asking informants whether they agree with what has been found, and triangulation (comparing conclusions derived from different data sources). Practical utility has been proposed as an important validity criterion. Stiles (1993, 1997) has also suggested that 'permeability' (the openness of the researcher to new insights) is one of the key characteristics of good qualitative research.

In an interesting and important recent paper, Madill, Jordan and Shirley (2000) applied criteria derived from three contrasting epistemological perspectives (realism, contextualism and radical social constructionism) to evaluate grounded theory analyses of a set of interview data carried out by two separate analysts. The realist position is derived from positivism (Kolakowski, 1993), and takes the view that different analyses should converge on a single, consensual, 'objective' version of findings. Contextualism, on the other hand, focuses attention on the extent to which an analysis is shaped by the situation in which it was produced, for example the individual attitudes and pre-dispositions of the analyst. Finally, a radical social constructionist perspective does not allow for any privileged external benchmark against which an analysis can be judged, and suggests instead that the most important indicator of the quality of an analysis lies in the extent to which it is internally coherent. Madill, Jordan and Shirley show that it is possible to use all three of these perspectives in evaluating the competing grounded theory analyses examined in their study. Their work illustrates the complexity of terms like 'objectivity' and 'reliability' in a field in which there are competing epistemological traditions. They emphasise that it important to assess any piece of qualitative research in accordance with the 'logic of justification' and epistemology adopted by its authors. While this conclusion (which is essentially the same as the position adopted by Reicher, 2000) may hold within the domain of academic discourse, but fails to recognise that, in an area like therapy research in which research aspires to have an impact on practice, judgements on the adequacy of studies will often be made by practitioners and policy-makers who may possess their own, quite different, criteria for assessing the value of a study.

Elliott, Fischer and Rennie (1999) have synthesised a wide range of criteria into what they have called 'Evolving guidelines for the publication of qualitative research studies in psychology and related fields'. The 'evolving guidelines', which are summarised in Table 11.1, have been subjected to an extensive consultation process across various professional groups, and represent the current consensus over what constitutes good practice in this field. It is perhaps worth noting that all three authors of the 'evolving guidelines' are psychotherapists and psychotherapy researchers, and their ideas have met with a certain amount of opposition from social psychologists committed to a discourse analysis perspective (Reicher, 2000). The 'evolving guidelines' presented in Table 11.1 are an abridged version. Interested readers are advised to consult the Elliott, Fischer and Rennie (1999) paper for a fuller account.

The 'evolving guidelines' provide invaluable assistance to qualitative researchers seeking to evaluate their work, by supplying a set of parameters and a language which may facilitate both further discussion and decision-making. However, it is clear that these guidelines are far from closing the debate. For example, if Guideline B1 *Owning one's perspective* were to be interpreted seriously, few of the papers discussed in earlier chapters of this book (including the work of Elliott, Fischer and Rennie) would be deemed publishable. The process of specifying 'theoretical orientations, personal anticipations . . . values, interests and assumptions' could go on for ever, in an endless recursive loop. The decision that a certain amount of reflexive self-disclosure is sufficient is dictated by stylistic conventions, including the current requirement in academic journals that reviewers of papers are not given the identity of the author(s) – how could this be possible if, in the paper, the author fully explicates his or her personal perspective? Also, who is to judge, or can judge, whether a perspective has been authentically conveyed? Similar points could be made in relation to Guidelines B2 *Situating the sample* and B3 *Grounding in examples*. How much situating and how many examples are sufficient?

The concept of 'credibility checks' (Guideline B4) has been promoted by many leading figures in qualitative research. One of the ways in which this kind of validation procedure can be carried out is through a procedure known as 'member checks': a report (written or oral) is presented by the researcher to informants or other members of the informant social group. These 'members' can then comment on the veracity of what the researcher has produced.

This procedure sounds fine in theory, but is enormously difficult in practice. Some of these difficulties are explored in a paper by the British

Table 11.1   *Guidelines for publishability of qualitative research studies*

---

**A   Publishability guidelines shared by both qualitative and quantitative approaches**

1   *Explicit scientific context and purpose.* The study is located within relevant literature; the intended purposes of the study are made explicit.
2   *Appropriate methods.* The methods or procedures used are appropriate or responsive to the intended purposes or questions of the study.
3   *Respect for participants.* Informed consent, confidentiality, welfare of participants, social responsibility and other ethical principles are fulfilled.
4   *Specification of methods.* Procedures for data collection and analysis are reported in sufficient detail to allow readers to see how to conduct a similar study themselves.
5   *Appropriate discussion.* Research data and understandings from them are discussed in terms of their relevance to theory, method and practice, in appropriately tentative and contextualised terms.
6   *Clarity of presentation.* The manuscript is clearly written and well-organised, with technical terms defined.
7   *Contribution to knowledge.* The manuscript contributes to an elaboration of a discipline's body of description and understanding.

**B   Publishability guidelines especially pertinent to qualitative research**

1   *Owning one's perspective.* Authors specify their theoretical orientations and personal anticipations, both as known in advance and as they become apparent during the research. In developing and communicating their understanding of the phenomenon under study, authors attempt to recognise their values, interests and assumptions and the role these play in the understanding. This disclosure of values and assumptions helps readers to interpret the researchers' data and understanding of them, and to consider possible alternatives.
2   *Situating the sample.* Authors describe the research participants and their life circumstances to aid the reader in judging the typicality of the data.
3   *Grounding in examples.* Authors provide examples of the data to illustrate both the analytic procedures used in the study and the understanding developed in the light of them. The examples allow appraisal of the fit between the data and authors' understanding of them; they also allow readers to conceptualize alternative meanings and understandings.
4   *Providing credibility checks.* Researchers may use any of several methods for checking the credibility of their categories, themes or accounts. Where relevant, these may include: (a) checking these understandings with the informants or others similar to them; (b) using multiple qualitative analysts, an additional analytic 'auditor', or the original analyst for a 'verification step' of reviewing the data for discrepancies, overstatements, or errors; (c) comparing two or more varied qualitative perspectives, or (d) where appropriate, 'triangulation' with external factors (e.g., outcome or recovery) or quantitative data.
5   *Coherence.* The understanding is represented in a way that achieves coherence and integration while preserving nuances in the data. The understanding fits together to form a data-based story/narrative, 'map', framework, or underlying structure for the phenomenon or domain.
6   *Accomplishing general vs specific research tasks.* Where a *general* understanding of a phenomenon is intended, it is based on an appropriate range of instances (informants or situations). Limitations to 'typicality' are specified in terms of context and informant characteristics. Where understanding a *specific* instance or case is the goal, it has been studied and described systematically and comprehensively enough to provide the reader

*continued*

Table 11.1   (*continued*)

with a basis for attaining that understanding. Such case studies also address limitations of 'typicality'.

7   *Resonating with readers.* The manuscript stimulates resonance in readers/reviewers, meaning that the material is presented in such a way that readers/reviewers, taking all other guidelines into account, judge it to have accurately represented the subject matter or to have clarified or expanded their appreciation and understanding of it.

sociologist Michael Bloor (1997). In sharing several examples of 'member checking' from his own work, he illustrates some basic difficulties in this technique. It can be difficult to engage informants in the task of reading a report closely or participating in a follow-up interview or discussion group. Some informants may be over-impressed by the 'authority' of what has been written by the researcher, and may thereby be inhibited from expressing their doubts and criticisms. Other informants may disagree but, out of respect for the researcher or through following the rules of polite conversation, be reluctant to articulate their disagreement openly. Yet other informants may be explicit about their disagreement, but be motivated by considerations other than those of scientific validity. For instance, in a study of a therapeutic community, Bloor found that some informants believed that his report had not sufficiently emphasised their psychodynamic perspective. On re-interviewing one of these informants some years later, Bloor found that this person could now see that the original report had been accurate and that his earlier comments had stemmed from a need to defend his position in the staff team.

For Bloor, the issue is that, in both member checking and triangulation, the validity of the new information being used to assess the accuracy of the primary data is uncertain. All the sources of error that might have been in place in the original data collection stage are possibly even more likely to occur in member checking or triangulation. Member checking is usually a fairly time-limited procedure in comparison with the main data collection phase of a study. It also involves informants entering a situation which may have particular meanings for them, as discussed earlier. Triangulation can take many forms, but may include information from a large data set being compared with contrasting information from a smaller set. For instance individual interviews are carried out with 20 informants and this is triangulated against focus-group material from a group of 8 new informants. The difficulty with both member checking and triangulation, viewed as validation techniques, is summed up by Bloor (1997: 49) in the following terms:

. . . all validating techniques are social products, constituted through particular and variable methodological processes. The very methodological frailties that lead sociologists to search for validating evidence are also present in the generation of that validating evidence.

In relation to the logic of research validity, this results in a paradox. If the new information from member checks or triangulation *corroborates* the original findings, then all is well. If, on the other hand, the new information *contradicts* the main study, then there is a problem; 'should the findings from the best available method be set aside on the basis of evidence generated by an inferior method?' (Bloor, 1997: 39). Clearly, it would not be justifiable to allow this to happen. On the other hand, a validation procedure cannot be a true test of validity if its conclusions are only acceptable in cases where the main findings are supported.

Most of the research that has been discussed in this book has been carried out within a psychological tradition that places great emphasis on convergent validity and consensus agreements (e.g., the widespread use of inter-rater and other reliability procedures in mainstream psychological research). In a qualitative study there may be pressure, therefore, to achieve consensus. It is always possible to explain away uncomfortable results from member checks or triangulation. If qualitative research in counselling and psychotherapy was taking place within a research tradition that encouraged the production of 'multi-voiced' texts and embraced relativism, then member checks might be more useful. As it is, there is a danger that, if regarded solely as validation procedures, member checking, triangulation and the use of external 'auditors' or 'adversaries' may function as validity rituals that serve little real purpose.

The point here is not to deny the value of checking categories and emerging themes against any and all available sources. This is essential. But, as Bloor (1997: 49) states: 'validation techniques are not tests, but opportunities for reflexive elaboration'. As qualitative researchers, we need to use what Glaser and Strauss (1967) called an attitude of 'constant comparison' as part of the actual process of the research. The key issue is whether the researcher or research team have genuinely looked for examples and evidence that might contradict their interpretation of the data. In a sense, the question of validity then comes back to a matter of whether the researcher is *plausible* and *trustworthy*. In practice, there is never the space in a qualitative report to unequivocally establish the 'truth value' of the description and analysis that are presented. In the end it comes down to a matter of trust. It seems to me that here, the *personal* qualities of the researcher, his or her integrity, courage, honesty and commitment to the task of inquiry, actually make a difference (McLeod, 1999a). Obviously there are many technical requirements that need to be met if a research study is to be regarded as competent. Appropriate choice and skilled implementation of method, presentation and analysis of data, and coherence of discussion are clearly necessary elements of good research. If a piece of research is carried out with integrity, then there is almost certainly something of value in it, there is *some truth* in it. Conversely, even though a study is technically or formally flawless, if it lacks personal integrity it is of limited value.

Any discussion of the personal qualities of researchers is highly embarrassing and goes against the grain of scientific method. But, to return to the 'evolving guidelines', the final item in this list is *resonating with readers*. Stiles (1993) also mentions various types of empowerment that can be associated with qualitative research, for example participation in the study acting as a catalyst and learning experience for both informants and researcher(s). My view is that research can only possess these kinds of meanings for readers and participants if it is approached in the right way, with sufficient openness and integrity on the part of the researcher. Mearns and McLeod (1984) have suggested that the facilitative therapist factors identified by Carl Rogers – empathy, congruence and acceptance – have an important role to play in qualitative research. There is certainly more to being a good researcher than this, but the Rogerian 'core conditions' at least begin to map some of the qualities that might be associated with personal validity. The 'human inquiry' genre of qualitative research (Reason, 1988a, 1994a) seeks to promote these qualities or virtues through the vehicle of a research group which is both supportive and challenging. The challenges associated with working collaboratively in research teams are examined by Erickson and Stull (1998) and Olesen et al. (1994).

In conclusion, it is clear that the issue of validity in qualitative research is far from simple. There are no straightforward 'quality criteria' that can be applied in any kind of automatic fashion. We all need to recognise that we are 'mucking about looking for truth' (Bochner, Ellis and Tillman-Healy, 1998) and that it is inevitable whatever we find will be partial, open to re-interpretation by others, and both culturally and historically constructed. Although the guidelines proposed by Elliott, Fischer and Rennie (1999) make an important contribution by offering an outline of some of the key elements of good practice in qualitative research, they do not really address the question of *quality*: what is it that makes a research report interesting, useful and evocative? This question is likely to become increasingly important as qualitative research becomes more widely accepted in the counselling and psychotherapy professional community. Quantitative research can, sometimes, generate a compelling authority through its demonstration of 'objectivity', 'facticity' and sheer weight of numbers. On what basis can qualitative research be persuasive enough to instigate changes in practice among therapists and agency administrators?

## The relationship between quantitative and qualitative research

Within the counselling and psychotherapy research community, there have been several calls for greater methodological *pluralism* (Howard, 1983; Greenberg, Elliott and Lietaer, 1994; Goss and Mearns, 1997a, b). What pluralism means, in this context, is a willingness to employ either (or both) qualitative or quantitative methods in research studies, with the choice of method being determined by the research question and purpose. It is hard to see how anyone could argue *against* this kind of broad definition of pluralism. We seek to live in a democratic society, and pluralism is a core value of the modern liberal democratic system. However, just as political pluralism is often difficult to achieve, so is methodological pluralism in therapy research.

The argument in support of methodological pluralism is based on the position that different methodologies have different strengths and weaknesses. For example, qualitative case studies are particularly sensitive at describing change processes, but do not yield convincing findings regarding outcomes. Randomised controlled trials, on the other hand, deliver robust conclusions around issues of efficacy and effectiveness, but are big, blunt instruments that miss the subtleties of process that shape these outcomes. Historically, an over-reliance on quantitative methods has led to gaps in the literature, which the new qualitative methods are able to fill.

There are, however, a number of problems associated with methodological pluralism:

• *Epistemological.* Qualitative research is rooted in a philosophical stance characterised by relativism, an image of the person as a reflexive agent, an image of the researcher as involved. Quantitative research implies, at a philosophical level, a knowable, single reality in which behaviour is controlled by cause-and-effect 'variables' and studied by detached, 'objective' scientists. Although several generations of philosophers and social scientists have sought to devise ways of resolving this polarity, there is nevertheless a basic contradiction in the ways in which the qualitative and quantitative research traditions have construed the world.

• *Methodological rules.* The contrasting aims and methodological stances associated with qualitative and quantitative approaches are linked to differences in the area of 'rules of method'. For example, in most instances large samples of subjects / participants are preferable in quantitative studies, because sample size generates statistical power (the capacity reliably to detect differences). In qualitative research, by contrast, a sample that is too large will yield too much 'text' to comprehend properly, with the danger of an analysis that is either superficial or incomplete. In quantitative research, it is good practice to specify hypotheses and procedures in advance, and stick to them. In some forms of qualitative research, procedural flexibility and openness to the emergence of new questions are recommended. In qualitative research, researcher reflexivity is a necessary element of good work. In quantitative research, researcher reflexivity is irrelevant. These are just some of the ways in which quantitative and qualitative research involve different sets of methodological 'rules', which take the researcher in different directions.

- *Researcher skills and 'mind-set'.* Qualitative and quantitative research involve different ways of 'seeing' the world. The experience of immersion in the meaning-systems of research participants, through interviewing and reading and re-reading transcripts, is quite different from the experience of analysing statistical data-sets on a computer. The 'logic' of quantitative researching is based on inference and hypothesis-testing. The logic of qualitative research also involves induction and abduction (see Chapter 5). Sometimes, students trained in quantitative methods in psychology or medicine just never 'see the point' of qualitative research, or ever achieve a stage of feeling comfortable or confident with textual material. Some students from humanities and arts backgrounds may never 'see the point' of quantification. Beyond these personal or attitudinal factors, there is also a matter of technical competence. It takes time to learn statistical methods, or qualitative approaches. For many students and researchers, it is not practically possible to acquire sufficient skills to achieve competence in both types of method.

- *Writing and reporting conventions.* A further barrier to pluralistic research resides in the problems involved in writing research reports that draw upon contrasting methodologies and different kinds of data. There are challenging issues for authors and journal editors around the relative emphasis and logical priority given to each method, and coping with the length restrictions of journal articles.

None of these barriers to methodological pluralism is insurmountable, but taken together they certainly represent a substantial disincentive to pluralism. It is certainly easier to carry out research, and compile research reviews, from a single-methodology perspective.

For anyone considering embarking on pluralistic research, it is important to take account of these issues and proceed with caution. There are four main strategies that have been employed by researchers combining qualitative and quantitative methods:

- Using qualitative methods in the initial phase of a research programme, to generate descriptive accounts and identify themes that can form the basis for subsequent quantification. This strategy is commonplace in many branches of applied psychology, and is an element of basic questionnaire design. For example, in a study where the management of a large organisation wished to evaluate staff perceptions of its in-house counselling provision, it might commission research which ran focus groups with staff to elicit the range of perceptions found in the organisation, and then transform these statements into a survey questionnaire (incorporating items drawn from a review of the relevant literature) that could be distributed to a large sample of employees. This approach combines the heuristic potential of qualitative research (discovering and describing attitudes and perceptions) with the capacity of the survey method to produce comparative and generalisable findings.

• Using quantitative findings as the basis for selecting cases for more intensive qualitative analysis. In therapy outcome research, the effectiveness of a form of therapy may be established, but insight into the factors which make it effective (or otherwise) are usually lacking. Where detailed case material (e.g., from tapes of therapy sessions, or from therapist notes) is available to supplement standard quantitative measures, it can be useful to conduct intensive case-study research on small numbers of representative cases, such as the two most successful cases and the two least successful cases. A good example of this kind of pluralism can be found in the 'Vanderbilt' study conducted by Hans Strupp and his colleagues in the 1970s and 1980s (Strupp, 1993). This principle of starting with quantitative data, from a survey or outcome study, and then using it to select representative cases for qualitative research, can be used in a variety of research situations.

• Using a combination of qualitative and quantitative techniques in case-study research. Good case-study research relies on the ability to integrate and compare different sources of evidence within the same case (Yin, 1989). The 'n = 1' or single-case design has been central to the development of cognitive-behavioural therapy. Most 'n = 1' studies contain a mix of quantitative (time-series) data and narrative descriptive data on the case (Morley, 1989). Other pluralistic approaches to single-case research include the Comprehensive Process Analysis approach devised by Elliott (see Chapter 8), the case studies published by Hill (1989), and the programme of case-based process research into the 'assimilation model' of therapeutic change (Honos-Webb and Stiles, 1998; Honos-Webb et al., 1998; Stiles et al., 1990; Stiles and Angus, 2000). All of these research genres illustrate the value of combining quantitative and qualitative data when studying individual cases. The tension between the two types of information, and the possibility of using quantitative data to anchor the case in a wider universe of cases, make pluralistic case studies more interesting than either wholly quantitative or wholly qualitative case analyses.

• Including open-ended questions in quantitative questionnaires. In surveys, client satisfaction scales, and other types of quantitative questionnaires, it can often be tempting for the researcher to include space for the respondent to add comments, or provide some open-ended items. This strategy is appealing for pluralistically-minded researchers who are essentially engaging in quantitative research. Although superficially attractive, it is a strategy that is very hard to implement successfully. Typically, once subjects have answered a series of 'tick-box' items, they either ignore an open-ended item, write cryptically, or repeat themes that were introduced in the scaled items. There is seldom enough space for participants to offer a full account of their experience. The brevity and incompleteness of such quasi-qualitative items makes them difficult to analyse at all, and seldom is it possible to do more than attempt a simple content analysis. A thoughtful critique of this kind of pluralism can be found in Rennie (1996).

It can be seen that methodological pluralism can produce practical research benefits, if pursued appropriately. One of the characteristics of successful pluralistic research is *conceptual coherence*: qualitative and quantitative findings can be more readily integrated if they are addressing the same (or similar) theoretical issues. The domain of humanistic/experiential approaches to counselling and psychotherapy is one which has, since the time of Carl Rogers, been an important site for methodological innovation and pluralism. The chapter by Greenberg, Elliott and Lietaer (1994) demonstrates how quantitative and qualitative findings can be integrated in a literature review. Further discussion of the issues associated with combining qualitative and quantitative methods can be found in Brannen (1992), Bryman (1984), McLeod (1994) and Sells, Smith and Sprenkle (1995).

Another significant dimension of the quantitative–qualitative debate is political. Methodological pluralism is not being constructed on level ground. The social and institutional power of numbers is such that there are strong forces pulling in the direction of quantitative methods. The location of psychotherapy research in psychology and psychiatry departments dominated by quantification has resulted in an at-best grudging acceptance of qualitative methods:

> We find ourselves adopting a kind of pluralism that does not throw out the virtues of the traditional approaches to research, but complements those with a variety of more flexible techniques for getting at the complexity of the phenomena we deal with. We anticipate seeing much more along this line in future. At the same time, we are not advocating a revision to nineteenth-century phenomenology and hermeneutics, but, rather, an objective approach to subjective phenomena that can be addressed qualitatively and descriptively using rigor and, in many cases, quantification. (Bergin and Garfield, 1994b: 626)

Allan Bergin and Sol Garfield have been leading figures in psychotherapy research for fifty years. The passage quoted above is taken from the concluding 'overview' chapter from their edited *Handbook of Psychotherapy and Behavior Change* (4th edn) (Bergin and Garfield, 1994a). The *Handbook* is widely regarded as the authoritative source of knowledge regarding all matters concerning psychotherapy research. Here, the relationship between quantitative and qualitative research is clear. It is 'complementary', an 'objective' approach that in many cases will lead to quantification.

The hegemony of quantitative research needs to be understood by those using qualitative methods to study therapy, or reading qualitative papers. Qualitative researchers in counselling and psychotherapy have consistently felt the need to accommodate the 'virtues of the traditional approaches'. Unlike qualitative research in sociology and anthropology, there has never existed a cogent vantage point from which *quantitative* research could be viewed as complementary. The potential of a truly human science approach to therapy research is, therefore, far from being fully realised.

## The role of computer software in qualitative analysis

The role of computer software packages in the analysis of qualitative research text has not been discussed in earlier sections of this book. In recent years, publishers such as Sage have developed and marketed a variety of software tools for qualitative researchers: NU-DIST, Code-a-Text, ATLAS-ti, and many others. Some researchers find these packages helpful, others do not. It is certainly possible to do first-rate qualitative research without the assistance of specialised software. Some researchers work with paper copies of qualitative text; others exploit the cut, paste and copy facilities in common wordprocessor tools such as WORD. To date, no one has claimed that their breakthrough research relied on the use of qualitative software. At best, qualitative software operates as a reliable clerical assistant (Morison and Moir, 1998). At worst, it can take up a lot of time (the system has to be learned) and then impose its own structure on the data.

It may be that software packages are in a transitional stage, and that the next generation of software tools will open up genuinely new possibilities in data analysis, rather than seeking merely to reproduce coding strategies taken from grounded theory or content analysis. For example, some packages can now allow the researcher to listen or view recordings of interviews, rather than merely work with transcripts. What difference will it make to researchers when the felt, embodied quality of the informant's voice and presence are available? What new possibilities will arise for reporting findings in vocal/visual as well as textual forms, for instance using CD-ROM or the Internet? Information technology should also enable innovation around dialogue between researchers and informants, and between members of a research team (including 'adversaries' and 'devil's advocates'). At some point, voice-translation devices should become efficient and cheap enough for transcribing to be a thing of the past. Will there eventually be voice-translation devices that render speech into stanzas, or conversation analysis formats? Finally, access to information about how to do qualitative research, and simple packages, may allow more people to do qualitative research. Will clients then be encouraged to do research into their own lives? Will clients do research on therapists?

## The development of critical reflexivity

> . . . a question that is often posed is:
> Why do research (if you cannot say that there is anything out there, and all research is self-reflexive)?
> My reply is:
> Why do research for which you must deny responsibility for what *you* have 'found'? (Steier, 1991b: 10)

It has been argued throughout this book that qualitative research is a *personal* activity, involving a personal struggle to challenge assumptions and achieve understanding, and usually also involving entering meaningful relationships with people who are the research 'informants' or 'participants'.

The intentionally personal nature of qualitative research is one of the characteristics that separates it from positivist research. In positivist research, the interests, passion and values of the researcher are put to one side: research is essentially a cognitive activity. In qualitative research, by contrast, the experience and identity of the researcher *always* influence the 'findings' that are produced. However, acknowledging the personal dimension of qualitative research, and knowing what to do about it, are two quite different things. Discussion of the issue of the personal nature of qualitative research has generally come to be referred to in terms of *reflexivity*. The idea of reflexivity implies a capacity for 'bending back' or 'turning back' one's awareness on oneself. No competent qualitative researcher would doubt that a capacity for self-reflection is a necessary component of effective qualitative researching, even if only at the level of thinking about how one's presence or manner might have an impact on people being interviewed. But the implications of the concept of reflexivity are potentially much further-reaching. It can be argued, as in the passage from Steier (1991b) quoted at the beginning of this section, that the personal dimension of qualitative research can be so all-powerful that all a qualitative researcher does is reflect on self, to the point where in the end there is nothing *out there*.

The question of reflexivity has special poignancy and significance for qualitative researchers in the area of counselling and psychotherapy. Therapy is an activity that has generated a multiplicity of ways of encouraging self-reflection, and has spawned an almost equal number of ideas about the nature or structure of the 'self' that does this reflecting. Yet, up until now, published qualitative therapy research has been highly cautious about acknowledging reflexivity. To some extent this caution may reflect the lag between qualitative research in therapy and the pace of development in qualitative research in other social science and health disciplines (see Chapter 1). It may also arise from a realisation that reflexivity represents a potential conceptual minefield which is perhaps best avoided. Reflexivity is a *contested* notion in psychology. At the extremes, it can be readily seen that psychoanalysts, humanistic psychologists, radical behaviourists and social constructionists have quite different ideas about what it means for a person to reflect on their own experience.

Some of the complexities that arise for certain social scientists in the notion of reflexivity can be appreciated by reading work such as Parker (1994) and the essays in Steier (1991a) and Hertz (1997). These debates might make one believe that it will never be possible to arrive at an understanding of reflexivity that could be used to inform practitioner-oriented research in counselling and psychotherapy. The aim in this section is to retrieve the concept of reflexivity from the realm of intellectual debate, and propose some principles, and a redefinition, that may contribute to the development of ways of using reflexivity to produce better research. The three key principles that follow from acknowledging the centrality of reflexivity in qualitative method are:

- Reflexivity implies awareness of the moral dimension of research.
- Reflexivity invites consideration of the processes through which text is co-constructed.
- Reflexivity opens up the necessity for new approaches to writing and communicating research findings.

These principles are discussed in turn. At the end of the section the concept of *critical reflexivity* is introduced.

Qualitative research in counselling and psychotherapy is a moral activity. Qualitative inquiry opens up the ways that people construct a moral world: what they believe is right or wrong, how they resolve dilemmas, how they feel about events. The narrative psychologist Arthur Frank (1992: 470) argues that 'the social sciences create and sustain society's morality as they legitimate ways of responding to the suffering of others'. He presents a powerful critique of the attempt of social science, influenced by the physical sciences, to 'stand outside morality'. In his review of psychological studies of cancer patients, Frank (1992) suggests that the denial of reflexivity produces a 'morality of distance' in which patients are not represented as real people, or allowed a voice, but are described in detached, 'distanced' language. More than other writers on this topic, he highlights the moral implications of failing to accept the possibility of the reflexive engagement of the researcher in the topic of study.

Many researchers might argue that the moral dimension of qualitative research is adequately addressed through attention to ethical guidelines. Of course, it is important for anyone carrying out research to be familiar with, and guided by, the ethical codes of the professional associations, universities, or organisations to which they belong. These ethical guidelines typically specify sensible rules of 'good practice' concerning informed consent, confidentiality and avoidance of harm. But this is not what Frank means. In recent years, it has become clear for Frank and other qualitative researchers that the work opens up a moral domain beyond that inscribed in ethical codes.

Areas of moral uncertainty that have been of particular concern include the impact of the research interview on the informant, and researchers' anxieties about the consequences for research participants of seeing their 'life' or 'story' in print.

An important theme in qualitative research, in therapy as in other areas of inquiry, has been the desire to encourage research informants to talk about their experience in ways that are complete, honest, rich or authentic. The goal for many researchers has been to get closer to what the person *really* experiences. In psychotherapy research, the use of recall interviews, where clients listen to or watch a tape of a session, and describe how and what they were thinking and feeling at each moment during that session, is an example of this kind of approach (Elliott, 1986; Rennie, 1990). Other researchers have carried out lengthy interviews in which participants have been invited to talk about experiences of therapy (Dale et al., 1998) or their memories of sexual abuse (Etherington, 1996, 2000). No one would doubt that taking part in such research can be upsetting and intrusive when the interview is badly handled. However, it is also apparent that being interviewed can have an even greater impact when it is handled *well* by the researcher. As Kvale (1996) has noted, one of the effects of a well-conducted qualitative interview is to give the informant new insight into the topic being explored. Lott (1999) has written about an observation that is well known to qualitative therapy researchers, which is the phenomenon of research participants recounting personal information and feelings to an interviewer (someone they had never met before) that they had been unable to talk about with their therapist (whom they might have been in therapy with for months or years).

It may be that poorly conducted research interviews have less impact on interviewees than might arise with skilled interviewing. In an inept interview, the probability is that the informant will 'close down' and defend himself or herself behind bland and uninformative answers. In the presence of a skilled qualitative interviewer the person may find that they are entering into new aspects of an issue, but with no chance to continue the conversation beyond the period of time set aside for the interview. Grafanaki (1996) has usefully emphasised the importance of *process consent* as a means of ensuring against unanticipated effects on research participants. Rather than merely seeking informed consent only at the ouset of a study, the research following a process consent procedure will build in to the research a series of 'consent negotiation-and-decision-points', for example, at the end of an interview, at the point of reading a transcript of the interview, and at the stage of receiving a copy of the final research report.

The adoption of a 'process consent' procedure may deal with the immediate moral dilemmas arising from the intensity of contact with informants. However, the essential dilemma does not go away. The act of *publishing* and disseminating work which is based on in-depth analysis of the life-stories of participants reopens the moral questions surrounding the relationship between the researcher and informant. In any kind of in-depth case-study research, no matter how much the identifying demographic details of the person (name, occupation, location) are disguised, the structure of their *story*, the specific concatenation of events that make them who they are, remains transparent, at least for the participant-as-reader. The collection of essays in Josselson (1996a) examines this issue in some depth. The normal ethical procedure of informed consent seems inadequate in relation to the possible consequences of publishing personal narratives. There are several examples in Josselson (1996a) of cases where participants freely agreed to publication but were surprised by how they felt when the paper or book was finally in the public domain, in the local bookshop. Josselson comments on the 'dread, guilt, and shame that go with writing about others':

> My guilt, I think, comes from my knowing that I have taken myself out of relationship with my participants (with whom, during the interview, I was in intimate relationship) to be in relationship with my readers. I have, in a sense, been talking about them behind their backs and doing so publicly. Where in the interview I had been responsive to them, now I am using their lives in the service of something else, for my own purposes, to show something to others. I am guilty about being an intruder and then, to some extent, a betrayer . . . And my shame is the hardest to analyse and the most painful of my responses. I suspect this shame is about my exhibitionism, shame that I am using these people's lives to exhibit myself, my analytic prowess, my cleverness. I am using them as extensions of my own narcissism and fear being caught, seen in this process. (Josselson, 1996b: 70)

These are honest words, which speak for many qualitative researchers who have found themselves paralysed and alone with their guilt and shame, unable for 'no good reason' to complete a dissertation or write up a paper for publication. For Josselson, the answer is not to turn away from narrative and qualitative methods, but to be willing to embrace these difficult and painful emotions: 'it is work we must do in anguish'.

This discussion can only illustrate in summary form one aspect of the moral landscape of qualitative research. For Frank (1992), there are troubling moral implications of conducting and publishing 'distanced' research. For Josselson (1996b) there are equally troubling consequences of the attempt to reduce that distance. In either case, the researcher is making moral decisions. The adoption of a critically reflexive approach to research involves developing an awareness of these moral dilemmas, and sharing them with readers.

## Critical reflexivity

The concept of *reflexivity* both resonates, and is contested, among qualitative researchers. Those who favour and promote reflexivity argue that the image of detached objectivity fostered by mainstream positivist research is an illusion when applied to research on human beings (Mair, 1989). The position here is that any researcher inevitably brings to a project his or her pre-understandings and assumptions, which in turn will shape the way that the research is conceived and carried out. From this perspective, it is good qualitative research practice for researchers to record and describe their reflections on the inquiry process. In recent times, an increasing number of qualitative therapy researchers have adopted the procedure of including in the Method section of their research papers and dissertations a short reflexive account. A typical example of such an account is taken from a study in which a team of researchers interviewed experienced therapists to collect accounts of 'impasses' in long-term psychotherapy (Hill et al., 1996):

> Five researchers participated in the study. The primary team of judges, who did all the major analyses, included one White female counseling psychologist and two White female graduate students in a counseling psychology doctoral program. The auditors were two White female psychologists (one counseling and one clinical) who were involved in the delivery of psychological services. The primary team recorded their biases and expectations about the outcomes of the study prior to collecting data. Qualitative researchers typically record their biases to ensure that they become aware of them and to try to set them aside and be objective when doing the analyses. Clara E. Hill expected that transference, countertransference, and client level of pathology (i.e., inability to form relationships) would all play major causal roles in impasses and that impasses would have a major negative impact on therapist self-esteem. Elizabeth Nutt-Williams believed that impasses would result from poor working alliances, poor matches, therapist countertransference, client pathology, therapist inexperience, or therapist lack of experience with own personal therapy. Kristin J. Heaton thought that therapists would generally be distressed by impasses, that male therapists would report fewer impasses than female therapists, and that therapists would tend to attribute responsibility for impasses to the clients rather than themselves. . . . To limit the potential distorting effects of group decision-making processes and to encourage us to work co-operatively, we strove to create a group atmosphere in which each person could express herself and the contributions of

everyone were valued. . . . Difficulties were examined in a spirit of compromise.
. . . (Hill et al., 1996: 208–9)

The extract above was chosen because this research group has been prominent in championing the use of this kind of reflexive writing in qualitative psychotherapy research papers. Prior to the incorporation of such reflexive sections, qualitative therapy research papers were typically published without any such first-person writing at all. In addition to the extract reproduced above, Hill et al. (1996) used the term 'we' several times in the Discussion section of this paper, possibly to emphasise their collective construction and 'ownership' of the findings and conclusions.

There appears to have been little discussion of the use of such brief reflexive inserts in counselling and psychotherapy research reports. Comparison of the 'reflexive statement' with the key points highlighted in the Abstract and Discussion parts of the paper suggests that the prior expectations of the research team were largely confirmed by the findings. However, there does not appear to be any comment on this linkage actually within the paper. It is of interest to look closely at what the researchers say in their reflexive statement, and how they say it. The topic of the study is an issue ('client–therapist' impasse or 'stuckness') that can be associated with feelings among therapists of inadequacy, powerlessness, and despair: it is potentially an emotionally 'hot' topic. Readers might wish to know whether the researchers themselves had experienced this type of event. Were they doing the research out of a personal drive to resolve their own experiences of impasse (as clients or therapists)? Other potentially relevant areas for researcher reflection are also omitted. The researchers chose not to reflect on the influence of their theoretical orientation or on the possible influence on informants of being interviewed by either a doctoral student or by a leading figure in the profession. The point here is not to question the value of the reflexive statement offered by Hill et al (1996); the statement greatly assists the reader in placing the analysis in context. The point, rather, is to ask the question: where does this kind of reflexivity end? There are many aspects of the theoretical, professional, personal and institutional identities of the researchers which could, in principle, be relevant to a full appreciation of the study and its findings.

Analysis of the approach to reflexivity found in Hill et al. (1996), and increasingly in other qualitative papers, highlights the objection that some social scientists would make, which is to question the status of such reflexive statements. In particular, from a discourse analysis perspective it might be argued that the reflexive account of the researcher is itself text to be analysed and 'deconstructed'. Why should the researcher be granted a privileged position, in being allowed to write anything he or she likes, without challenge? After all, from a discursive point of view, such a reflexive account expresses and exhibits discourses through which the reality of the researcher is constructed. The reflexive vignette placed in the heart of a Method section is a rhetorical device, designed to invoke agreement, perhaps by alluding to humanistic notions of authenticity, trustworthiness or transparency.

However, the position adopted by discourse-analytic writers is itself open to challenge. Do they believe that there is *nothing* outside the text? Is there nothing 'personal' in what they write themselves? Do their passions and desires stand aside when they write and conduct research? These are deep issues, which lie at the heart of contemporary debates over the nature of human science, regarding relativism vs. objectivity, the possibility of human agency, and the nature of knowledge itself.

In the spirit of Fay (1996) it may be possible to avoid being caught between the two poles of these dichotomies by affirming the validity of both. On the one hand, qualitative research is indeed personal, and the promotion and communication of the reflexive awareness of the expectations and experiences of the researcher contribute to the meaningfulness of a research report. On the other hand, the subjectivity of the researcher does not command a privileged position. Personal statements made by researchers are themselves positioned within discourses.

Gergen and Gergen (1991) make a distinction between constructivist and constructionist approaches to reflexivity. Constructivism and constructionism both share the (anti-positivist) view that there is no objective social world. However, for constructivists the 'constructed world' is constituted through individual cognitive activity, while for the constructionist it is constituted through historical, micro-social and cultural collective action. So, while both perspectives agree that attention to reflexivity is important and necessary, as a means of making sense of how the process of constructing happens, these positions lead to quite contrasting understandings of the meaning of reflexivity:

> Regarding the problem of reflexivity in research, a constructivist approach tends to lead inward. For if there is no exit from personal subjectivity, then we find individuals looking back at themselves in an infinite regress of cognitive dispositions. Each attempt at self-understanding (or of understanding of one's research efforts) can only lead to a replication of the same dispositions one attempts to transcend through self-replication. . . . In contrast, a social constructionist view invites the investigator outward – into the fuller realm of shared languages. The reflexive attempt is thus relational, emphasizing the expansion of languages of understanding. (Gergen and Gergen, 1991: 79)

Returning to the research by Hill et al (1996) mentioned earlier, it is possible to see that the reflexive statement offered by that research team was *constructivist*, in the sense of listing a set of 'cognitive dispositions' in the form of beliefs and expectations about the topic. For Gergen and Gergen (1991), from a constructivist perspective the only way to improve the Hill et al (1996) reflexive summary would be to explain their chosen

cognitive dispositions in terms of other cognitive constructs. This procedure could continue through several iterations, taking the reflexive
statement to greater levels of 'inward' subjectivity, and with each cycle of
reflexive exploration taking the emphasis further and further away from
the topic and inexorably refocusing it on the personal realities and inner
worlds of the members of the research team. Presumably this is why
therapy researchers such as Hill and her colleagues do not pursue their
reflexive inquiries beyond a relatively superficial level – they can see that to
take it any further would be irrelevant and a distraction from the task in
hand.

An alternative approach, recommended by Gergen and Gergen (1991), is
to move reflexively *outwards*, into the language and culture within which
one lives. Staying with the idea of a research study into therapeutic
'impasses', it is easy to see many fertile horizons of cultural meaning which
might valuably be explored. The researcher is positioned within a cultural
context within which certain ways of understanding therapeutic progress
prevail. What are the dominant stories of 'progress' (versus impasses) that
the researcher knows about? These could be stories in the literature,
personal stories, or mythic stories told by trainers or supervisors. Beyond
these therapy stories, what other broader cultural narratives might be
relevant, for instance stories of achievement, time, courage, grace?

A notion of *critical reflexivity* therefore takes to heart the ideas of
Gadamer and Heidegger, and seeks to open out for the reader not only the
personal experience of the researcher, but the *historical consciousness*
which he or she brings to the research task. The aim of critical reflexivity is
to place a piece of research within a cultural tradition, so that what
becomes visible includes both the way in which the tradition constructs the
topic, and the way in which an engagement with the topic changes the
tradition.

## Future directions in qualitative research in counselling and psychotherapy

There have been several distinct threads running through the evidence and
argument presented in this book. There are always great dangers in
attempting to reduce complex discussions to sets of action points – the risk
of oversimplifying the situation, closing down the debate, appearing
grandiose and dogmatic. Nevertheless, there seems to be some merit in
making an attempt to conclude this book with some concrete suggestions
concerning how best we might collectively proceed. Counselling and
psychotherapy are applied, professional disciplines, and the great bulk of
research in these fields needs to be tied to practical action rather than to
open-ended theorising and speculation.

This section seeks to summarise the main themes of the book in terms of a set of suggestions for the future of qualitative research in counselling and psychotherapy. These suggestions are not placed in any order of priority, and are best seen as interdependent and interlocking.

## Become philosophically informed

It may be possible to do good quantitative research without knowing much about epistemology or the philosophy of (social) science, but good qualitative research requires an informed awareness of philosophical perspectives. Qualitative psychotherapy researchers tend to use ideas from phenomenology and hermeneutics without much apparent knowledge of the origins, development and complexity of these perspectives. Awareness of philosophical issues is essential because it is clear that qualitative inquiry does not constitute a fixed, agreed method. It keeps changing, in response to individual and social circumstances. Even an apparently systematised approach such as grounded theory can be seen to include within it divergent notions of how to interpret hermeneutic and phenomenological knowledge construction moves. Ultimately, qualitative research relies on the capacity of the individual, or members of a team, to struggle with the task of knowing. To do this effectively requires possessing some kind of philosophical vocabulary for reflecting on the nature of knowing. There are many ways in which the qualitative research community can become more philosophically informed, such as the inclusion of philosophy courses in postgraduate research training, opening up areas for philosophical discussion within the literature, and inviting professional philosophers to review papers and contribute to conferences.

## Employ a broader range of writing strategies

Possibly the most important skill involved in qualitative research, and the one that is hardest to acquire, it that of *writing*. Too many published qualitative studies in counselling and psychotherapy are written in an opaque technical language that is hard going. Sometimes researchers, their attitudes shaped by the quantitative tradition, either do not perceive writing as important, or regard good writing with suspicion ('mere rhetoric'). There is little guidance or training for writers of qualitative research (but see Wolcott, 1990). There are also institutional constraints that hinder good writing. Not all qualitative research can be faithfully translated into the APA standard format. Sometimes, journals give qualitative writers too much space, or too little space. There is a growing corpus of brief (2,500-word) and highly effective qualitative research reports published in medical journals such as the *British Medical Journal* and *British Journal of General Practice*. The discipline of writing within such word limits forces authors to be clear about aims, method and findings. On the other hand, some qualitative writing needs a *lot* of space. Typically, ethnographic studies are published as research monographs or books that may be 30,000 words or more in length. There are some qualitative studies that require this kind of length in order to provide sufficient textual detail and to do justice to its analysis. Examples of book-length qualitative studies of psychotherapy include the ethnographic studies reported in Chapter 4, and also the books by O'Neill (1998) and Lott (1999). Significantly, Deborah Lott describes herself as a professional writer; her book is engaging and informative. Increasingly, also, there are possibilities for new forms of writing associated with the Internet and other electronic media. For instance, it is now quite feasible to let 'readers' *hear* or even *see* interview material. Hypertext links make it possible to give readers the option to call up textual detail, without cluttering the mainline narrative report. The openness of the Internet makes new kinds of dialogical presentation of findings, member checks and collaborative research a practical reality. The much-noted 'gap' between research and practice in counselling and psychotherapy will not be closed by replacing quantitative studies by qualitative ones, but by producing qualitative research that practitioners *want to read*.

One of the challenges facing qualitative researchers in counselling and psychotherapy is that of how best to write reflexively. No one wants to read research reports that are little better than narcissistic, disguised autobiographies. On the other hand, if critical reflexivity is acknowledged as essential to the practice of tradition-informed, hermeneutic inquiry, then researchers need to learn how to write personally and dialogically. Some of the possibilities for reflexive, dialogical writing can be seen in the new qualitative sociology, for example Kiesinger (1998) and Tillmann-Healy (1996), in the counselling research of Etherington (2000), and in the work of Richardson (1991, 1992, 1994).

## Adopt a knowledge-in-context approach

Critical reflexivity is not a psychological process of self-reflection. The implication of Gadamer's (1975) work, and also that of Gergen (1985), is to make it clear that all awareness is *historical*: we exist and make sense of things from within a culture that is itself historically constituted. What this means for research in counselling and psychotherapy is an encouragement for researchers to be more modest, and descriptive, about their findings. Very often, influenced by the conventions of laboratory science, qualitative research papers are given titles which draw attention to abstract conceptual factors or 'variables' which the researcher has observed. Also, the methods sections of papers typically provide little information about the social and institutional context of the study. The effect of all this is to emphasise what is supposedly generalisable and universal in a study, and downplay what is local and contextual. Yet, it is all but impossible for a reader to evaluate the relevance of a set of findings in the absence of rich contextual information (McLeod, 1999a). For example, in an (imaginary) study of 'the impact of counsellor self-disclosure on client outcome' it is *very* unlikely that the results of the investigation would be so clear-cut, or could be placed alongside findings of previous studies, in such a way as to lead to an unambiguous conclusion such as 'counsellor self-disclosure is useful but not in the first session'. Everyone knows that the use of self-disclosure (or any other counsellor activity) depends on the moment, the timing, the readiness of the client, the quality of the relationship, the type of expectations engendered by the counselling agency, etc., etc. Any counsellor disclosing personal information to a client will do so in an awareness of these contextual meanings. Any reader of a research paper who is *really interested* in the phenomenon will also be aware of these contextual details, and want to know as much as possible about them. It is only by placing a study in a social and historical context that the reader can fully appreciate what has been found. If one researcher finds that self-disclosure is a 'good thing' and another that it is harmful, then the explanation for these contradictory findings must be in the different contexts of the studies. However, if only thin contextual detail is supplied, the reader is left with little evidence on which to base a considered appraisal of the significance of contrasting findings. The ethnographic research tradition has always been strong on contextual detail. Knowledge about specific people, places and their history represents a fundamental dimension of knowing that has been largely eliminated from qualitative therapy research. In qualitative research in counselling and psychotherapy, the effect of including much more contextual detail would be that research papers would become more interesting and relevant for practitioners, and that tensions between apparently conflicting findings from different studies could be more readily understood.

## Invite and facilitate replication and the development of community knowledge

One of the themes running through this book has been that relatively little qualitative research has been published in the area of counselling and psychotherapy. However, as more research of this kind is carried out, it will become important to ensure that a sufficiently 'joined-up' body of work emerges. All too often, qualitative researchers carry out research which makes little productive use of the findings of previous studies into the topic. This produces a fragmented and unsatisfactory basis for knowledge around which practice can be built. Some qualitative researchers, influenced by phenomenology, try to avoid being too influenced by the literature before commencing data collection. Their goal is to be as open to the data as possible, and to produce findings that are grounded in that data rather than determined by pre-existing assumptions. However, even in phenomenologically oriented research it is possible to report findings in a form that facilitates comparisons with other studies. For example, in the exemplar study by Fischer and Wertz (1979) discussed in Chapter 3, a summary phenomenological description was produced. In principle, another team of researchers independently studying the same phenomenon could generate their own summary description, which could then be systematically compared with the one written by Fischer and Wertz. One of the most powerful and influential tools developed within quantitative research has been the technique of *meta-analysis*, which allows the findings of several studies to be aggregated statistically. Qualitative meta-analysis will always involve some degree of interpretation of findings, rather than following a strict formula. However, many qualitative studies are written in such a style that any kind of sensible meta-analysis would be almost impossible, because findings are not clearly specified but buried in a loose discussion. The vagueness of some qualitative research also inhibits replication, because it is not at all clear what could be added to what has already been 'found'. The more explicitly qualitative findings are reported, the more room there should be for subsequent researchers to identify gaps or contradictions that can be usefully clarified in further work on the topic. Another possible strategy for overcoming the fragmentation in qualitative research in therapy is through the idea of *knowledge communities*. A community of knowledge is a network of people who collectively share, in their language and practice, the knowledge of how to do something. Typically, most of this knowledge is implicit, with only part of it being formally codified in the form of research findings. If qualitative research was published in a format that made it possible for people to support, disagree with or modify findings on the basis of their implicit practical knowledge, then the scope of qualitative research could be widened. For example, if research papers were published on the Internet in a format that included a discussion forum beside each article, it might be feasible to generate a knowledge community around the topic.

## Become interdisciplinary

It is essential for psychotherapy researchers to become more familiar with examples of qualitative research in fields such as sociology, social anthropology, education, management, and health studies. Colleagues in these disciplines have more experience of qualitative research and possess a wide repertoire of methodological strategies from which counselling and psychotherapy researchers can learn. Researchers trained within conventional psychology departments are usually indoctrinated into a kind of 'methodolatry' in which methodological rigour is more important than relevance. Researchers trained in other disciplines are often more relaxed about the role of method. It is important to bring in non-psychologists to do research on therapy. Qualitative inquiry involves 'bracketing-off' assumptions about the nature of the phenomenon being studied, as far as possible. This process is very difficult for qualitative therapy researchers who are psychologists or therapists and who have spent years becoming socialised into their chosen therapeutic meta-perspective or discourse system. Researchers who do not owe professional allegiance to the therapy business may be more open to 'seeing' what is happening, particularly in relation to the experience of clients in therapy.

## Develop a review literature

In Chapter 9, a brief discussion was offered of the parallels between qualitative research and art. Both qualitative research studies and works of art can be regarded as representations of the world. However, it is possible to find two different kinds of writing in the art world. There are books and articles for artists, and books and articles for consumers of art. In all probability, the second category is more important, in numerical terms, than the first. Newspapers, magazines and television provide coverage of art exhibitions and competitions. In addition, there are many commercially successful art books. This consumer-oriented literature helps to promote interest in and awareness of art. It creates and sustains a critical language, so that people are able to talk about art – they have access to frameworks with which they can evaluate what they see. In the therapy research world, we only have the equivalent of books for artists. The literature on qualitative psychotherapy research, with very few exceptions, is concerned with how to do research. There is very little published material that comments on specific examples of research that has appeared in books or journals, or on the value and characteristics of genres of research. If an artist exhibits in a well-known gallery, there can easily be twenty or more widely disseminated critical pieces that circulate around the community of people interested in that kind of art. The existence of this group of professional critics makes it easier for ordinary art enthusiasts to engage with the exhibition, to talk about it, and to assimilate its meaning into their lives. Could it be useful for counsellors and psychotherapists to have similar access to an on-going critical discourse? Would it be useful to regard a piece of qualitative research by an important researcher such as David Rennie, Clara Hill or Robert Elliott as similar to a work of art, that is exhibited and written about by critics?

## Do outcome research

Qualitative research in counselling and psychotherapy will continue to be marginalised and undervalued until qualitative researchers get to grips with the single most important research question in the discipline, that of outcome. As long as qualitative researchers restrict themselves to studies of process, leaving quantitative investigators a monopoly on outcome, qualitative methods will continue to be regarded as second best. The issue of the effectiveness of therapy is what drives the policy agenda both for health service managers and ultimately for users/clients. People want to know how much, and in what ways, various forms of therapy *make a difference*. The counselling and psychotherapy research community is doing the public a disservice by not conducting systematic qualitative outcome studies. Existing quantitative methods occlude the true nature of outcomes, and have provided a conservative and impoverished picture of the ways in which people engage with therapy and use it to change their lives for good or ill. Qualitative outcome studies have the potential to open up important new understandings of the relationship between therapy and the everyday lives of those who make use of it.

## Forget method

Doing good qualitative research is not a matter of following a set of procedures. To accomplish worthwhile findings requires engaging as fully as possible in the topic, and then employing specific methods and techniques, in the spirit of the *bricoleur*, to bring the project to fruition. There are no hard and fast methodological rules that guarantee validity; the truth value of findings depends on achieving a successful balance between a number of factors. Qualitative researchers need to know about *methodological issues* rather than learn how to conform to step-by-step instructions on 'how to do grounded theory' or 'how to do phenomenology'. A secure basis in relevant aspects of the philosophy and sociology of social science supplies the basis for making methodological choices appropriate to the task in hand. Useful findings do not result from following a recipe, but from knowing what each step in the recipe is intended to achieve. Those who doubt this assertion might consult a paper by Chard, Lilford and Court (1997). These medical researchers carried out a citation count in relation to the impact of qualitative studies in the field of medical sociology. They discovered, not surprisingly, that qualitative papers were cited much less often than quantitative articles. What is more significant, in the context of this discussion of the role of method, is that the work that was cited most often was that of Erving Goffman, particularly *Asylums* (first in the list of qualitative 'citation classics') and *Stigma* (fourth in the list). Goffman, it should be noted, was light on method. Member checks, specifying personal assumptions, employing auditors, presenting category definitions – these are notably absent in Goffman's writings. Yet it is clear that Goffman *knew what he was doing* and also that he *had something to say*. These are virtues that we all might do well to cultivate.

# References

Aanstoos, C.M. (ed.) (1984) *Exploring the Lived World: Readings in Phenomenological Psychology*. Carrollton, GA: West Georgia College.

Allport, G. (1942) *The Use of Personal Documents in Psychological Science*. New York: Social Science Research Council.

Angus, L.E. and Rennie, D.L. (1988) 'Therapist participation in metaphor generation: collaborative and noncollaborative styles', *Psychotherapy*, 25: 552–60.

Angus, L.E. and Rennie, D.L. (1989) 'Envisioning the representational world: the client's experience of metaphoric expressiveness in psychotherapy', *Psychotherapy*, 26: 373–9.

Archer, M. (1997) *Art since 1960*. London: Thames and Hudson.

Arthern, J. and Madill, A. (1999) 'How do transition objects work? The therapist's view', *British Journal of Medical Psychology*, 72: 1–21.

Atkinson, J.M. and Heritage, J.C. (eds) (1984) *Structures of Social Action*. Cambridge: Cambridge University Press.

Atkinson, P. and Hammersley, M. (1994) 'Ethnography and participant observation', in N.K. Denzin and Y.S. Lincoln (eds), *Handbook of Qualitative Research*. London: Sage.

Bachelor, A. (1995) 'Clients' perception of the therapeutic alliance: a qualitative analysis', *Journal of Counseling Psychology*, 42: 323–37.

Barker, C. (1985) 'Interpersonal Process Recall in clinical training and research', in F.N. Watts (ed.), *New Developments in Clinical Psychology*. Chichester: Wiley/BPS.

Barthes, R. (1972) *Mythologies*. New York: Hill & Wang.

Bazerman, C. (1988) *Shaping Written Knowledge: The Genre and Activity of the Experimental Article in Science*. Madison, WI: University of Wisconsin Press.

Benjamin, W. (1970) *Illuminations*. London: Jonathan Cape.

Berger, J. (1972) *Ways of Seeing*. Harmondsworth: Penguin.

Bergin, A.E. and Garfield, S.L. (eds) (1994a) *Handbook of Psychotherapy and Behavior Change* (4th edn). Chichester: Wiley.

Bergin, A.E. and Garfield, S.L. (1994b) 'Overview, trends and future issues', in A.E. Bergin and S.L. Garfield (eds), *Handbook of Psychotherapy and Behavior Change* (4th edn). Chichester: Wiley.

Billig, M. (1987) *Arguing and Thinking: A Rhetorical Approach to Social Psychology*. Cambridge: Cambridge University Press.

Billig, M. (1997) 'The dialogic unconscious: psychoanalysis, discursive psychology and the nature of repression', *British Journal of Social Psychology*, 36: 139–59.

Billig, M. (1999) 'Whose terms? Whose ordinariness? Rhetoric and ideology in Conversation Analysis', *Discourse and Society*, 10: 543–82.

Billig, M., Condor, S., Edwards, D., Gane, M., Middleton, D. and Radley, A. (1988) *Ideological Dilemmas*. London: Sage.

Bloor, M. (1997) 'Techniques of validation in qualitative research: a critical commentary', in G. Miller and R. Dingwall (eds), *Context and Method in Qualitative Research*. London: Sage.

Bloor, M., McKeganey, N. and Fonkert, D. (1988) *One Foot in Eden: A Sociological Study of the Range of Therapeutic Community Practice*. London: Routledge.

Bochner, A.P., Ellis, C. and Tillman-Healy, L. (1998) 'Mucking about looking for truth', in B.M. Montgomery and L.A. Baxter (eds), *Dialectical Approaches to Studying Personal Relationships*. Mahwah, NJ: Lawrence Erlbaum.

Boothe, B., von Wyl, A. and Wepfer, R. (1999) 'Narrative dynamics and psychodynamics', *Psychotherapy Research*, 9: 258–73.

Brannen, J. (ed.) (1992) *Mixing Methods: Qualitative and Quantitative Research*. Aldershot: Avebury.

Branthwaite, A. and Lunn, T. (1983) 'Projective techniques in social and market research', in R. Walker (ed.), *Applied Qualitative Research*. Aldershot: Gower.

Bristol, T. and Fern, E.F. (1996) 'Exploring the atmosphere created by focus group interviews: comparing consumers' feelings across qualitative techniques', *Journal of the Market Research Society*, 38: 185–95.

Brown, S.D. (1999) 'Stress as regimen: critical readings of self-help literature', in C. Willig (ed.), *Applied Discourse Analysis: Sociological and Psychological Interventions*. Buckingham: Open University Press.

Bruner, E.M. (1993) 'Introduction: the ethnographic self and the personal self', in P. Benson (ed.), *Anthropology and Literature*. Urbana, IL: University of Illinois Press.

Bruner, J.S. (1986) *Actual Minds, Possible Worlds*. Cambridge, MA: Harvard University Press.

Bruner, J.S. (1990) *Acts of Meaning*. Cambridge, MA: Harvard University Press.

Bruner, J.S. (1993) 'Loyal opposition and the clarity of dissent: commentary on Donald P. Spence's "The Hermeneutic Turn"', *Psychoanalytic Dialogues*, 3: 11–19.

Bryman, A. (1984) 'The debate about quantitative and qualitative research: a question of method or epistemology?' *British Journal of Sociology*, 35 (1): 75–93.

Bullington, J. and Karlsson, G. (1984) 'Introduction to phenomenological psychological research', *Scandinavian Journal of Psychology*, 25: 51–63.

Caputo, J.D. (1993) *Demythologizing Heidegger*. Bloomington, IN: Indiana University Press.

Chard, J.A., Lilford, R.J. and Court, B.V. (1997) 'Qualitative medical sociology: what are its crowning achievements?' *Journal of the Royal Society of Medicine*, 9: 504–9.

Charity, A. (1995) *Doing Public Journalism*. New York: Guilford Press.

Charmaz, C. (1990) 'Discovering chronic illness: using grounded theory', *Social Science and Medicine*, 30: 1161–72.

Charmaz, C. (1995) 'Grounded theory', in J. Smith, R. Harré and L. van Langenhove (eds), *Rethinking Methods in Psychology*. London: Sage.

Christopher, J.C. (1996) 'Counseling's inescapable moral visions', *Journal of Counseling and Development*, 75: 17–25.

Cohen, L.H., Sargent, M.M. and Sechrest, L.B. (1986) 'Use of psychotherapy research by professional psychologists', *American Psychologist*, 41: 198–206.

Colaizzi, P.F. (1978) 'Psychological research as the phenomenologist views it', in R.S. Valle and M. King (eds), *Existential-Phenomenological Alternatives for Psychology*. New York: Oxford University Press.

Crotty, M. (1996) *Phenomenology and Nursing Research*. South Melbourne, Australia: Churchill Livingstone.

Cummings, A.L., Hallberg, E.T. and Slemon, A.G. (1994) 'Templates of client change in short-term counseling', *Journal of Counseling Psychology*, 41 (4): 464–72.

Cushman, P. (1990) 'Why the self is empty: toward a historically-situated psychology', *American Psychologist*, 45: 599–611.

Cushman, P. (1992) 'Psychotherapy to 1992: a historically-situated interpretation', in D.K. Freedheim (ed.), *History of Psychotherapy: a Century of Change*. Washington, DC: American Psychological Association.

Cushman, P. (1995) *Constructing the Self, Constructing America: A Cultural History of Psychotherapy*. New York: Addison-Wesley.

Czarniawska, B. (1998) *A Narrative Approach to Organization Studies*. Thousand Oaks, CA: Sage.

Dale, P., Allen, J. and Measor, L. (1998) 'Counselling adults who were abused as children: clients' perceptions of efficacy, client–counsellor communication, and dissatisfaction', *British Journal of Guidance and Counselling*, 26: 141–58.

Davis, B. and Harré, R. (1990) 'Positioning the discursive production of selves', *Journal for the Theory of Social Behaviour*, 20: 42–63.

Davis, K. (1986) 'The process of problem (re)formulation in psychotherapy', *Sociology of Illness and Health*, 8: 44–74.

Danziger, K. (1990) *Constructing the Subject: Historical Origins of Psychological Research*. Cambridge: Cambridge University Press.

Danziger, K. (1997a) *Naming the Mind: How Psychology Found its Language*. Thousand Oaks, CA: Sage.

Danziger, K. (1997b) 'The varieties of social construction', *Theory and Psychology*, 7: 399–416.

de Rivera, J. (ed.) (1976) *Field Theory as Human Science*. New York: Gardner Press.

de Rivera, J. (1981) *Conceptual Encounter: A Method for the Exploration of Human Experience*. Washington, DC: University Press of America.

de Rivera, J. (1989) 'Choice of emotion and ideal development', in L. Cirillo, B. Kaplan and S. Wapner (eds), *Emotions in Ideal Human Development*. Hillsdale, NJ: Erlbaum.

de Rivera, J. (1991) 'The structure and dynamics of emotion', in A.J. Stewart, J.M. Healy, Jr. and D. Ozer (eds), *Approaches to Understanding Lives. Perspectives in Personality*, Vol. 3, Part A. London: Jessica Kingsley.

de Rivera, J. (1997) 'The construction of false memory syndrome: the experience of retractors', *Psychological Inquiry*, 8: 271–92.

Delbecq, A.L., Van de Ven, A.H. and Gustafson, D.H. (1975) *Group Techniques for Program Planning: A Guide to Nominal Group and Delphi Techniques*. Glenview, IL: Scott, Foresman.

Dennis, M., Fetterman, D.M., and Sechrest, L. (1994) 'Integrating qualitative and quantitative evaluation methods in substance abuse research', *Evaluation and Program Planning*, 17: 419–27.

Denzin, N.K. (1997) *Interpretive Ethnography: Ethnographic Practices for the 21st Century*. Thousand Oaks, CA: Sage.

Denzin, N.K. and Lincoln, Y.S. (eds) (1994a) *Handbook of Qualitative Research*. Thousand Oaks, CA: Sage.

Denzin, N.K. and Lincoln, Y.S. (1994b) 'Introduction: Entering the field of qualitative research', in N.K. Denzin and Y.S. Lincoln (eds), *Handbook of Qualitative Research*. Thousand Oaks, CA: Sage.

Dinnage, R. (1988) *One to One: The Experience of Psychotherapy*. London: Viking.

Douglass, B. and Moustakas, C. (1985) 'Heuristic inquiry; the internal search to know', *Journal of Humanistic Psychology*, 25: 39–55.

Edwards, D. (1995) 'Two to tango: script formulations, dispositions, and rhetorical symmetry in relationship troubles talk', *Research on Language and Social Interaction*, 28: 319–50.

Elliott, R. (1983a) 'That in your hands . . .': a comprehensive process analysis of a significant event in psychotherapy', *Psychiatry*, 46: 113–29.

Elliott, R. (1983b) 'Fitting process research to the practicing psychotherapist', *Psychotherapy*, 20 (1): 47–55.

Elliott, R. (1984) 'A discovery-oriented approach to significant change events in psychotherapy: Interpersonal Process Recall and Comprehensive Process Analysis', in L.N. Rice and L.S. Greenberg (eds), *Patterns of*

*Change: Intensive Analysis of Psychotherapy Process.* New York: Guilford Press.

Elliott, R. (1986) 'Interpersonal Process Recall (IPR) as a psychotherapy process research method', in L.S. Greenberg and W.M. Pinsof (eds), *The Psychotherapeutic Process: A Research Handbook.* New York: Guilford Press.

Elliott, R. (1993) *Comprehensive Process Analysis: Mapping the Change Process in Psychotherapy.* Unpublished manual. Available from Dept of Psychology, University of Toledo, Toledo, Ohio, USA.

Elliott, R. and Shapiro, D.A. (1988) 'Brief Structured Recall: a more efficient method for studying significant therapy events', *British Journal of Medical Psychology,* 61: 141–53.

Elliott, R. and Shapiro, D.A. (1992) 'Client and therapist as analysts of significant events', in S.G. Toukmanian and D.L. Rennie (eds), *Psychotherapy Process Research: Paradigmatic and Narrative Approaches.* London: Sage.

Elliott, R., Fischer, C.T. and Rennie, D.L. (1999) 'Evolving guidelines for the publication of qualitative research studies in psychology and related fields', *British Journal of Clinical Psychology,* 38: 215–29.

Elliott, R., Hill, C.E., Stiles, W.B., Friedlander, M.L., Mahrer, A. and Margison, F. (1987) 'Primary therapist response modes: A comparison of six rating systems', *Journal of Consulting and Clinical Psychology,* 55: 218–23.

Elliott, R., Shapiro, D.A., Firth-Cozens, J., Stiles, W.B., Hardy, G.E., Llewelyn, S.P. and Margison, F.R. (1994) 'Comprehensive Process Analysis of insight events in cognitive-behavioral and psychodynamic-interpersonal psychotherapies', *Journal of Counseling Psychology,* 41: 449–63.

Ellis, C. and Bochner, A. (eds) (1996) *Composing Ethnography: Alternative Forms of Qualitative Writing.* Thousand Oaks, CA: Sage.

Ellis, C. and Flaherty, M. (eds) (1992) *Investigating Subjectivity: Research on Lived Experience.* Thousand Oaks, CA: Sage.

Ellis, C., Kiesinger, C.E. and Tillmann-Healy, L.M. (1997) 'Interactive interviewing: talking about emotional experience', in R. Hertz (ed.), *Reflexivity and Voice.* Thousand Oaks, CA: Sage.

Ericsson, K.A. and Simon, H. (1984) *Protocol Analysis: Verbal Reports as Data.* Cambridge, MA: MIT Press.

Erickson, K. and Stull, D. (1998) *Doing Team Ethnography: Warnings and Advice.* Thousand Oaks, CA: Sage.

Etherington, K. (1996) 'The counsellor as researcher: boundary issues and critical dilemmas', *British Journal of Guidance and Counselling,* 24 (3): 339–46

Etherington, K. (2000) *Narrative Approaches to Working with Adult Male Survivors of Child Sexual Abuse: The Clients', the Counsellor's and the Researcher's Story.* London: Jessica Kingsley.

Fay, B. (1996) *Contemporary Philosophy of Social Science: a Multicultural Approach*. Oxford: Blackwell.

Fessler, R. (1983) 'Phenomenology and the "talking cure": research on psychotherapy', in A. Giorgi, A. Barton and C. Maes (eds), *Duquesne Studies in Phenomenological Psychology, Vol. 4*. Pittsburgh, PA: Duquesne University Press.

Fetterman, D.M. (1998) 'Ethnography', in J.L. Bickman and D.J. Rog (eds), *Handbook of Social Research Methods*. Thousand Oaks, CA: Sage.

Fielding, N. (1993) 'Ethnography', in N. Gilbert (ed.), *Researching Social Life*. London: Sage.

Fischer, C.T. (1984) 'A phenomenological study of being criminally victimized: contributions and constraints of qualitative research', *Journal of Social Issues*, 40: 161–78.

Fischer, C.T. and Wertz, F.J. (1979) 'Empirical phenomenological analyses of being criminally victimized', in A. Giorgi, R. Knowles and D.L. Smith (eds), *Duquesne Studies in Phenomenological Psychology, Vol. 3*. Pittsburgh, PA: Duquesne University Press.

Fischer, C.T., Eckenrod, J., Embree, S.M. and Jarzynka, J.F. (2000) 'Empirical phenomenological research in psychotherapy: Duquesne dissertations', in J. Frommer and D.L. Rennie (eds), *Qualitative Psychotherapy Research: Methods and Methodology*. Berlin: Pabst.

Fish, L.S. and Busby, D.M. (1996) 'The Delphi method', in D.H. Sprenkle and S.M. Moon (eds), *Research Methods in Family Therapy*. New York: Guilford Press.

Flick, U. (1998) *An Introduction to Qualitative Research*. London: Sage.

Fonteyn, M.E., Kuipers, B. and Grobe, S.J. (1993) 'A description of think aloud method and protocol analysis', *Qualitative Health Research*, 3: 430–41.

Frank, A.W. (1992) 'The pedagogy of suffering: moral dimensions of psychological therapy and research with the ill', *Theory and Psychology*, 2: 467–85.

Frank, J. (1974) 'Psychotherapy: the restoration of morale', *American Journal of Psychiatry*, 131: 271–4.

Frommer, J., Reissner, V., Tress, W. and Langenbach, M. (1996) 'Subjective theories of illness in patients with personality disorders: qualitative comparison of twelve diagnostic interviews', *Psychotherapy Research*, 6: 56–69.

Frontman, K.C. and Kunkel, K.A. (1994) 'A grounded theory of counselors' construal of success in the initial session', *Journal of Counseling Psychology*, 41: 492–9.

Gadamer, H. (1975) *Truth and Method* (2nd edn). New York: Continuum.

Gale, J.E. (ed.) (1991) *Conversation Analysis of Therapeutic Discourse: The Pursuit of a Therapeutic Agenda*. Norwood, NJ: Ablex.

Gale, J.E. and Newfield, N. (1992) 'A conversation analysis of a solution-focused marital therapy session', *Journal of Marital and Family Therapy*, 18: 153–65.

Gale, J., Chenail, R., Watson, W.L., Wright, L.M. and Bell, J.M. (1996) 'Research and practice: a reflexive and recursive relationship – three narratives, five voices', *Marriage and Family Review*, 24: 275–95.

Garfinkel, H. (1967) *Studies in Ethnomethodology*. Englewood Cliffs, NJ: Prentice-Hall.

Gee, J.P. (1986) 'Units in the production of narrative discourse', *Discourse Processes*, 9: 391–422.

Gee, J.P. (1991) 'A linguistic approach to narrative', *Journal of Narrative and Life History*, 1: 15–39.

Geertz, C. (1973) *The Interpretation of Culture: Selected Essays*. New York: Basic Books.

Geertz, C. (1983) *Local Knowledge: Further Essays in Interpretive Anthropology*. New York: Basic Books.

Gergen, K.J. (1985) 'The social constructionist movement in modern psychology', *American Psychologist*, 40: 266–75.

Gergen, K.J. (1988) 'If persons are texts', in S.B. Messer, L.A. Sass and R.L. Woolfolk (eds), *Hermeneutics and Psychological Theory: Interpretive Perspectives on Personality, Psychotherapy and Psychopathology*. New Brunswick, NJ: Rutgers University Press.

Gergen, K.J. (1994a) *Toward Transformation in Social Knowledge* (2nd edn). London: Sage.

Gergen, K.J. (1994b) *Realities and Relationships: Soundings in Social Construction*. Cambridge, MA: Harvard University Press.

Gergen, K.J. (1997) 'Who speaks and who replies in human science scholarship?' *History of the Human Sciences*, 10 (3): 151–73.

Gergen, K.J. and Gergen, M.M. (1991) 'Toward reflexive methodologies', in F. Steier (ed.), *Research and Reflexivity*. London: Sage.

Giorgi, A. (1970) *Psychology as a Human Science*. New York: Harper and Row.

Glaser, B.J. (1978) *Theoretical Sensitivity: Advances in the Methodology of Grounded Theory*. Mill Valley, CA: Sociology Press.

Glaser, B.J. (1982) *Emerging vs. Forcing: The Basics of Grounded Theory Research*. Mill Valley, CA: Sociology Press.

Glaser, B.J. and Strauss, A. (1967) *The Discovery of Grounded Theory*. Chicago: Aldine.

Goffman, E. (1968a) *Asylums: Essays on the Social Situation of Mental Patients and Other Inmates*. Harmondsworth: Penguin.

Goffman, E. (1968b) *Stigma*. Harmondsworth: Penguin.

Goldstein, A.E., Safarik, L., Reibolt, W., Albright, L. and Kellett, C. (1996) 'An ethnographic approach to understanding service use among ethnically diverse low income families', *Marriage and Family Review*, 24: 297–321.

Goss, S. and Mearns, D. (1997a) 'A call for a pluralistic epistemological understanding in the assessment and evaluation of counselling', *British Journal of Guidance and Counselling*, 25: 189–98.

Goss, S. and Mearns, D. (1997b) 'Applied pluralism in the evaluation of employee counselling', *British Journal of Guidance and Counselling*, 25: 327–44.

Grafanaki, S. (1996) 'How research can change the researcher: the need for sensitivity, flexibility and ethical boundaries in conducting qualitative research in counselling / psychotherapy', *British Journal of Guidance and Counselling*, 24 (3): 329–38.

Grafanaki, S. and McLeod, J. (1999) 'Narrative processes in the construction of helpful and hindering events in experiential psychotherapy', *Psychotherapy Research*, 9: 289–303.

Greenbaum, T.L. (1998) *The Handbook for Focus Group Research* (2nd edn). Thousand Oaks, CA: Sage.

Greenberg, G. (1994) *The Self on the Shelf: Recovery Books and the Good Life*. Albany, NY: State University of New York Press.

Greenberg, L.S. (1984a) 'A task analysis of intrapersonal conflict resolution', in L.N. Rice and L.S. Greenberg (eds), *Patterns of Change: Intensive Analysis of Psychotherapy Process*. New York: Guilford Press.

Greenberg, L.S. (1984b) 'Task analysis: the general approach', in L.N. Rice and L.S. Greenberg (eds), *Patterns of Change: Intensive Analysis of Psychotherapy Process*. New York: Guilford Press.

Greenberg, L.S. (1992) 'Task analysis: identifying components of interpersonal conflict resolution', in S.G. Toukmanian and D.L. Rennie (eds), *Psychotherapy Process Research: Paradigmatic and Narrative Approaches*. London: Sage.

Greenberg, L.S., Elliott, R.K. and Lietaer, G. (1994) 'Research on experiential psychotherapies', in A.E. Bergin and S.L. Garfield (eds), *Handbook of Psychotherapy and Behavior Change* (4th edn). Chichester: Wiley.

Greenberg, L.S., Rice, L.N. and Elliott, R. (1993) *Facilitating Emotional Change: The Moment-by-Moment Process*. New York: Guilford Press.

Greene, J.C. (1998) 'Qualitative, interpretive evaluation', in A.J. Reynolds and H.J. Walberg (eds), *Advances in Educational Productivity*, Vol. 7, *Evaluation Research for Educational Productivity*. Greenwich, CT: JAI Press.

Guba, E.G. and Lincoln, Y.S. (1994) 'Competing paradigms in qualitative research', in N.K. Denzin and Y.S. Lincoln (eds), *Handbook of Qualitative Research*. London: Sage.

Gubrium, J.F. (1992) *Out of Control: Family Therapy and Domestic Disorder*. Newbury Park, CA: Sage.

Hammersley, M. (ed.) (1993) *Social Research: Philosophy, Politics and Practice*. London: Sage.

Hammersley, M. (1999) 'Not bricolage but boatbuilding: exploring two metaphors for thinking about ethnography', *Journal of Contemporary Ethnography*, 28: 574–85.

Haraway, D. (1988) 'Situated knowledges: the science question in feminism and the privilege of partial perspective', *Feminist Studies*, 14: 575–99.

Hardy, G.E., Rees, A., Barkham, M., Field, S.D., Elliott, R. and Shapiro, D.A. (1998) 'Whingeing versus working: Comprehensive Process Analysis of a "vague awareness" event in psychodynamic-interpersonal therapy', *Psychotherapy Research*, 8: 334–53.

Harré, R. (1995) 'Discursive psychology', in J.A. Smith, R. Harré and L. van Langenhove (eds), *Rethinking Psychology*. London: Sage.

Hasenfeld, Y. (1992) 'Theoretical approaches to human service organizations', in Y. Hasenfeld (ed.), *Human Services as Complex Organizations*. Thousand Oaks, CA: Sage.

Hayes, J.A., McCracken, J.E., McClanahan, M.K., Hill, C.E., Harp, J.S. and Carozzini, P. (1998) 'Therapist perspectives on countertransference: qualitative data in search of a theory', *Journal of Counseling Psychology*, 45: 468–82.

Heath, A.E., Neimeyer, G.J. and Pedersen, P.B. (1988) 'The future of cross-cultural counselling: a Delphi poll', *Journal of Counseling and Development*, 67: 27–30.

Heidegger, M. (1962) *Being and Time*. Oxford: Blackwell.

Hener, T., Weisenberg, M., and Har-Even, D. (1996) 'Supportive versus cognitive-behavioral intervention programs in achieving adjustment to home peritoneal dialysis', *Journal of Consulting and Clinical Psychology*, 64 (4): 731–41.

Heritage, J. (1984) *Garfinkel and Ethnomethodology*. Cambridge: Polity.

Heritage, J. (1997) 'Conversation Analysis and institutional talk: analysing data', in D. Silverman (ed.), *Qualitative Research: Theory, Method and Practice*. London: Sage.

Herman, S.E., Marvenko, M.O. and Hazel, K.L. (1996) 'Parents' perspectives on quality in family support programs', *Journal of Mental Health Administration*, 23: 156–69.

Heron, J. (1996) *Co-operative Inquiry: Research into the Human Condition*. London: Sage.

Hertz, R. (ed.) (1997) *Reflexivity and Voice*. Thousand Oaks, CA: Sage.

Hill, C.E. (1989) *Therapist Techniques and Client Outcomes: Eight Cases of Brief Psychotherapy*. London: Sage.

Hill, C.E., Nutt-Williams, E. and Thompson, B.J. (1997) 'A rejoinder to Stiles's, Hoshmand's and Tinsley's comments about "A guide to conducting consensual qualitative research"', *Counseling Psychologist*, 25: 606–14.

Hill, C.E., Thompson, B.J. and Nutt-Williams, E. (1997) 'A guide to conducting consensual qualitative research', *Counseling Psychologist*, 25: 517–72.

Hill, C.E., Nutt-Williams, E., Heaton, K.J, Thompson, B.J. and Rhodes,

R.H. (1996) 'Therapist retrospective recall of impasses in long-term psychotherapy: a qualitative analysis', *Journal of Counseling Psychology*, 43: 207–17.

Hingley, S.M. (1995) 'Cognition, emotion and defence: processes and mechanisms of change in a brief psychotherapy for depression', *Clinical Psychology and Psychotherapy*, 2: 122–33.

Honos-Webb, L. and Stiles, W.B. (1998) 'Reformulation of assimilation analysis in terms of voices', *Psychotherapy*, 35: 23–33.

Honos-Webb, L., Surko, M. and Stiles, W.B. (1998) *Manual for Rating Assimilation in Psychotherapy*. Unpublished manual. Available from Dept of Psychology, Miami University, Ohio, USA.

Hoshmand, L.T. and Martin, J. (eds) (1994) *Method Choice and Inquiry Process: Lessons from Programmatic Research in Therapeutic Psychology*. New York: Teachers' Press.

Hoshmand, L.T. (1997) 'The normative context of research practice', *Counseling Psychologist*, 25: 599–605.

Howard, G.S. (1983) 'Toward methodological pluralism', *Journal of Counseling Psychology*, 30 (1): 19–21.

Howard, G.S. (1985) 'The role of values in the science of psychology', *American Psychologist*, 40: 255–65.

Howe, D. (1989) *The Consumer's View of Family Therapy*. Aldershot: Gower.

Howe, D. (1996) 'Client experiences of counselling and treatment interventions: a qualitative study of family views of family therapy', *British Journal of Guidance and Counselling*, 24: 367–76.

Huberman, A.M. and Miles, M.B. (1994) 'Data management and analysis methods', in N.K. Denzin and Y.S. Lincoln (eds), *Handbook of Qualitative Research*. London: Sage.

Husserl, E. (1960) *Cartesian Meditations: An Introduction to Phenomenology*. Translated by Dorion Cairns. The Hague: Nijhoff.

Hycner, R.H. (1985) 'Some guidelines for the phenomenological analysis of interview data', *Human Studies*, 8: 279–303.

Hyde, C. (1994) 'Reflections on a journey: a research story', in C.K. Riessman (ed.), *Qualitative Studies in Social Work Research*. Thousand Oaks, CA: Sage.

Jackson, A.P. and Patton, M.J. (1992) 'A hermeneutic approach to the study of values in counseling', *Counseling and Values*, 36: 201–19.

Josselson, R. (ed.) (1996a) *Ethics and Process in the Narrative Study of Lives*. Thousand Oaks, CA: Sage.

Josselson, R. (1996b) 'On writing other people's lives: self-analytic reflections of a narrative researcher', in R. Josselson (ed.), *Ethics and Process in the Narrative Study of Lives*. Thousand Oaks, CA: Sage.

Josselson, R. and Lieblich, A. (eds) (1993) *The Narrative Study of Lives*, Vol. 1. London: Sage.

Josselson, R. and Lieblich, A. (eds) (1995) *Interpreting Experience: The Narrative Study of Lives*, Vol. 3. London: Sage.

Josselson, R. and Lieblich, A. (eds) (1999) *Meaning Making of Narratives: Narrative Study of Lives*, Vol. 6. Thousand Oaks, CA: Sage.

Josselson, R., Lieblich, A., Sharabany, R. and Wiseman, H. (1997) *Conversation as Method: Analyzing the Relational World of People who were Raised Communally*. Thousand Oaks, CA: Sage.

Kagan, N. (1980) 'Influencing human interaction: 18 years with IPR', in A.K. Hess (ed.), *Psychotherapy Supervision: Theory, Research and Practice*. Chichester: Wiley.

Kagan, N. (1984) 'Interpersonal Process Recall: basic methods and recent research', in D. Larsen (ed.), *Teaching Psychological Skills*. Monterey, CA: Brooks/Cole.

Kiesinger, C.E. (1998) 'From interview to story: writing Abbie's life', *Qualitative Inquiry*, 4: 71–95.

Knox, S., Hess, S.A., Petersen, D.A. and Hill, C.E. (1997) 'A qualitative analysis of client perceptions of the effects of helpful therapist self-disclosure in long-term therapy', *Journal of Counseling Psychology*, 44: 274–83.

Kolakowski, L. (1993) 'An overall view of positivism', in M. Hammersley (ed.), *Social Research: Philosophy, Politics and Practice*. London: Sage.

Kools, S., McCarthy, M., Durham, R. and Robrecht, L. (1996) 'Dimensional analysis: broadening the conception of grounded theory', *Qualitative Health Research*, 6: 312–30.

Kovel, J. (1981) 'The American mental health industry', in D. Ingleby (ed.), *Critical Psychiatry: the Politics of Mental Health*. Harmondsworth: Penguin.

Krueger, R. (1994) *Focus Groups: A Practical Guide for Applied Research*. London: Sage.

Kuehl, B.P., Newfield, N.A. and Joanning, H. (1990) 'A client-based description of family therapy', *Journal of Family Psychology*, 3: 310–21.

Kuhn, T.S. (1962) *The Structure of Scientific Revolutions*. Chicago: University of Chicago Press.

Kuhnlein, I. (1999) 'Psychotherapy as a process of transformation: the analysis of posttherapeutic autobiographical narrations', *Psychotherapy Research*, 9: 274–88.

Kvale, S. (1996) *InterViews: An Introduction to Qualitative Research Interviewing*. London: Sage.

Kvale, S. (2000) 'The psychoanalytic interview as qualitative research', in J. Frommer and D.L. Rennie (eds), *Qualitative Psychotherapy Research: Methods and Methodology*. Berlin: Pabst.

Labott, S.M., Elliott, R. and Eason, P.S. (1992) '"If you love someone, you don't hurt them": a Comprehensive Process Analysis of a weeping event in therapy', *Psychiatry*, 55: 49–62.

Labov, W. and Fanshel, D. (1977) *Therapeutic Discourse*. New York: Academic Press.

Labov, W. and Waletzky, J. (1967) 'Narrative analysis: oral versions of personal experience', in J. Helm (ed.), *Essays on the Verbal and Visual Arts*. Seattle, WA: University of Washington Press.

Ladany, N., O'Brien, K., Hill, C.E., Melincoff, D., Knox, S. and Petersen, D. (1997) 'Sexual attraction toward clients, use of supervision, and prior training: a qualitative study of psychotherapy predoctoral interns', *Journal of Counseling Psychology*, 44: 413–24.

Laing, R.D. (1960) *The Divided Self: An Existential Study in Sanity and Madness*. Harmondsworth: Penguin.

Laing, R.D. (1961) *Self and Others*. Harmondsworth: Penguin.

Laing, R.D. and Esterson, A. (1964) *Sanity, Madness and the Family: Families of Schizophrenics*. Harmondsworth: Penguin.

Laing, R.D., Phillipson, N. and Lee, A.R. (1966) *Interpersonal Perception: A Theory and a Method of Research*. London: Tavistock.

Lieblich, A. and Josselson, R. (eds) (1994) *Exploring Identity and Gender: The Narrative Study of Lives*, Vol. 2. London: Sage.

Lincoln, Y.S. (1995) 'The sixth moment: emerging problems in qualitative research', *Studies in Symbolic Interaction*, 19: 37–55.

Lincoln, Y.S. and Denzin, N.K. (1994) 'The fifth moment', in N.K. Denzin and Y.S. Lincoln (eds), *Handbook of Qualitative Research*. Thousand Oaks, CA: Sage.

Lindsay-Hart, J., de Rivera, J. and Mascolo, M.F. (1995) 'Differentiating shame and guilt and their effects on motivation', in J.P. Tangnay and K.W. Fischer (eds), *Self-Conscious Emotions: The Psychology of Shame, Guilt, Embarrassment and Pride*. New York: Guilford Press.

Llewelyn, S.P., Elliott, R., Shapiro, D.A., Hardy, G. and Firtu-Cozens, J. (1988) 'Client perceptions of significant events in prescriptive and exploratory periods of individual therapy', *British Journal of Clinical Psychology*, 27: 105–14.

Lofland, J. (1971) *Analyzing Social Settings: A Guide to Qualitative Observation and Analysis*. Belmont, CA: Wadsworth.

Lott, D.A. (1999) *In Session: The Bond between Women and their Therapists*. New York: W.H. Freeman.

Macdonald, K. and Tipton, C. (1993) 'Using documents', in N. Gilbert (ed.), *Researching Social Life*. London: Sage.

Madill, A. and Barkham, M. (1997) 'Discourse analysis of a theme in one successful case of brief psychodynamic-interpersonal psychotherapy', *Journal of Counseling Psychology*, 44: 232–44.

Madill, A. and Docherty, K. (1994) '"So you did what you wanted then": discourse analysis, personal agency, and psychotherapy', *Journal of Community and Applied Social Psychology*, 4: 261–73.

Madill, A., Jordan, A. and Shirley, C. (2000) 'Objectivity and reliability in qualitative analysis: realist, contextualist and radical constructionist epistemologies', *British Journal of Psychology*, 91: 1–20.

Mair, M. (1989) *Between Psychology and Psychotherapy: A Poetics of Experience*. London: Routledge.

McClelland, D.C. (1980) 'Motive dispositions: the merits of operant and respondent measures', in L. Wheeler (ed.), *Review of Personality and Social Psychology*. Thousand Oaks, CA: Sage.

McKenna, P.A. and Todd, D.M. (1997) 'Longitudinal utilization of mental health services: a time-line method, nine retrospective accounts, and a preliminary conceptualization', *Psychotherapy Research*, 7: 383–96.

McLeod, J. (1994) *Doing Counselling Research*. London: Sage.

McLeod. J. (1997) *Narrative and Psychotherapy*. London: Sage.

McLeod, J. (1999a) *Practitioner Research in Counselling*. London: Sage.

McLeod, J. (1999b) 'Counselling as a social process', *Counselling*, 10: 217–22.

McLeod, J. and Balamoutsou, S. (1996) 'Representing narrative process in therapy: qualitative analysis of a single case', *Counselling Psychology Quarterly*, 9: 61–76.

McLeod, J. and Balamoutsou, S. (2000) 'A method for qualitative narrative analysis of psychotherapy transcripts', in J. Frommer and D.L. Rennie (eds), *Qualitative Psychotherapy Research: Methods and Methodology*. Berlin: Pabst.

Mearns, D. and McLeod, J. (1984) 'A person-centred approach to research', in R. Levant and J. Shlien (eds), *Client-Centered Therapy and the Person-Centered Approach: New Directions in Theory, Research and Practice*. New York: Praeger.

Melia, K. (1996) 'Rediscovering Glaser', *Qualitative Health Research*, 6: 368–78.

Messer, S.B., Sass, L.A. and Woolfolk, R.L. (eds) (1988) *Hermeneutics and Psychological Theory: Interpretive Perspectives on Personality, Psychotherapy and Psychopathology*. New Brunswick: Rutgers University Press.

Miles, M. and Huberman, A. (1994) *Qualitative Data Analysis: A Sourcebook of New Methods* (2nd edn). London: Sage.

Miller, G. and Silverman, D. (1995) 'Troubles talk and counselling discourse: a comparative study', *Sociological Quarterly*, 36: 725–47.

Miller, T., Velleman, R., Rigby, K., Orford, J., Tod, A., Copello, A. and Bennett, G. (1997) 'The use of vignettes in the analysis of interview data: relatives of people with drug problems', in N. Hayes (ed.), *Doing Qualitative Analysis in Psychology*. Hove: Psychology Press.

Mishler, E.G. (1986) *Research Interviewing: Context and Narrative*. Cambridge, MA: Harvard University Press.

Moodley, R. (1998) '"I say what I like": frank talk(ing) in counselling and psychotherapy', *British Journal of Guidance and Counselling*, 26: 495–508.

Moran, D. (2000) *Introduction to Phenomenology*. London: Routledge.

Morison, M. and Moir, J. (1998) 'The role of computer software in the analysis of qualitative data: efficient clerk, research assistant or Trojan horse?' *Journal of Advanced Nursing*, 28: 106–16.

Morley, S. (1989) 'Single-case research', in G. Parry and F. Watts (eds), *Behavioural and Mental Health Research: a Handbook of Skills and Methods*. London: Lawrence Erlbaum.

Morrow-Bradley, C. and Elliott, R. (1986) 'Utilization of psychotherapy research by practicing psychotherapists', *American Psychologist*, 41 (2): 188–97.

Moustakas, C. (1967) 'Heuristic research', in J. Bugental (ed.), *Challenges of Humanistic Psychology*. New York: McGraw-Hill.

Moustakas, C. (1990a) *Heuristic Research: Design, Methodology and Applications*. Thousand Oaks, CA: Sage.

Moustakas, C. (1990b) 'Heuristic research, design and methodology', *Person-Centered Review*, 5: 170–90.

Moustakas, C. (1994) *Phenomenological Research Methods*. London: Sage.

Mueller-Vollmer, K. (1985) 'Language, mind and artifact: an outline of hermeneutic theory since the Enlightenment', in K. Mueller-Vollmer (ed.), *The Hermeneutics Reader: Texts of the German Tradition from the Enlightenment to the Present*. Oxford: Blackwell.

Natanson, M. (1973) *Edmund Husserl: Philosopher of Infinite Tasks*. Evanston, IL: Northwestern University Press.

Neimeyer, G.J. and Norcross, J.C. (1997) 'The future of psychotherapy and counseling psychology in the USA: Delphi data and beyond', in S. Palmer and V. Varma (eds), *The Future of Counselling and Psychotherapy*. London: Sage.

Neufeldt, S.A., Karno, M.P. and Nelson, M.L. (1996) 'A qualitative study of experts' conceptualization of supervisee reflexivity', *Journal of Counseling Psychology*, 43: 3–9.

Newfield, N.A., Kuehl, B.P., Joanning, H.P. and Quinn, W.H. (1990) 'A mini ethnography of the family therapy of adolescent drug abuse: the ambiguous experience', *Alcoholism Treatment Quarterly*, 7: 57–79.

Nightingale, D.J. and Cromby, J. (eds) (1999) *Social Constructionist Psychology: A Critical Analysis of Theory and Practice*. Buckingham: Open University Press.

O'Callaghan, J. (1998) 'Grounded theory: a potential methodology', in P. Clarkson (ed.), *Counselling Psychology*. London: Routledge.

O'Hanlon, W.M. (1991) Foreword, in J.E. Gale (ed.), *Conversation Analysis of Therapeutic Discourse: The Pursuit of a Therapeutic Agenda*. Norwood, NJ: Ablex.

Olesen, V., Droes, N., Hatton, D., Chico, N. and Schatzman, L. (1994) 'Analyzing together: recollections of a team approach', in A. Bryman and R.G. Burgess (eds), *Analyzing Qualitative Data*. London: Routledge.

O'Neill, P. (1998) *Negotiating Consent in Psychotherapy*. New York: New York University Press.

Osborne, J.W. (1994) 'Some similarities and differences among phenomenological and other methods of psychological qualitative research', *Canadian Psychology*, 35: 167–89.

Ossorio, P.G. (1985) 'An overview of descriptive psychology', in K.J. Gergen and K.E. Davis (eds), *The Social Construction of the Person*. New York: Springer-Verlag.

Packer, M. (1985) 'Hermeneutic inquiry in the study of human conduct', *American Psychologist*, 40: 1081–93.

Packer, M. and Addison, R.B. (eds) (1989) *Entering the Circle: Hermeneutic Investigation in Psychology*. Albany, NY: State University of New York Press.

Parker, I. (1994) 'Reflexive research and the grounding of analysis: social psychology and the psy-complex', *Journal of Community and Applied Social Psychology*, 4: 239–52.

Parker, I. (1997) *Psychoanalytic Culture: Psychoanalytic Discourse in Western Society*. London: Sage.

Parker, I. (ed.) (1999) *Deconstructing Psychotherapy*. London: Sage.

Perakyla, A. and Silverman, D. (1991) 'Reinterpreting speech-exchange systems: communication formats in AIDS counselling', *Sociology*, 25: 627–51.

Perakyla, A. (1995) *AIDS Counselling: Institutional Interaction and Clinical Practice*. Cambridge: Cambridge University Press.

Pogge, D.L. and Dougher, M.J. (1992) 'Evaluation of psychotherapeutic interpretations: an example of the application of the phenomenological method to discovery-based psychotherapy reesarch', *Journal of Psychotherapy Practice and Research*, 1: 248–58.

Polkinghorne, D.E. (1988) *Narrative Knowing and the Human Sciences*. Albany, NY: State University of New York Press.

Polkinghorne, D.E. (1989) 'Phenomenological research methods', in R.S. Valle and S. Halling (eds), *Existential-Phenomenological Perspectives in Psychology*. New York: Plenum Press.

Polkinghorne, D.E. (1995) 'Narrative configuration in qualitative analysis', in J.A. Hatch and R. Wisniewski (eds), *Life History and Narrative*. London: Falmer.

Potter, J. (1997) 'Discourse Analysis as a way of analysing naturally occurring talk', in D. Silverman (ed.), *Qualitative Research: Theory, Method and Practice*. London: Sage.

Potter, J. and Wetherell, M. (1987) *Discourse and Social Psychology: Beyond Attitudes and Behaviour*. London: Sage.

Potter, J. and Wetherell, M. (1994) 'Analyzing discourse', in A. Bryman and R.G. Burgess (eds), *Analyzing Qualitative Data*. London: Routledge.

Potter, J. and Wetherell, M. (1995) 'Discourse analysis', in J.A. Smith, R. Harré and L. van Langenhove (eds), *Rethinking Methods in Psychology*. London: Sage.

Powell, R.A., Single, H.M. and Lloyd, K.R. (1996) 'Focus groups in mental health research: enhancing the validity of user and provider questionnaires', *International Journal of Social Psychiatry*, 42: 193–206.

Psathas, G. (ed.) (1979) *Everyday Language: Studies in Ethnomethodology*. New York: Irvington.

Radnitzky, G. (1970) *Contemporary Schools of Metascience*. Göteborg: Akademiforlaget.

Reason, P. (ed.) (1988a) *Human Inquiry in Action: Developments in New Paradigm Research*. London: Sage.

Reason, P. (1988b) 'Introduction', in P. Reason (ed.), *Human Inquiry in Action: Developments in New Paradigm Research*. London: Sage.

Reason, P. (1988c) 'Whole person medical practice', in P. Reason (ed.), *Human Inquiry in Action: Developments in New Paradigm Research*. London: Sage.

Reason, P. (ed.) (1994a) *Participation in Human Inquiry*. London: Sage.

Reason, P. (1994b) 'Three approaches to participative inquiry', in N.K. Denzin and Y. Lincoln (eds), *Handbook of Qualitative Research*. London: Sage.

Reason, P. and Heron, J. (1986) 'Research with people: the paradigm of cooperative experiential inquiry', *Person-Centered Review*, 1 (4): 456–76.

Reason, P. and Rowan, J. (eds) (1981) *Human Inquiry: A Sourcebook of New Paradigm Research*. Chichester: Wiley.

Reason, P., Chase, H.D., Desser, A., Melhuish, C., Morrison, S., Peters, D., Wallstein, D., Webber, V. and Pietroni, P.C. (1992) 'Towards a clinical framework for collaboration between general and complementary practitioners: discussion paper', *Journal of the Royal Society of Medicine*, 85: 161–4.

Reicher, S. (2000) 'Against methodolatry: some comments on Elliott, Fischer and Rennie', *British Journal of Clinical Psychology*, 39: 1–6.

Rennie, D.L. (1990) 'Toward a representation of the client's experience of the psychotherapy hour', in G. Lietaer, J. Rombauts and R. Van Balen (eds), *Client-Centered and Experiential Therapy in the Nineties*. Leuven: University of Leuven Press.

Rennie, D.L. (1992) 'Qualitative analysis of the client's experience of psychotherapy: the unfolding of reflexivity', in S.G. Toukmanian and D.L. Rennie (eds), *Psychotherapy Process Research: Paradigmatic and Narrative Approaches*. London: Sage.

Rennie, D.L. (1994a) 'Clients' deference in psychotherapy', *Journal of Counseling Psychology*, 41: 427–37.

Rennie, D.L. (1994b) 'Storytelling in psychotherapy: the client's subjective experience', *Psychotherapy*, 31: 234–43.

Rennie, D.L. (1994c) 'Clients' accounts of resistance in counselling: a qualitative analysis', *Canadian Journal of Counselling*, 28: 43–57.

Rennie, D.L. (1994d) 'Human science and counselling psychology; closing the gap between science and practice', *Counselling Psychology Quarterly*, 7: 235–50.

Rennie, D.L. (1994e) 'Strategic choices in a qualitative approach to psychotherapy process research: a personal account', in L. Hoshmand and J. Martin (eds), *Method Choice and Inquiry Process: Lessons from Programmatic Research in Therapeutic Psychology*. New York: Teachers' Press.

Rennie, D.L. (1995) 'On the rhetorics of social science: let's not conflate natural science and human science', *Humanistic Psychologist*, 23: 321–32.

Rennie, D.L. (1996) 'Commentary on "clients' perception of treatment for depression: I and II"', *Psychotherapy Research*, 6 (4): 263–8.

Rennie, D.L. (1998a) 'Grounded theory methodology: the pressing need for a coherent logic of justification', *Theory and Psychology*, 8: 101–19.

Rennie, D.L. (1998b) *Person-centred Counselling: An Experiential Approach*. London: Sage.

Rennie, D.L. (1999) 'Qualitative research: a matter of hermeneutics and the sociology of knowledge', in M. Kopala and L. Suzuki (eds), *Using Qualitative Methods in Psychology*. Thousand Oaks, CA: Sage.

Rennie, D.L. (2000a) 'Experiencing psychotherapy: grounded theory studies', in D. Cain and J. Seeman (eds), *Handbook of Research in Humanistic Psychotherapies*. Washington: American Psychological Association.

Rennie, D.L. (2000b) 'Aspects of the client's conscious control of the psychotherapeutic process', *Journal of Psychotherapy Integration*, 10: 151–67.

Rennie, D.L. (2000c) 'Grounded theory methodology: the pressing need for a coherent logic of justification', in J. Frommer and D.L. Rennie (eds), *Qualitative Psychotherapy Research: Methods and Methodology*. Berlin: Pabst.

Rennie, D.L. (2000d) 'Grounded theory methodology as methodological hermeneutics: reconciling realism and relativism', *Theory and Psychology*, 10 (4): 481–502.

Rennie, D.L. and Toukmanian, S.G. (1992) 'Explanation in psychotherapy process research', in S.G. Toukmanian and D.L. Rennie (eds), *Psychotherapy Process Research: Paradigmatic and Narrative Approaches*. London: Sage.

Rennie, D.L., Phillips, J.R. and Quartaro, J.K. (1988) 'Grounded theory: a promising approach for conceptualization in psychology?' *Canadian Psychology*, 29: 139–50.

Rhodes, R., Hill, C.E., Thompson, B.J. and Elliott, R. (1994) 'A retrospective study of client perceptions of misunderstanding events', *Journal of Counseling Psychology*, 41: 473–83.

Rice, L.N. and Greenberg, L.S. (eds) (1984a) *Patterns of Change: Intensive Analysis of Psychotherapy Process*. New York: Guilford Press.

Rice, L.N. and Greenberg, L.S. (1984b) 'The new research paradigm', in L.N. Rice and L.S. Greenberg (eds), *Patterns of Change: Intensive Analysis of Psychotherapy Process*. New York: Guilford Press.

Richardson, L. (1991) *Writing Strategies: Reaching Diverse Audiences*. London: Sage.

Richardson, L. (1992) 'The consequences of poetic representation: writing the other, rewriting the self', in C. Ellis and M.G. Flaherty (eds), *Investigating Subjectivity: Research on Lived Experience*. New York: Sage.

Richardson, L. (1994) 'Writing: a method of inquiry', in N.K. Denzin and Y.S. Lincoln (eds), *Handbook of Qualitative Research*. Thousand Oaks, CA: Sage.

Riches, G. and Dawson, P. (1996) 'Making stories and taking stories: reflections on researching grief and marital tension following the death of a child', *British Journal of Guidance and Counselling*, 24 (3): 3357–66.

Riessman, C.K. (1993) *Narrative Analysis*. London: Sage.

Riessman, C. (1994) 'Making sense of marital violence: one woman's narrative', in C. Riessman (ed.), *Qualitative Studies in Social Work Research*. London: Sage.

Roberts, J. (1996) 'Perceptions of the significant other of the effects of psychodynamic psychotherapy: implications for thinking about psychodynamic and systems approaches', *British Journal of Psychiatry*, 168: 87–93.

Rodriguez, M.A., Quiroga, S.S. and Bauer, H.M. (1998) 'Breaking the silence: battered women's perspectives on medical care', *Archives of Family Medicine*, 5: 153–8.

Rogers, C.R. (1961) *On Becoming a Person*. London: Constable.

Rose, N. (1990) *Governing the Soul: The Shaping of the Private Self*. London: Routledge.

Roth, A. and Fonagy, P. (1996) *What Works for Whom? A Critical Review of Psychotherapy Research*. New York: Guilford Press.

Rowland, N. and Goss, S. (eds) (2000) *Evidence-Based Counselling and Psychological Therapies: Research and Applications*. London: Routledge.

Russell, R.L. (ed.) (1994) *Reassessing Psychotherapy Research*. New York: Guilford Press.

Sacks, A., Schegloff, E.A. and Jefferson, G. (1974) 'A simplest systematics for the organization of turn-taking in conversation', *Language*, 50: 696–735.

Sacks, H. (1972) 'An initial investigation of the usability of conversational materials for doing sociology', in D.N. Sudnow (ed.), *Studies in Social Interaction*. New York: Free Press.

Sandell, R. and Fredelius, G. (1997) 'Prioritizing among patients seeking subsidized psychotherapy', *Psychoanalytic Psychotherapy*, 11: 73–86.

Sass, L.A. (1988) 'Humanism, hermeneutics, and the concept of the human subject', in S.B. Messer, L.A. Sass and R.L. Woolfolk (eds), *Hermeneutics and Psychological Theory: Interpretive Perspectives on Personality, Psychotherapy and Psychopathology*. New Brunswick: Rutgers University Press.

Schegloff, E.A. (1968) 'Sequencing in conversational openings', *American Anthropologist*, 70: 1075–95.

Schegloff, E.A. (1997) 'Whose text? Whose context?' *Discourse and Society*, 8: 165–87.

Schegloff, E.A. (1999) '"Schegloff's texts" as "Billig's data": a critical reply', *Discourse and Society*, 10: 538–72.

Schwartz, N. (1996) *Cognition and Communication: Judgemental Biases, Research Methods, and the Logic of Conversation*. Mahwah, NJ: Lawrence Erlbaum.

Searle, J.R. (1969) *Speech Acts: An Essay in the Philosophy of Language*. Cambridge: Cambridge University Press.

Sells, S.P., Smith, T.E. and Sprenkle, D.H. (1995) 'Integrating qualitative and quantitative research methods: a research model', *Family Process*, 34: 199–218.

Sells, S.P., Smith, T.E., Coe, M.J., Yoshioka, M. and Robbins, J. (1994) 'An ethnography of couple and therapist experiences in reflecting team practice', *Journal of Marital and Family Therapy*, 20: 247–66.

Shapiro, D.A., Barkham, M., Hardy, G. and Morrison, L. (1990) 'The Second Sheffield Psychotherapy project: rationale, design and preliminary outcome data', *British Journal of Medical Psychology*, 63: 97–108.

Silverman, D. (1997) *Discourses of Counselling: HIV Counselling as Social Interaction*. London: Sage.

Silverman, D. (1998) *Harvey Sacks: Social Science and Conversation Analysis*. New York: Oxford University Press.

Smagorinsky, P. (ed.) (1994) *Speaking about Writing: Reflections on Research Methodology*. London: Sage.

Smith, J.K. and Heshusius, L. (1986) 'Closing down the conversation: the end of the quantitative–qualitative debate among educational inquirers', *Educational Researcher*, 15: 4–12.

Smith, M., Glass, G. and Miller, T. (1980) *The Benefits of Psychotherapy*. Baltimore, MD: Johns Hopkins Press.

Spence, D.P. (1989) 'Rhetoric vs. evidence as a source of persuasion: a critique of the case study genre', in M.J. Packer and R.B. Addison (eds), *Entering the Circle: Hermeneutic Investigation in Psychology*. Albany, NY: State University of New York Press.

Spence, D.P. (1993) 'The hermeneutic turn: soft science or loyal opposition?' *Psychoanalytic Dialogues*, 3: 1–10.

Steier, F. (ed.) (1991a) *Research and Reflexivity*. London: Sage.

Steier, F. (1991b) 'Research as self-reflexivity, self-reflexivity as social process', in F. Steier (ed.), *Research and Reflexivity*. London: Sage.

Stern, P. (1994) 'Eroding grounded theory', in J.N. Morse (ed.), *Critical Issues in Qualitative Research Methodology*. Thousand Oaks, CA: Sage.

Stewart, D.W. and Shamdasani, P.N. (1998) 'Focus group research: exploration and discovery', in J.L. Bickman and D.J. Rog (eds), *Handbook of Social Research Methods*. Thousand Oaks, CA: Sage.

Stiles, W.B. (1993) 'Quality control in qualitative research', *Clinical Psychology Review*, 13: 593–618.

Stiles, W.B. (1997) 'Consensual qualitative research: some cautions', *Counseling Psychologist*, 25: 586–98.

Stiles, W.B. and Angus, L. (2000) 'Qualitative research on clients' assimilation of problematic experiences in psychotherapy', in J. Frommer and D.L. Rennie (eds), *Qualitative Psychotherapy Research: Methods and Methodology*. Berlin: Pabst.

Stiles, W.B., Elliott, R., Llewelyn, S.P., Firth-Cozens, J.A., Margison, F.R., Shapiro, D.A. and Hardy, G. (1990) 'Assimilation of problematic experiences by clients in psychotherapy', *Psychotherapy*, 27: 411–20.

Strauss, A. and Corbin, J. (1990) *Basics of Qualitative Research: Grounded Theory Procedures and Techniques*. London: Sage.

Strauss, A. and Corbin, J. (1994) 'Grounded Theory methodology: an overview', in N.K. Denzin and Y.S. Lincoln (eds), *Handbook of Qualitative Research*. London: Sage.

Strupp, H. (1993) 'The Vanderbilt psychotherapy studies: synopsis', *Journal of Consulting and Clinical Psychology*, 61: 431–3.

Stuhr, U. and Wachholz, S. (2000) 'In search for a psychoanalytic research strategy: the concept of ideal types', in J. Frommer and D.L. Rennie (eds), *Qualitative Psychotherapy Research: Methods and Methodology*. Berlin: Pabst.

Taylor, C. (1971) 'Interpretation and the sciences of man', *Review of Metaphysics*, 25: 3–51.

Thompson, C.E. and Jenal, S.T. (1994) 'Interracial and intraracial quasi-counseling interactions when counselors avoid discussing race', *Journal of Counseling Psychology*, 41: 484–91.

Tillman-Healy, L. (1996) 'A secret life in a culture of thinness: reflections on body, food and bulimia', in C. Ellis and A.P. Bochner (eds), *Composing Ethnography: Alternative Forms of Qualitative Writing*. Thousand Oaks, CA: Sage.

Todd, T.A., Joanning, H., Enders, L., Mutchler, L. and Thomas, F.N. (1991) 'Using ethnographic interviews to create a more cooperative client–therapist relationship', *Journal of Family Psychotherapy*, 1: 51–63.

Tress, W., Frommer, J., Langenbach, M. and Schmitz, N. (1997) 'Research in psychotherapeutic diagnosis and the concept of socio-empirical markers', *Psychotherapy Research*, 7: 71–82.

Turner, B.A. (1981) 'Some practical aspects of qualitative data analysis: one way of organising the cognitive processes associated with the generation of grounded theory', *Quality and Quantity*, 15: 225–47.

Turner, R. (ed.) (1974) *Ethnomethodology*. Harmondsworth: Penguin.

Valle, R.S. and Halling, S. (eds) (1989) *Existential-Phenomenological Perspectives in Psychology: Exploring the Breadth of Human Experience*. New York: Plenum.

Valle, R.S. and King, M. (eds) (1978) *Existential-Phenomenological Alternatives for Psychology*. New York: Oxford University Press.

van den Berg, J.H. (1961) *The Changing Nature of Man*. New York: WW Norton.

van den Berg, J.H. (1972) *A Different Existence*. Pittsburgh: Duquesne University Press.

van den Berg, J.H. (1974) *Divided Existence and Complex Society*. Pittsburgh: Duquesne University Press.

van Kaam, A. (1969) *Existential Foundations of Psychology*. New York: Image Books.

Van Maanen, J. (1988) *Tales of the Field: On Writing Ethnography*. Chicago: University of Chicago Press.

Vaughn, S., Schumm, J.S. and Sinagub, J.M. (1996) *Focus Group Interviews in Education and Psychology*. Thousand Oaks, CA: Sage.

von Wright, G.H. (1993) 'Two traditions', in M. Hammersley (ed.), *Social Research: Philosophy, Politics and Practice*. London: Sage.

Wachholz, S. and Stuhr, U. (1999) 'The concept of ideal types in psychoanalytic follow-up research', *Psychotherapy Research*, 9: 327–41.

Walsh, R.A. (1995) 'The approach of the human science researcher: implications for the practice of qualitative research', *Humanistic Psychologist*, 23: 332–44.

Walsh, R.A. (1996) 'The problem of unconsciousness in qualitative research', *British Journal of Guidance and Counselling*, 24: 377–84.

Walsh, R., Perrucci, A. and Severns, J. (1999) 'What's in a good moment? A hermeneutic study of psychotherapy values across levels of psychotherapy training', *Psychotherapy Research*, 9: 304–26.

Warnke, G. (1987) *Gadamer: Hermeneutics, Tradition and Reason*. Cambridge: Polity Press.

Watson, J.C. and Rennie, D.L. (1994) 'Qualitative analysis of clients' subjective experience of significant moments during the exploration of problematic reactions', *Journal of Counseling Psychology*, 41: 500–9.

Weinstein, D. and Weinstein, M.A. (1991) 'Georg Simmel: sociological *flâneur bricoleur*', *Theory, Culture and Society*, 8: 151–68.

Wertz, F.J. (1984) 'Procedures in phenomenological research and the question of validity', in C.M. Aanstoos (ed.), *Exploring the Lived*

*World: Readings in Phenomenological Psychology*. Carrollton, GA: West Georgia College.

West, W.S. (1996) 'Using human inquiry groups in counselling research', *British Journal of Guidance and Counselling*, 24: 347–55.

West, W.S. (1997) 'Integrating counselling, psychotherapy, and healing: an inquiry into counsellors and psychotherapists whose work includes healing', *British Journal of Guidance and Counselling*, 25: 291–312.

Wetherell, M. (1998) 'Positioning and interpretive repertoires: Conversation Analysis and post-structuralism in dialogue', *Discourse and Society*, 9: 387–412.

Wolcott, H.F. (1990) *Writing up Qualitative Research*. London: Sage.

Wolcott, H.F. (1992) 'Posturing in qualitative inquiry', in M.D. LeCompte, W.L. Millroy and J. Preissle (eds), *The Handbook of Qualitative Research in Education*. New York: Academic Press.

Wolcott, H.F. (1994) *Transforming Qualitative Data: Description, Analysis, Interpretation*. London: Sage.

Wolcott, H.F. (1995) *The Art of Fieldwork*. London: Sage.

Woolfolk, R.L., Sass, L.A. and Messer, S.B. (1988) 'Introduction to hermeneutics', in S.B. Messer, L.A. Sass and R.L. Woolfolk (eds), *Hermeneutics and Psychological Theory: Interpretive Perspectives on Personality, Psychotherapy and Psychopathology*. New Brunswick: Rutgers University Press.

Worthen, V. and McNeill, B.W. (1996) 'A phenomenological investigation of "good" supervision events', *Journal of Counseling Psychology*, 43: 25–34.

Yin, R.K. (1989) *Case Study Research: Design and Methods*. London: Sage.

# Index